American Epic

American Epic

Reading the US Constitution

GARRETT EPPS

OXFORD
UNIVERSITY PRESS

OXFORD

UNIVERSITY PRESS

Oxford University Press is a department of the University of Oxford.
It furthers the University's objective of excellence in research,
scholarship, and education by publishing worldwide.

Oxford   New York

Auckland   Cape Town   Dar es Salaam   Hong Kong   Karachi
Kuala Lumpur   Madrid   Melbourne   Mexico City   Nairobi
New Delhi   Shanghai   Taipei   Toronto

With offices in

Argentina   Austria   Brazil   Chile   Czech Republic   France   Greece
Guatemala   Hungary   Italy   Japan   Poland   Portugal   Singapore
South Korea   Switzerland   Thailand   Turkey   Ukraine   Vietnam

Oxford is a registered trade mark of Oxford University Press
in the UK and certain other countries.

Published in the United States of America by
Oxford University Press
198 Madison Avenue, New York, NY 10016

Library of Congress Cataloging-in-Publication Data
Epps, Garrett.
American epic : reading the U.S. Constitution / Garrett Epps.
p.   cm.
Distinguished legal scholar and award-winning novelist Garrett Epps walks the
reader through all the articles and sections of the Constitution, presenting
an analysis of what their various 'takeaways' are.
ISBN 978-0-19-997474-0 (hardback)
1. Constitutional law—United States. 2. Constitutions—United States. 3. United States. Constitution. I. Title.
KF4550.E67   2013
342.7302—dc23   2012049750

1 3 5 7 9 8 6 4 2

Printed in the United States of America
on acid-free paper

For the many dedicated teachers who taught me to read, and especially
for R.H.W. Dillard,
best teacher ever

We have had founded for us the most positive of lands. The founders have pass'd to other spheres—but what are these terrible duties they have left us?

"Democratic Vistas"
Walt Whitman

CONTENTS

PREFACE

How to Read a Constitution

In 1987, the American novelist E. L. Doctorow observed the Bicentennial of the United States Constitution by sitting down to read it from start to finish. Doctorow is a profound and affectionate student of American history, and a writer who can (as he did in his famous novel *Ragtime*) wring pure poetry from a description of the early twentieth century interurban streetcar system.

But Doctorow found no poetry in his nation's Constitution. "It is five thousand words long but reads like fifty thousand," he reported sadly. "It lacks high rhetoric and shows not a trace of wit, as you might expect, having been produced by a committee of lawyers. It uses none of the tropes of literature to create empathetic states in the mind of the reader."[1]

Doctorow quickly moved from the Constitution to more welcoming turf—the soaring words of the Declaration of Independence—"as alive with passion and the juices of outrage as the work of any single artist"—and the stirring history of the Revolution and the Framing of the Constitution.

Doctorow is one of America's finest writers and readers, but I think on this occasion he missed a good deal of high rhetoric, many literary tropes, and even a trace of, if not wit, at least irony. But Doctorow did tackle the text, read it as a whole, and tried to make something of it. In that attempt, he outdid many of his fellow patriots; many of them insistently proclaim fidelity to a Constitution they seem to have barely read.

The United States Constitution turned 225 years old in 2012. It is the central document of American history and politics. From all sides of the political spectrum, from ranks of society low and high, it is ceaselessly venerated, admired, and invoked. But all too seldom is it read. It sometimes seems that Americans worship the Constitution so deeply that they find its actual text a distraction.

When I started teaching law students twenty years ago, I was surprised to realize that my students had no more interest in actually reading the Constitution than does the ordinary person. When I ask them to read the Constitution from start to finish, they quickly skim its 7,500 words. (Doctorow undercounted, by the way; he apparently made the common American error of assuming that the amendments somehow don't "count.") They then arrive in class, expecting that I will now tell them what it means.

They are disappointed when I tell them that I don't know the answer, and that other scholars and judges don't really know it either. As a people, Americans are like my students: we have little interest in what the Constitution says; but, as befits the culture that spawned *The Da Vinci Code*, we are obsessed with what it *means*.

The *meaning* of the Constitution is a national obsession, pursued in a number of ways. For my apprentice lawyers, those words signify what the Supreme Court has said it means. That is the Philosopher's Stone lawyers seek, in order to manipulate it to the advantage of their clients.

There are at least three problems with this Court-centered approach. To begin with, even the Court that issues a decision may not know what the decision "means." These hard-working federal employees can really only *know* what *words*—written by a law clerk, edited by a justice, and circulated to all nine chambers—can get five votes on this day of this term of court. It may take the legal system a generation to settle on an agreed meaning of even a single case—that is, on the ideas for which a lawyer can cite it to a later court. And as time goes on, that agreed meaning will change. Meanwhile, lawyers must not only cite but argue the case, using its fact pattern and specific wording to shed light on widely varying situations in new cases. What lawyers learn is cases, not meanings.

Second, part of a lawyer's job—and for that matter, part of any citizen's—is to decide whether the Court is right. "We are not final because we are infallible," the late Justice Robert Jackson once wrote. "But we are infallible only because we are final."[2] Jackson, a man of great intellectual integrity, understood that the infallibility of the Court was limited and temporary; a Court decision resolves a specific dispute among specific parties at a specific time. What it does not do is end the debate.

Within the legal system, lawyers and judges will criticize and defend the Court's decisions; and in the larger political system, the correctness of a decision—whether it is *Roe v. Wade* or *Citizens United v. Federal Election Commission*—is always legitimate grounds for debate. "I do not forget the position assumed by some that constitutional questions are to be decided by the Supreme Court, nor do I deny that such decisions must be binding in any case upon the parties to a suit as to the object of that suit, while they are also entitled to very high respect and consideration in all parallel cases by all other departments of the

Government," Abraham Lincoln explained in his first inaugural address. "At the same time, the candid citizen must confess that if the policy of the government upon vital questions affecting the whole people is to be irrevocably fixed by decisions of the Supreme Court, the instant they are made, in ordinary litigation between parties, in personal actions, the people will have ceased to be their own rulers, having, to that extent, practically resigned their Government into the hands of that eminent tribunal."[3] Criticism by "candid citizens" often has eventual effect—years or even generations later, the Court itself may reexamine its precedent, and even overturn it.

Third, many important parts of the Constitution are never tested in any court. The other two branches of government make decisions all the time, and not all of them can give rise to a lawsuit. As an example, consider the decision by President Barack Obama to allow U.S. aircraft to participate in the NATO intervention in the 2011 Libyan civil war. Many people—including me—believed that the Constitution required him to get congressional approval. Obama, on the advice of some of his executive branch lawyers, chose not to do so. A group of members of the House brought a federal lawsuit against the president, and were unceremoniously tossed out of court. War and peace is just one of the great constitutional questions that courts don't usually touch.

In 1998, the House of Representatives impeached President Bill Clinton and brought him to trial in the Senate on the charge of having lied in a deposition about his affair with the intern Monica Lewinski. Many people—including me—believed that a president's sexual behavior, and his efforts in a private lawsuit to cover it up, simply did not match the standard of "high crimes and misdemeanors" the Constitution sets for impeachment of a federal official. But no one was foolish enough to ask a court to stop the impeachment. Article I, Section Two, Clause Six of the Constitution gives to the House "the sole power of impeachment"; a court involving itself in the case would be wandering far off its Article III reservation. Again, the grounds of impeachment is a great constitutional question that will always be outside courts' jurisdiction.

In deciding whether Obama violated the Constitution in Libya, or the House violated the Constitution in impeaching Clinton, then, we are on our own, and must rely on the Constitution itself.

But the quest for the *meaning* of the Constitution is not limited to lawyers. Citizens seek it as well. To them the secret code is not what the courts have said, but *What the Framers Intended*. The words on the parchment, to many Americans, are much less important than what the Framers were thinking when they said them. If we knew these secret thoughts, they would answer all our questions. So persistent is this popular belief that best-selling novelist William Martin recently wrote a book entitled *The Lost Constitution*, a Dan Brown–style thriller about the quest for a copy of the Constitution "annotated by the Founding

Fathers" that can answer all of our current constitutional riddles.[4] If we could just get our hands on some *other* words the Founders wrote, they would tell us the meaning of the words we already have.

The Constitution, as Doctorow noted, is not light reading. The drafters of the Napoleonic Code intended their handiwork to be a central document of French identity, to be read before every Gallic hearth. The Framers of our Constitution had less lofty ambitions. Unlike the drafters of the Code, the Framers were not academics concerned with consistency and elegance. (There was one exception: America's first law professor, George Wythe of Virginia, was a delegate to Philadelphia, but Wythe left the Convention only ten days after it convened, called home to tend to his sick wife, and never returned; his signature does not appear on the Constitution.) They were practical men of affairs (contrary to popular belief, only about half were actually lawyers); most lacked the talent or literary ambition of a Jefferson or even a John Adams. They were worried less about generations to come than about the about the immediate future of the country. They knew what they were doing would not matter centuries hence if the document they wrote did not win ratification in the next eighteen months.

The Constitution, nonetheless, has its moments of metaphor, even of grace. Its text offers us at the most basic level the means we can employ today to create a "more perfect union . . . to ourselves and our posterity"; at a deeper level, it tells us much about who we are and how we got here. It is a tool kit of our politics and a testament of our history.

It is worth reading. So I propose that we read it together, even the "boring" parts, and try to understand it both as a whole and in detail.

How then shall we read it? This question is not as easy to answer as it seems. The usual way for a legal scholar to write about the text is, as noted, to *explain it*. The explanation sometimes draws on Supreme Court doctrine, treating that as authoritative explanation. Or, equally often, it may consist of a history of each clause and phrase, guiding us through the author's version of the thought of the Framers and the vagaries of interpretation.

I don't want to explain the Constitution to you. I do not want to tell you what it *means*. If I were to do that, you would then know something about what I think, but perhaps not much about what the Constitution says.

Besides, I don't *know* what it means. I can carefully read what it says; and as I do so, I find many parts that have no clear, definite, single meaning. I find no single overarching philosophy, but some hints at underlying ideas. Some of those ideas are self-contradictory, some are profound, some are repulsive. Some seem to relate to other parts; sometimes the parts don't fit together at all. Most of all, I find, as Hamlet did in his book, words, words, words—words that spark memories, thoughts, and imaginings in me, that remind me of other documents of American history and works of American literature, and of events that I have read about and sometimes seen. The words stir thoughts in me, but they do not tell me which thoughts are correct.

I read the Constitution as I do because of who I am. I am a constitutional scholar and a teacher. I have also been a lawyer in both constitutional and ordinary cases, and have seen the effect of the law and the Constitution on ordinary people as they confront the daunting power of government. In my own writing, I have studied the development of religious freedom in particular, and of democratic ideas in general, through the work not only of the courts but of Congress and of social movements from the anti-slavery movement of the 1840s to the women's movement of the 1970s.

But like any reader, I bring to the text more than my job title. I am a former journalist; my fifteen-year career with newspapers large and small has given me a practical, non-lawyer's respect for the Constitution, and particularly for the First Amendment. I am a novelist, a literary critic, and even a published poet, with an overwhelming fascination and concern for words in themselves and the ways they can combine to stir wonder, admiration, anger, and despair in the minds of those who read them.

By birth, I am a white Southerner, born at the midpoint of the last century. I came of age in a society that was in the process of being transformed from a racial dictatorship into a full part of America's flawed democracy. That change was wrought by the devotion of ordinary citizens to the ideas of the Constitution and by the willingness of the legal system to follow those ideas into areas that at first seemed impossible and even terrifying. To my mind, the most profound constitutional statement uttered during the 1950s is found not in the words of the Supreme Court in *Brown v. Board of Education* but in those of Martin Luther King Jr. two years later, when he stood before a crowd at the Holt Street Baptist Church and inaugurated the Montgomery bus boycott by saying, "If we are wrong, then the Supreme Court of this nation is wrong. If we are wrong, the Constitution of the United States is wrong. If we are wrong, God Almighty is wrong."[5]

To grow up in those years was an extraordinary experience; southern society was consumed with a debate about the Constitution, and everyone understood that underlying the debate was the threat of private violence and civil chaos. That experience made me very skeptical of much of what is claimed for "state's rights," of the idea that local beliefs should prevail over national values, and of the rhetoric that exalts the work of the Framers but slights the democratic changes the amendment process has made in the Constitution's text.

(I am the first, however, to say that my experience may make me insensitive to other dangers—centralization, standardization, the potential tyranny of the majority—that you, my reader, may find more salient than I.)

And before I was any of the things I describe, I was a bookish, bespectacled boy who at an early age decided that words and books were the finest things on earth, and who treasured more than anything else the time to sit alone with a book—whether it was the Bible or Charles Dickens's *David Copperfield*—and marvel at the way words could change me and change the world.

How do I, the product of those experiences, read the Constitution? I count no fewer than four ways.

First, and perhaps most obvious, I have learned to read the Constitution like the Bible. Americans have had, over the years, a more intense relationship with Christian Scripture than perhaps any other people on earth. American constitutional theory, for much of our history, has often been nothing more than slightly retooled Protestant biblical interpretation. (In fact, I sometimes think that I love the Constitution and its interpretation so much because studying it takes me back to my elementary school days, which included a daily "Sacred Studies" in which we read the stories of the kings of Israel and of the parables of Jesus.)

The idea of a single meaning, available to all, is a uniquely Protestant idea. Throughout the history of Christianity, the faithful have read the Bible in many ways: as an allegory of divine love, for example (as in the seemingly erotic *Song of Songs*) or as an "anagogy," a deliberately concealed key to events in another world, to be understood only by those who had by study gained mystical access to God.

The idea of a single, literal, intended meaning gained primacy only during the Reformation. The religious historian Jaroslav Pelikan writes that Martin Luther and the other Reformers believed that what mattered was "the original intent and *sensus literalis* (literal meaning)" of the words of the Bible.[6] Pelikan sees in Luther's biblicism a direct forebear of American constitutional interpretation.

For Americans in particular, this general Protestant notion of "original intent" was strengthened and elaborated a century ago, when a group of American Evangelicals published a set of theological essays on "the fundamentals" of Christian belief that have given rise to the movement we call "Fundamentalism."[7] Fundamentalism was fueled by opposition to was called the "higher criticism"—scholarship that analyzed the Bible as a human work of literature, without any assumptions of divine origin or authority. Higher critics, for example, viewed some books of the Bible as blends of earlier books, or as appropriations from other early religions of the region. They studied the Bible stories as they studied non-Christian myths, and they refused to take stories like the deliverance from Egypt or the raising of Lazarus as fact.

Fundamentalists rejected the "higher criticism." The Bible, they wrote, is the Word of God. This means that all parts of it are *inspired*. The inspiration is not general, but verbal—meaning that God has fixed for all times not just the ideas in the Bible but the precise words. There are no mistakes or inconsistencies in the Bible, and nothing it says—whether about the Sun standing still, the "gift of tongues" at Pentecost, or the coming apocalypse described in Revelation—is false. The Bible is *true*. It says it is true, and the prophecies of the Old Testament have been fulfilled in the New.

Thus every word has a meaning; that meaning is invariably correct and immune from question by history or contemporary morality; and all the words fit together into one divine whole.

So influential has Fundamentalism been in this country that these attitudes are now cultural rather than specifically religious values. Many Americans profoundly believe that the Framers in Philadelphia made no mistakes or omissions; that every provision in the Constitution is there for a clear reason; that the Framers of the Constitution, like Isaiah and St. John the Divine, saw forward in time and made prophecies that have been miraculously fulfilled; and that nothing in the Constitution—not even its provisions recognizing slavery—can be wrong, or more properly "wrong for its time." They often test the constitutionality of a measure by asking whether they think the Framers foresaw it. They say, "If the Founding Fathers could see what we are doing today, they'd be appalled."

The Founders actually had no idea what America would become 225 years after Philadelphia and weren't thinking about it much; they were trying to write a set of rules that would work for the moment, not to foretell and control the future. Some Americans—by no means only those of a Fundamentalist background—find this idea threatening, in much the way the writers of *The Fundamentals* feared the insights of the "higher criticism."

We are all influenced by this school of reading—even though a moment's conscious reflection should convince us, no matter what our religious beliefs, that a human document like the Constitution cannot be read as if it were written by God. As we confront the text, the "fundamentalist" reading may prevent us from seeing everything that is there; that's because much of the Constitution is in fact confusing and ambiguous. Some of it seems in fact to be wrong, and some is even, as far as I can tell, meaningless.

But the biblical reading of the Constitution cannot be put aside. That's because for Americans, reading the Bible and reading itself are closely intertwined. The high levels of literacy in early America can be traced to the ambition of ordinary people to read the Word of God. Every time we interpret any text, we are drawing on our culture's rich history of biblical interpretation. For that reason, we should bring to reading the Constitution all the resources of readers of Scripture. The literal mode of reading exists beside other traditions—those that see the Bible as a source of poetic inspiration, of divine allegory, and historical understanding. These too are a part of any American reader's palette, and they can show us the ways in which parts of the Constitution may resemble the laws of Leviticus, the Psalms of David, or the Sermon on the Mount—similarities that may illuminate the proper application of those parts to practical problems.

Lawyers have a great deal of experience in reading texts that are ambiguous and contradictory. Many of these texts are called statutes. And the second way you and I can read the Constitution is in fact as a set of rules written to operate as law, to be read as law using the methods lawyers use.

Statutes have only become dominant in the legal field in the past century; when the Constitution was written, most lawyers most of the time studied the "common," or unwritten, law, or read large theoretical volumes by scholars of English and international law. But even in the eighteenth century, statutes were a part of their trade; rules for reading them had been evolving for at least a century. Today, the "science" of statutory construction has evolved its own techniques and doctrines, including a set of Latin "canons" that can be wheeled out when they favor one side or another. Lawyers like to intone solemnly that "*expressio unius exclusio alterius est*" (to express one concept in a statute is to exclude all others) or "*noscitur a sociis*" (a word in a statute can draw its meaning from those around it). These "canons" rarely, however, settle anything in a court of law, because, as the famous scholar Karl Llewellyn once wrote, "there are two opposing canons on almost every point,"[8] each accepted maxim contradicting another.

The term "strict construction" is an example. Presidents and senators like to intone that they are seeking justices who will "strictly construe" the Constitution. But they'd be appalled if they actually found one. "Strict construction" is a statutory, not a constitutional term; it directs a court to read a statute as narrowly as possible, disturbing the unwritten, common law as little as it can. That presupposition makes no sense in the context of a written Constitution, which was inspired by a desire to change the unwritten law and substitute for the British Constitution an entirely new one.

By a "strict construction" of the Constitution, it seems to me, Congress would have no power to establish an Air Force—the Constitution authorizes only an Army and a Navy. For that matter, Congress wouldn't have the power to designate a national flag—American forces would be required to march under one of fifty state flags—because there is no textual "flag power" in the document.

Of course this makes no sense. No less a conservative icon than Justice Antonin Scalia says, "A text should not be construed strictly, and it should not be construed leniently; it should be construed reasonably."[9]

Any introduction to statutory construction will state that its aim is to discern "what the legislature intended." The quest for "legislative intent," however, is by and large a much more formalized (indeed almost ritualized) pursuit than is constitutional interpretation. Statutory intent is to be derived first from the text, and when that is unclear, from "legislative history," a complex bundle of official committee reports, hearing transcripts, and floor speeches compiled by Congress during the writing of a statute. Judges are expected to scry this chaotic mass of words and conclude which way the legislature would have applied the statute to the specific case had it considered it.

In fact, the pursuit of "intent" usually seems half-hearted at best, and increasingly some judges question its utility at all. Justice Scalia has written that "I reject intent of the legislature as the proper criterion of law."[10] To Scalia, the only sound basis of statutory construction is *the precise literal meaning of the words* (sound familiar?), supplemented, if necessary, by a nice, thick dictionary.

Justice Scalia contends that constitutional interpretation differs from statutory interpretation only slightly. It "is distinctive not because special principles of interpretation apply, but because the usual principles are being applied to an unusual text," he says.[11] Thus it falls particularly to judges to "give words and phrases an expansive rather than narrow interpretation—though not an interpretation that the language will not bear."[12]

Here again we see the quest for the "literal sense" of the words. The special quality that Scalia gives to this endeavor is his insistence that the only criterion is "the original meaning of the text, not what the original draftsmen intended." And among judges and scholars, the term "originalism" today applies to that kind of reference— to what some scholars call "the original public meaning" of constitutional language, what an ordinary American at the time of the ratification would have thought the words meant—rather than to the "original intent" of "the Founding Fathers."

A statutory approach to reading the Constitution is important because it reminds us of the background against which it was written; but applied too enthusiastically, it can thus lead us in one of two directions—neither of them, to me at least, wholly satisfactory. One the one hand, we can extract meaning from the document using traditional statutory construction. The problem with this is twofold: first, it applies highly artificial principles developed *after* the Constitution was written—since the "age of statutes," as Judge Guido Calabresi calls it, began in earnest only in the twentieth century.[13] Second, it seeks meaning from "legislative history" that doesn't exist.

A number of people (including, at times, Justice Scalia) claim to divine the "original intent" (or "understanding") from Madison's *Notes of Debates* in the Philadelphia Convention and from the essays published in 1787 and 1788 as *The Federalist*. But the debates were never intended to be part of public record; the delegates swore themselves to strictest secrecy. The *Notes* were a private project of Madison's, not an official record of the Convention. They were not published until Madison's death in 1836, largely because Madison did *not* want people to rely on them for constitutional interpretation. In fact, Madison said repeatedly that the "intent" of the Philadelphia delegates was largely irrelevant to interpreting the document they wrote.

The Federalist, the second common source of "original intent" or "original understanding," is a bracing and fascinating work of political theory. It was not written as a book, but as a series of what we today might call "op ed" articles for newspapers. A current volume of *The Federalist* contains eighty-five essays hastily written by one of three major figures: Madison, who was present every day of the Convention; Hamilton, who attended very few of the sessions; and John Jay, who was not a delegate at all.

These essays were also a private project—the authors did not ask the Convention for permission to write them or show them to other delegates for their approval. The essays were most assuredly not designed as an explanation of "intent" to future generations; they were aimed at influencing the voters of one state, New York. They are, in short, a partisan document.

There's reason to think that *The Federalist*'s authors, pressed by a desperate political struggle, said some things they did not really mean. We know for a fact that Madison's defense in Federalist 62 of equal representation in the Senate, lukewarm as it was, was written between clenched teeth. His friend Thomas Jefferson tried to console him for the unpleasant task of explaining parts of the Constitution he despised: "With respect to *The Federalist*," Jefferson wrote Madison from Paris after reading the essays, "[i]n some parts it is discoverable that the author means only to say what may be best said in defence of opinions in which he did not concur."[14]

Nonetheless, because the authors write brilliantly, because they pretend to be one person named "Publius," and because "Publius" displays the good salesman's certainty that every aspect of the product is perfect in every way, many people who prize "original intent" or "understanding" have come to regard the essays also as a kind of secondary scripture, a set of divine epistles, with Publius in the role of St. Paul. One scholar recently explained that *The Federalist* should be viewed in almost precisely the terms often used of the Bible: "Use of a single pseudonym suggested that *The Federalist* possessed a uniformity of intent: that *The Federalist* was to be read as the work of one mind, not three, and was coherent throughout."[15] Not only coherent, he adds, but also eternal: "The teaching of *The Federalist* was intended to be true for all times and all places."[16]

This scriptural faith rests on even shakier ground than does a belief in what we might call the inerrancy of the Constitution. As a mild gesture toward proper reading, I pledge here and now that nowhere in these pages will you find a quote from *The Federalist*. We are here to read the Constitution itself.

Anyway, even if we could somehow find the "legislative history" of the Constitution (like William Martin's imaginary "lost Constitution"), there is a further question dogging this way of reading the Constitution. If a court misconstrues the "intent of Congress" in reading a statute, Congress can always change the statute. This happens regularly, when Congress changes a law's wording to "overrule" a judicial reading of it.

But the Constitutional Convention does not sit. Its members are all dead, and so are the members of the ratifying conventions that approved it. We cannot revise what they wrote, without great effort. Why should their long-ago "intent" or "understanding" bind us today? If their intent was that we should not interpret the Constitution for ourselves, then their intent was undemocratic, immoral, and just plain silly. Our Constitution today is binding because of our living allegiance to it, not because of its pedigree. And our intentions and understandings matter far more than those of the dead.

Finally, the quest for "original intent" or "original public meaning" involves minute and highly technical discussions of etymology of words, the evolution of language, and the intellectual history of Anglo-American society. It is, in short, a scholastic activity; it does not just smell, but actually reeks, of the lamp. Ordinary citizens have no standing to engage in this pursuit. If we accept it as determining the meaning of the Constitution, we are thus delivered into the hands of those, like historians, who have special knowledge of these things, or justices, who usually do not but believe they do.

The document binds us, the living, together as a nation today, and perhaps thus what should matter is what the words mean to us, the living, today. And if we take Justice Scalia at his word, then "reasonable construction" of the words does not deliver our fundamental law into the hands of a priesthood. If "reasonable construction" of written law is the intent of statutory construction, surely we should not aim for less when we read the Constitution as law.

Bible or statute—these two, however, do not exhaust the ways of reading a text. I can name some others—certainly you can too. In any text, an engineer may see a blueprint, a chef a recipe, a doctor a disease. "Law, say the gardeners, is the sun," the poet W. H. Auden once wrote.[17] Each of us sees in the world around us what we love and understand in it, and reading is no different from seeing.

Before I loved the law I loved literature and poetry, and as I read the Constitution—despite Doctorow's dour evaluation—I do hear poetry. Does that sound outlandish? Some would think so. "The federal Constitution is not a poem, a novel (chain or otherwise), a manifesto, or a treatise. The federal Constitution is a blueprint—an instruction manual, if you will—for a particular form of government," two legal scholars wrote recently.[18] Another eminent scholar rather grandly christened the idea of Constitution as poetry "the Aesthetic Fallacy," explaining that "people in the grip of this fallacy suppose that the Constitution is like a poem, a symphony, or a great work of political philosophy. Each word and every phrase must come together to form a harmonious and pleasing composition."[19]

The later "definition" of poetry tempts me to ask, "Are you sure you understand what a poem is?" No one who has read widely in poetry could imagine that "each word and every phrase must come together to form a harmonious and pleasing composition." By tradition, poetry can express a narrative (as in ancient epics), embody drama (as in classic drama), or give vent to emotion. Most of the poetry we read today is *lyric* poetry, poetry descended from ancient songs sung to the accompaniment of a lyre. Today's "literary lyrics carry their own music,"[20] and the combination of sense and sound is designed to evoke an evoke an emotional response in the reader. Even within the lyric genre, good poetry is not all lonely clouds and daffodils any more than good music is all "moon" and June. Lyric poetry may be jagged, unharmonious, partial, confusing, deliberately or unintentionally misleading, and even horrifying; consider, for example, Allen Ginsberg's masterwork *Howl*, which begins,

> I saw the best minds of my generation destroyed by madness, starving
> hysterical naked,
> dragging themselves through the negro streets at dawn looking for an
> angry fix. . . .[21]

Poetry is, as the famous literary scholar Harold Bloom has written, characterized not so much by airy beauty as by "figurative language, concentrated so that its form is both expressive and evocative."[22]—words that in novel combination stand for or suggest meanings beyond those we find for them in dictionaries. I see figures—metaphors, analogies, and others—in the Constitution's text. Moreover, some of the text really does carry its own music, much like a lyric poem.

The wider genre of poetry throughout literary history has also included other forms, most particularly epic poetry, whose wide sweep and narrative drive are the very expression of a civilization's soul. An ancient epic was, like the Constitution, the work of many hands—oral bards elaborating and refining the stories of figures like Gilgamesh or Achilles. The heroes' deeds embody their cultures, as the Constitution embodies ours. Epic poems, like the Constitution, are assembled in part from "formulas" already known to poet and audience. Homer's "wine-dark sea" has some kinship to legal terms used by the Framers, such as "due process of law" and "life or limb"—they are brief evocations of complex cultural ideas, of the evolving Anglo-American idea of law and the history of criminal punishment in our culture.

Homer's verse in particular is often constitutional: much of *The Iliad* and *The Odyssey* depict law and government in his imagined version of Bronze Age Greece. Agamemnon presiding over the assembly of warriors on the beach before Troy is perhaps the earliest model we have of a deliberative body like the US Congress. Penelope and Telemachus, in their struggle against the suitors who demand the wealth and throne of Ithaca, are dealing with potential violence in the transfer of ultimate power, a problem that bedeviled the Framers of Article II and those of the Twelfth, Twentieth, and Twenty-Fifth Amendments.

Homer's broad vision, his sweeping diction, and his raw enthusiasm for all of human life make him to this day the greatest poet in Western culture. Walt Whitman, who consciously aspired to that kind of greatness, is America's Homer. Whitman was also deeply influenced by the Constitution, which he studied during his years as an editor and a political journalist. In many ways, he considered his great, much revised epic *Leaves of Grass* a companion work to the Constitution, a document that would constitute the American soul much as the Constitution brings into being its government. Generations of children have learned such verses as "I Hear America Singing"; their vision and diction are part of our heritage as surely as the Bible and the Constitution. Whitman's poems often consciously depict the process of "singing" America—putting our nation into words. What better metaphor for constitution-making could there be?

"I am large. . . . I contain multitudes,"[23] Whitman wrote—and the multitudes he sought to contain were us, and our country, and "the song of the throes of Democracy."[24] We can learn a good deal from comparing the Constitution to Whitman's work, and noting both what is in the text and, as all good readers of poetry must do, what is not.

These examples propose four modes of reading—scriptural, legal, lyric, and epic. In what follows, I will return to them over and over—not so much because they are the *right* ways of reading as because they are the ways of reading I delight in and partially understand. What follows is my own reading of the Constitution. It is in part a lawyer's reading, to be sure, focused some of the time on the meaning of clauses and commas; but it also supplies some means of interpretation that lawyers often do not use. Lawyers enjoy splitting texts up into pieces; when they are done with them, they too rarely stitch them up into a whole again. It is common in legal analysis, for example, to take Congress's Article I Power "To regulate Commerce with foreign Nations, and among the several States, and with the Indian Tribes" and divide it solemnly into three self-contained entities—the "interstate commerce" power, the "Indian commerce" power, and the "foreign commerce" power—then consider one of them in isolation. In literary terms—that is in terms that seek an understanding of a text beyond an immediate, specific application—this makes no more sense than trying to analyze, in the quote from Ginsberg's "Howl," which of the "best minds of my generation" were "starving," which were "hysterical," and which were "naked."

Readers of poetry, epic, and Scripture, at their best, look for the whole as well as the part. They remember to ask themselves what sort of text they are reading—invocation, elegy, psalm, commandment—and they ask how it fits into other parts of the work.

Let me emphasize what this book is not. It is not a formal legal commentary, of the sort written by Chief Justice Joseph Story in 1833 and carried forward by brilliant scholars like Akhil Reed Amar today. These are wonderful books either for browsing for an evening of reading; but I have been as careful as possible not to absorb their reading and instead offer my own. A scholarly monograph would quickly become a dialogue between me and those who have written before me; I want this book to be a conversation among author, reader, and text.

Second, I will not explain, as some scholars do, the *real meaning* of the Constitution. After two decades of study, I don't know it and often doubt that it exists. I certainly do not propose to offer comprehensive explanations drawn from history—*this is what the Framers said, this is what they were thinking, this is what they must have meant.* Nor is my subject a detailed explanation of Court precedent. There are many very fine books that offer this kind of analysis. I read them with pleasure but also with some bemusement.

They bemuse me because, to begin with, they do not agree one with another, and to accept any of them I must often deny what I read in the text. For another, too much of this kind of historical and doctrinal reading can make a reader weary, with the fatigue Whitman depicts in "When I Heard the Learn'd Astronomer." After listening to a recitation of the astronomer's proofs, figures, charts and diagrams, the poet writes that, "tired and sick," he left the crowded lecture-room and

> *wander'd off by myself,*
> *In the mystical moist night-air, and from time to time,*
> *Look'd up in perfect silence at the stars.*[25]

After twenty years of late nights under the lamp, and many hours in the crowded lecture hall, I confess that the Constitution for me sometimes still seems as distant as the stars. But every time I look at it in "perfect silence"—not as a learn'd astronomer but as a reader capable of wonder and confusion—it shows me new and surprising things.

I am approaching the reading ahead, then, as a reader in the mystical moist night-air. I know what I think I know; I am well aware of what I do not know. As a reader, I don't know more than you do, and I want us to read together.

In his essay, "Good Writers and Good Readers," the novelist Vladimir Nabokov suggested that readers should read great texts without critical theory or specialized training, but armed with a dictionary, some imagination, a good memory, and some artistic sense.[26] I have, as best I can, strapped this armor on, and I will battle the text only as someone who aspires to be Nabokov's good reader.

From time to time, I will consult a dictionary—particularly, when I encounter specialized legal terms. I may mention the Supreme Court, particularly when I think the Court has read the text wrong (or at least oddly), and I will even look into history, not because this is a historical guide but because some of the phrases in the Constitution are so opaque that any sane reader would wonder what its framers thought they were talking about. (History shows us that in some cases, they didn't know what they meant any more than we do.)

Never if I can avoid it will I tell you the reader what *the meaning* of the words is. Instead, I will ask myself, and you, "What *could* this mean? What meanings could we draw from this? How many of them are plausible, and how would we decide which of them is best?"

I expect that readers will not agree with much of what I say. Some things I consider clear will seem murky to you. In other places, you may think I am introducing ambiguity into provisions any child should understand. So be it. Constitution reading is, like baseball, an American national pastime. Kids love baseball because any American can stand up and boo the ump. Feel free to boo or cheer as we move along.

I do not aspire to be your teacher, but to be what Whitman would have called your *camerado*, a companion on the open road. We will wander through the Constitution, and loaf and invite our souls.

To paraphrase *Leaves of Grass*, do I contradict myself? Very well, I contradict myself. And if you contradict me, very well. For every atom belonging to me as good belongs to you.

ACKNOWLEDGMENTS

This project began as a private pursuit, with no notion of publication. I am grateful to David McBride of Oxford University Press for his willingness, two years later, to wade into the result and help carve an actual book out of it. His patience in shepherding the project cannot be overstated or overvalued. David's assistant, Sarah Rosenthal, read with a sharp eye and provided many valuable suggestions. I also got useful readings, in whole or part, from some of the people closest to me in my life: my son Daniel, my dear friends David Ignatius and David Schuman, my old friend and University of Baltimore colleague Elizabeth Samuels, and my prized ex-student, the brilliant Credence Sol. All their reactions were valuable, and some helped me avoid serious mistakes. Professor Paula Blank of the College of William and Mary helped me catch up on changes in literary theory in the years since I was an English major many years ago. Rafe Sagalyn, a friend of forty years' standing, gave me useful feedback on the vexing issues of publishing contracts.

One of the privileges of being a law professor is the chance to work with research assistants of diverse interests and broad talents, and many of them helped with this project over the years of its gestation. In particular, I thank Adam Lynn, Juliana Bell, Josh Swanner, and Taylor Novak at the University of Baltimore. Also at UB, Douglas Nivens, Class of 2013, was heroic in helping finish the project. Shavaun O'Brien, my assistant at UB, keeps everything running smoothly. The UB Law School supported me with a one-semester research leave, which I used by reading the Constitution over and over and then gazing at the ceiling.

Finally, I was lucky enough to be invited to speak on successive Constitution Days by the University of Cincinnati School of Law and by St. Mary's College of Maryland. Audiences on both occasions heard a variation of a talk called "What Does the Constitution Really *Say*?" Their reactions gave me a chance to work on some of the ideas herein, and to profit from the comments of an engaged audience of lawyers and laypeople.

American Epic

Preamble

"Tell me, Muse, how it all began"

"We the people." Whatever it is, it is not a statement of fact; and whatever else it is, it is also a distraction.

Many Americans remember nothing of the Constitution's Preamble but those words. They burst into the mind; they tell us we are reading no ordinary document, indeed not even an ordinary law. We are being addressed by ourselves, looking into our own faces; we are being welcomed to a party where we are not only honored guests but also hosts. Who remembers what is *said* at a party? Often we don't even remember the occasion—was it a birthday, a wedding? What we remember are smiling faces, warmth, and the feeling of belonging.

There are two problems with these words. First, the Constitution may not be in fact our party; and, second, in this context, both the occasion and the speeches matter as much as the glow of fellowship. The claim that "we" wrote the document is false. Someone has written a Constitution, and done so for specific reasons. We need to understand both hosts and occasion.

What is meant by "we the people"? In no real sense was the original Constitution written by the people. As every American schoolchild learns, the authors were a group of some fifty-five men, distinguished in the new nation by their wealth and prominence, meeting in the Pennsylvania State House in Philadelphia between May 25 and September 17, 1787. The "United States" already existed as a society and an independent country. In fact, the Convention was held in the eleventh year of Independence, the sixth since Britain had recognized American freedom as an accomplished fact.

The Convention assembled under conditions of strictest secrecy. The "people" were to take no part in the drafting; indeed, they were not even represented there. The delegates were sent by their individual state legislatures, and each state, whether tiny Delaware or mammoth Virginia, had one vote. The people had not summoned them; the convention had been called by the Congress, a body in which again the states, not the people, were represented. The people had no notice that the meeting would write a new constitution in their name; the formal purpose of the meeting was to "propose amendments" to the existing constitution, the Articles of Confederation.

No one was told that these men might, in contemporary terms, "go rogue" and write a new fundamental law. And when their work was done, they instructed (in Article VII) "the people" to approve or disapprove. No changes; no amendments. Just a simple "yes" or "no."

Nonetheless, they presumed to speak in the voice of "the people." The choice may have been adventitious. The first draft of the Preamble, reported by a committee on August 6, 1787, read, "We the people *of the States*," then listed each by name.[1]

That has a very different sound. More modest? Perhaps—though equally false. Not every state named in the draft was even present in Philadelphia. (Rhode Island scorned the Convention, and later was slow to ratify the Constitution.) Beyond that, what of those places that were not yet states? Would the Constitution have established an order of precedence, a sort of First Family of states, with others implicitly inferior? Would it have spoken as powerfully as it does to the people of Vermont, then independent, or Kentucky or Ohio, then being formed, or Louisiana or Oregon, undreamt of? The words "we the people" have a contemporary sound; in 1787 they were positively futuristic. The words, "we the people of the states" would instead have been archaic on the day of publication and would emphasize to any contemporary reader the historical distance between the Framing and today. Whatever impulse led the drafters to make the change has led to profound consequences, certainly in rhetoric and probably in politics. It was an inspired act of ventriloquism.

But it was more than pretense. It was aspirational. The Constitution is not a prayer—prayers are addressed to someone, a superior, either an earthly king or a divine lord, and great care is taken to name the addressee and less to characterize the speaker. The Preamble does the reverse. The speaker is "the people," the words are addressed to the world at large. But if not a prayer, what? Consider these words: "Goddess, sing the rage of Peleus' son, Achilles . . ."[2] Or these: "Tell me, Muse, how it all began."[3] These sound like prayers, addressed to Calliope, the Muse of poetry, who was herself a goddess. But they are in fact, just like "we the people," a deceptive claim of authorship. It is not I, the poet, who brings you the tale of Achilles and Hector, but Calliope herself. I did not see Aeneas's meeting with Dido in Hades, but Calliope surely did. In epic poetry, the poet speaks the Goddess's words; in constitution-making, the drafters speak to us in our own voice.

"We the people" are thus not precisely impersonated but invoked. The act is not one of imposture but of aspiration—let me speak in the voice of the Muse, let me give voice to the spirit of the people. In "By Blue Ontario's Shore," Walt Whitman writes of being accosted by a grim phantom (probably history):

> Chant me the poem, it said, that comes from the soul of America,
> chant me the carol of victory,
> And strike up the marches of Libertad, marches more powerful yet,
> And sing me before you go the song of the throes of Democracy.[4]

So successful has the Preamble's invocation been that the generations that came after have heard the words as their own, have come to believe the fiction that they gave birth to the Constitution, that it issued from, rather than being all but imposed upon, "the people." It has been too successful, in fact—for the Preamble was not only designed to give a kind of epic authorship to the Constitution but to spell out its purpose, to explain why "we the people" had brought it into being. Those purposes are as important as the invocation.

Therein lies the distraction. Quick—what are the purposes of the Constitution as laid out in the Preamble? Most people cannot recite them by memory. Here they are: "to form a more perfect union, establish justice, insure domestic tranquility, provide for the common defence, promote the general welfare, and secure the blessings of liberty to ourselves and our posterity." These purposes are as relevant as the claim of "authorship," but the brilliant rhetoric of "we the people" all too often dims their importance. This passage has some striking qualities that should bear on our understanding of the Constitution.

First and most important, they are national purposes. Americans often think of the Constitution as a defensive document, designed to shield "the people" against the reach of government and "the states" against federal authority. But where is either in the list of purposes? In fact, the purposes are active—"form, establish, insure, provide, promote, secure"; strong verbs that signify governmental power, not restraint. "We the people" are to be *bound*—into a stronger union. We will be *protected* against internal disorder—that is, against ourselves—and against foreign enemies. The "defence" to be provided is "common," general, spread across the country. The Constitution will *establish* justice; surely this means not merely the Aristotelian ideal of giving each her own, but a system of justice, courts, judges, and jails. The new Constitution will promote the "general" welfare, not welfare varying by condition or by place of residence. It will *secure* our liberties—against whom?

There's an ambiguity here; liberty could be secured against foreign enemies and domestic subversives, or against the new government itself. The latter interpretation is soothing to American ears; but in this context, it seems far-fetched. The clause appears in a list of things government is to do, not things it is not to do; a list of powers, not of prohibitions. The new government, it would appear, is not the enemy of liberty but its chief agent and protector.

The purpose then, in its most plausible reading, is to create a strong, active, national government, one whose benefits will flow directly to the people who create it. "Limited government" as an idea receives at best an incidental nod; the states are nowhere to be found. It would seem legitimate to interpret the rest of the Constitution *purposively*, as a remedial statute is interpreted in terms of the evil it seeks to remedy. If one interpretation of the document will further these national and public purposes more fully than another, we have no obligation to be "neutral" between them, or to finely parse the grammar of other constitutional provisions considered in isolation from the entire text. The purposes laid out in the Preamble are broad and general; but they are not meaningless. They might constitute for constitutional interpretation what Aristotle called "special topics" peculiar to a specific field of discourse, mental "places" that orators and advocates could visit to find subjects for their speeches and writings, means of persuasion directed at the particular audience. These "special topics" may not answer constitutional questions; but they can shape the way we ask them.

Some things are conspicuous by their absence from this list of topics. (Remember, we read poems by what they do not say as well as by what they do.) Constitutional historians often see the Constitution as first and foremost an economic or commercial pact, creating a continental free-trade zone and an authority that could regulate and foster the economy by coining money and protecting commerce. There is no question that such purposes were in the mind of the Framers in Philadelphia. From the oldest, the diplomat and commercial printer Franklin, to the youngest, the lawyer and land speculator Jonathan Dayton, these prosperous men were caught up in the world marketplace and aspired to extend its reach and ease impediments to its workings. (In that, as in other things, they were not fully representative of "we the people"; many Americans in 1787 lived on small landholdings, grew food crops, and sought no place in the thickening web of eighteenth-century global trade.)

But when they spelled out their purpose, "trade" and "prosperity" were not mentioned. The document's stated aims are wholly public, not private. "We the people" hope for justice, security, and liberty, not for wealth.

Another idea is strikingly absent. "All men are created equal," the Declaration of Independence had said. The Preamble makes no such claim. The new nation is to have security, order, law, liberty—but these things can exist without equality. In North America, vast inequalities by law were not only tolerated but enforced— between slave and free, between apprentice and master, between woman and man, between Native American and white, between "free black" and "free white." "We the people" show no disposition to disturb this state of affairs.

In fact, it is not just the Preamble but the entire Constitution of 1787 that is silent on the subject. Human equality as an explicit concept will not appear in the document until 1868, eight decades after the Federal Convention.

(The word "equal" appears in the Convention's Constitution, but it refers almost exclusively to equality among states.)

Finally, "we the people . . . *ordain* and *establish* this Constitution for the United States of America." The two words can be seen as boilerplate, like a lawyer's claim that his client did not commit fraud "in any way, shape, fashion, or form." But taken separately, the words have different connotations. "Ordination" is sacerdotal; priests and rabbis enter into their sacred functions by way of ordination. The Christian sacrament of ordination for many believers even today refers to a physical touch that brings in an unbroken chain the authority of Christ's own Apostles. To "ordain" a Constitution or a government is more than simply to set it up.

"Establish" is already making its second appearance in the Constitution. The people seek to "establish" justice, and in order to do so they do now—not in the future but at the moment they speak—"establish" the Constitution. To "establish" a government means to set it up; but it means something more, and in 1787 meant it even more strongly. "Establishment" referred to churches—more than half of the thirteen states had established churches, official links between God and the state supported by tax funds. Not very long before, established churches had enforced conformity with fire and the rope. Later the First Amendment would spell out that there was to be no national establishment—religious establishment, that is. The new Constitution, however, is brought to us by a Muse, ordained by the authority of the People, and established at the center of our common life. We can read these words as creating a national religion, one at which we still worship.

Surely the Preamble, no matter how scholars may grumble, is a poem. In 1950, the poet Charles Olson defined a poem as "energy transferred from where the poet got it . . . by way of the poem itself to, all the way over to, the reader . . . a high-energy construct and, at all points, an energy-discharge."[5] Beyond invoking the Muse, beyond specifying a purpose, the Preamble crackles with that "energy-discharge." As the lightning brings life to Frankenstein's monster, the Preamble quickens the structural provisions that follow.

In the beginning, the nation is without form and void. There is darkness; then someone speaks in our voice: *Let there be law.*

Article I

A Tale of Two Cities

"We the people" have spoken. Now it is the Framers' turn to speak as themselves. Article I is the longest and most complex in the Constitution, and in many ways it is the Philadelphia Framers' best work: intricate, self-confident, and far less tentative than their discussions of the presidency in Article II and the judiciary in Article III. Representative government, eighteenth-century political theory held, involved creating a kind of mirror that reflected the image of the people; Article I, which creates the representative body of the Constitution, Congress, is a kind of mirror of the United States. It is at once specific and lofty; it uses dry lawyers' language to evoke the future America it was designed to create.

Traditionally, where kings or tyrants did not govern, assemblies did. Ancient Athens, whose example all educated Americans revered, reposed power in an assembly of citizens. Until late in its history, the Roman Empire maintained the fiction that power lay in the Senate and was only delegated to figures like Augustus or Hadrian. Epic poems often begin with the story of what happened in assembly. *The Iliad* in particular depicts over and over the process of deliberation in a group.[1] Even Mycenaean kings were constrained to ask consent from their warrior-subjects and listen to their counsel, whether they were as wise as Nestor or as volatile as Achilles.

Before the Revolution, the colonies had been under the authority of the British Parliament. For as long as the United States had existed apart from Britain, it had been loosely governed by "the United States, in Congress assembled." Under the Articles of Confederation, there was no president and no federal courts.

Little wonder, then, that the legislative branch may have seemed to the Framers the most important to define. Article I sets up the structure and powers of the Congress, and in so doing offers not only a picture of America's assembly but of the nation it is assembled from.

Here is the structure: Sections One through Six set up the ways in which Congress is to be elected and empowers each House to set up its own internal structure. Section Seven describes how a legislative measure is to become law. Section Eight sets out an epic catalogue of congressional powers; Section Nine lists actions Congress is not permitted to take; and Section Ten lists things the states are not permitted to do, or may do only with congressional consent.

SECTION ONE. At the outset, words of limitation, or at least potential limitation, enter the document: "All legislative Powers herein granted shall be vested in a Congress of the United States, which shall consist of a Senate and House of Representatives." The words affirm, but they also possibly deny: powers are vested in Congress, but some powers somewhere are not "herein granted," though it does not say what they are or where we should look for them. Some powers are not legislative; they are not vested in Congress by the text. The text doesn't say that nonlegislative powers are not or could not be vested in Congress. It says only that if a power is legislative, it is vested in Congress. There could be legislative powers not "herein granted" that Congress *also* has. In this reading, the legislative powers "herein granted" would be *in addition* to the legislative powers that Congress, for whatever reason, already possesses. The reading is not a popular one; most interpreters think that the "herein" language signifies limitation and not addition. But the text does not say "All *and only* those powers herein granted."

In addition, what does "herein granted" mean? It begins Article I, and we could read it to mean all legislative powers granted in Article I, leaving legislative powers granted elsewhere in the Constitution up for grabs. This may seem like a very pernickety question. But consider that much of the constant warfare between Congress and the president in our system concerns whether certain presidential programs involve "legislation" by the executive—for example, in writing regulations to implement new government programs. Perhaps there are "legislative" powers granted in the president's article, Article II?

Article I could easily have said, "all legislative powers pertaining to the federal government." Elsewhere in Article I, we will learn, there is mention of powers that belong to the federal government but not to the Congress. In addition, there might be "implied" legislative powers, powers of lawmaking possessed by every government through its very existence as a government. If so, might they lie in other branches?

Could they be powers granted to no legislative body? That is one reading— powers that in the United States no government may have. If so, the Constitution offers little hint what they are (remember that at this point there was no Bill of Rights). The conclusion must depend on what each reader considers the implication of the words: are they words of limitation, or of empowerment? The Constitution does not pause—it moves forward to the internal organization of Congress.

SECTION TWO. First to be defined is the House of Representatives. In the Preamble, "We the people" were author and source of the Constitution. In setting up the House, the Constitution offers a definition of "the people" that owes nothing to the idea that "all men are created equal."

Only in the House do the people as such take part in government. The Senate will be chosen by state legislatures; the president by electors chosen by the legislatures. Alone among the branches of the new government, the House is to be elected by the "the People of the Several States." That is not precisely the same "people" as "We the People," though, because the states have the power to determine who belongs: "the Electors in each State shall have the Qualifications requisite for Electors of the most numerous Branch of the State Legislature." In other words, states would decide which of their own people could vote in state elections, and that choice would bind the federal government as well. If a voter could vote for the "most numerous Branch of the State Legislature," then he could vote for the House; if not, not.

States varied widely in what proportion of their population they chose to allow to vote. They could impose that choice on the federal government as well. Equivocal as it is, this is the only reference in the original Constitution to anything like a "right" to vote.

But no matter how many of their people the states chose to disfranchise, their representation in the House remained the same. Here the Constitution offers a picture of "the people" that snubs equality. Members of the House are to be awarded to states by "respective numbers," that is, population, not by number of voters or of citizens. Even today, noncitizens, including "illegal" aliens, are counted in the division of House seats among the states. In numbers, if not in votes, the House represents not states, not citizens, not voters, but natural persons.

But in Article I, the raw numbers of people within each state's borders go through a pernickety mathematical function before they yield political power:

> Representatives . . . shall be apportioned among the several States which may be included within this Union, according to their respective Numbers, which shall be determined by adding to the whole Number of free Persons, including those bound to Service for a Term of Years, and excluding Indians not taxed, three fifths of all other Persons.

Most Americans learn in school about the "three-fifths ratio." We take it quite properly as a sign of the racial hierarchy created by slavery. But the ratio is only part of a complex table of inequalities. Under Article I, those natural persons were divided into four classes: first came (1) "free persons," who were their own masters; to them were added (2) persons of the second class, those "bound to service for a term of years," meaning indentured servants and apprentices, who were not their own masters, not first-class persons, but who could expect to become so when their indentures expired. These were counted one for one.

The third class was (3) "Indians not taxed," which referred to the many Native people still living within the borders of the states under the authority of their own tribal governments (which by 1787 were in many places quite elaborate). These were under the nominal protection of the United States and had no relationship to state governments They were not counted at all.

Finally, (4) "other persons." We all know who they were—persons bound to service not for a "term of years" but for life, and for longer than life, because their status was hereditary. Slaves were to count at the ratio of three-fifths to one.

Where did this "federal ratio" come from? It was not in the Articles of Confederation—no need for it; each state there had one and only one vote in Congress. But it had been proposed by the Confederation Congress as an amendment to the Articles. It would provide a formula for deciding what share of the Confederation's expenses each state should pay. Under the Articles, each state's share was based on its wealth. Thus slave "property" would be counted just as real property would. The proposed amendment to the Articles was designed to shift allocation of contributions to population—but it would cut slave states a break by counting a slave as less than a free person, meaning a slave state's share of the contribution would be smaller. This proposal, though, had fallen afoul of the Articles' requirement that any amendment be unanimously approved.

The "federal ratio" was thus simply an idea that had been discussed. Now it was ensconced at the very basis of the new legislature. Giving states additional legislative representation for slaves was a very different thing from fine-tuning their financial obligations. (For one thing, many states under the Articles simply tore up the bills sent them by Congress anyway.) The three-fifths ratio now gave the slaveholding states more power, and that imbalance became a fixed feature of the new system.

Representation was important. It fixed the level of a state's influence, not merely in the House but, as we shall see, in the selection of the president. The Framers were scrupulous about ensuring that the states' levels of representation would be awarded based on their actual population. The British Parliament was apportioned with grotesque inequality. British authors like Anthony Trollope and William Makepeace Thackeray have great fun with these "rotten boroughs." Some of them would elect one Member even though there were fewer than a dozen qualified voters; giant cities would have only one Member, or even worse be lumped in with rural counties in a single district. That was not to happen in the new American system: the federal government was required to hold a census every ten years; a reapportionment according to the new "respective numbers" would ensue.

But House seats are not strictly apportioned by population, because every state has one. Today, if the entire nation were divided into equal House districts, each district would have roundly 700,000 residents. But Wyoming, with about 532,000 residents, gets one House seat even though in an equal apportionment it would not be entitled to one.

Even that limited principle of equal representation applied only between states. Nothing in Article I required the states to divide themselves into districts to elect representatives; they could, if they chose, elect them all at large. And if states did create congressional districts, they could certainly have made the districts unequal. That would be up to the state legislatures. The requirement of equal districting entered the picture much later, through the Fourteenth Amendment's norm of "equal protection."

The states define the qualifications of voters and create districts. But state legislatures and governors play no role in selecting representatives. When a seat falls vacant between elections, state governors are required to order special elections. Unlike the Senate, there can be no interim appointments.

Who may serve in the people's house? The requirements are specific: members must be twenty-five years old; they must have been a citizen for at least seven years; and they must be "inhabitants" (note that at law this is not necessarily the same as being a "resident") of the districts they represent. But note the peculiar language the Constitution uses to spell out these requirements: "No Person shall be a Representative who shall not" possess the specified qualifica tions. It does not say that anyone who does possess the qualifications may be a representative. In later years, some have argued that this means state governments may impose additional qualifications for members—most recently, in the case of state-imposed term limits. The more logical reason for the peculiar wording, however, is that it means that members of the House must be qualified voters in their states. This requirement would refer, as does the specification of who may vote in House elections, to the election laws of each state.

Obviously women, and slaves, could not vote and thus could not serve. But beyond this, in some states the vote was limited by property requirements; a citizen who could be a member of the House from one state might find himself ineligible if he moved to another.

All told, the new "people's house" was not very close to the people. When it was created, it existed against and reinforced a careful backdrop of legal and constitutional inequality, and empowered state governments to define the "people" who would elect it.

SECTION THREE. But even so, the House was more egalitarian than the Senate, in which the smallest state was equal to the largest, and the members were chosen by the political elites in both states. Senators from a state "chosen by the Legislature thereof." When Senate seats fell vacant, the governor could, if he chose, name a temporary replacement "until the next Meeting of the Legislature, which shall then fill such Vacancies."

Senators were (and still are) required to be thirty years old, to have been citizens for nine years, and to be "inhabitants" of the state they represent. They serve for six years, in staggered terms. This meant that at the outset some members of the first Senate would only receive two-year terms, others four-year terms, and others the full six years. In the provision empowering this division, the Constitution uses the term "equal" for the first time—the first Senate is to be divided "as equally as may be" into three groups.

Each House was given some authority over its own membership and affairs. Each would have "*sole* power" to determine whether a claimant to membership was eligible under the Constitution, and whether he had been duly elected. (Both bodies to this day must often adjudicate the disputed results of elections.) But in 1969, the Supreme Court held that the House could not add qualifications—in effect, by deciding that a duly elected candidate, who met the age, residency, and citizenship requirements was not morally fit to serve. If two-thirds voted to expel such a member, so be it; but a mere majority could not prevent him or her from taking a seat.[2]

The House was required to choose "a Speaker." This makes the leader of the House a constitutional officer—probably the most important in the legislative department. The Senate was to be led by the vice president, the first reference to that office. The vice president, unlike the Speaker, was not chosen by the members of the House he would lead. The Senate's top elected official was a second banana to a second banana: the Senate would choose a president pro tempore to preside when the vice president was absent—or when, it notes in highly ambiguous language, "he shall exercise the Office of President." It does not say, as we would think, when "he becomes President," but when he shall "exercise the office." (Right away, a kind of sullen, hangdog ambiguity begins to cloud the language describing the vice president.)

Article I also lays out the responsibility in cases of impeachment. The House has "sole Power of Impeachment," meaning that it alone can vote to require a trial of the impeached official on charges of the House's choice; the Senate has "sole Power to try" impeachments, meaning that the Senate sits as a court after the House has brought a successful impeachment. Note the limitations: the House may agree unanimously on an official's guilt; but all it can do is pass the decision on to the Senate. As a jury of sorts, the Senate may only decide whether the official is guilty of the offenses the House has charged; no matter what emerges during an impeachment trial, it cannot add new charges.

Senators sitting to hear articles of impeachment are required to take a special oath, emphasizing that they are acting in a judicial capacity. Two-thirds of the senators present must vote "aye" for any impeachment to be sustained. When the Senate sustains the House, it can assess only two penalties: removal from office and disqualification to hold any federal office again. An official successfully impeached, however, cannot plead double jeopardy against a subsequent trial in a regular court; the Constitution states that such a person is subject to "Indictment, Trial, Judgment, and Punishment, according to Law."

Impeachment was not a remedy solely directed at the president. Parliament had used the device of impeachment to strike at the king's ministers, and even (once) the queen. The text shows that impeachment is available against other officials: "the Chief Justice shall preside" over any trial of a *presidential* impeachment. The reason is obvious—the vice president, as president of the Senate, would otherwise be in charge of a proceeding that might let him take the president's place. So since the chief justice presides only when the president is a defendant, clearly others may be impeached—exactly who is laid out later in the Constitution.

SECTION FOUR. States were, in the first instance, to have authority to conduct congressional elections; but the Framers reserved to Congress the power to "make or alter such Regulations." Congress has since set one uniform day for congressional elections around the country. As long as state legislatures elected senators, however, the Constitution prohibited Congress from specifying when legislatures must meet to choose new ones. State legislative sessions are usually fixed by state law, and a congressional power to schedule them might have permitted future Congresses more control over the state legislatures than they needed.

One of the most important and least well designed sections of the Constitution requires that "Congress shall assemble at least once in every Year, and such Meeting shall be on the first Monday in December." By writing a required annual meeting into the Constitution, the Framers sought to forestall a situation in which a president would prevent Congress from meeting. However, by so doing, they inadvertently created a deeply problematic timetable for the new government. The December date is the only one prescribed in the original Constitution for any governmental function. Congress is allowed to vary this date; but it did not do so, even though the December date fit weirdly into the timeline that grew up after the Constitution was ratified.

The Constitution was proposed in the fall of 1787, and the process of ratification by state conventions took until late in 1788. (North Carolina did not finally ratify until the fall of 1789, by which time Washington had taken office; Rhode Island held out until the spring of 1790, and the new state of Vermont ratified in early 1791.) Once ratification began to seem likely, the Continental Congress passed a statute setting up a timetable for beginning the new government. Members of Congress were elected at various times as set by their sending states. The presidential electors were to be selected on January 7, 1789; the electors would select the president on February 4; and the new government was to begin a month later, with the new bicameral Congress taking office on March 4, 1789. Technically the president's term began then, although the electoral votes were not counted before a joint session until April 6, 1789, designating George Washington as president; logistical delays prevented Washington from formally beginning his term until April 30.[3]

After that, the March 4 date, even though set by a statute and not the Constitution, took on constitutional significance. The president serves a "Term of Four Years." Washington's first term had to end exactly four years after it began, and so on, quadrennium by quadrennium. The same was true of members of Congress.

Meanwhile, the Congress was elected in the fall of every even-numbered year and was to meet each December. But members elected in November did not take office until March. As a result, the Constitution required a meeting of the existing Congress in December of each even-numbered year even though its successor had already been chosen during the previous fall. And that new Congress, chosen in the fall of even-numbered years, was not required to meet until December of the next odd-numbered year, more than a year after it had been selected.

This strange timetable made the new government a more rickety affair than it need have been. The departing Congress and president, even if repudiated by the voters, met in what came to be known as the "lame duck" Congress. These departing officials might make important decisions in December which, in the normal course, the new Congress and president would not have a chance to address until a year later. This problem could have been averted had the Framers specified the timetable more closely. But in fact the Constitution did give Congress the power "by Law appoint a different day." It didn't do so, probably because of a combination of institutional inertia, the growing reverence for constitutional text—and the fact that it was much safer for politicians to schedule legislative sessions months before elections, giving voters time to forgive and forget before they had to vote.

SECTION FIVE. Each House of Congress was given wide authority to govern its internal matters. Though the Constitution required a majority of members as a quorum to do official business, it allowed each House to set "a smaller Number" to close meetings, or to convene and then demand (by force if necessary, as was often the case in the early history of parliaments) that members attend. Each house would be the final judge of election results for its seats; but once a member was seated, he (or she) could only be expelled by a two-thirds vote. Each house could also set its own rules and discipline its own members in unspecified ways short of expulsion.

Neither house was required to conduct its business in public. Parliament by tradition met in secret, and to publish what was said in its sessions was punishable by law. The eighteenth-century British essayist Samuel Johnson for years earned his living by reconstructing debates in Parliament from smuggled notes. Disguised as the debates of the Parliament of "Lilliput," these appeared in *The Gentleman's Magazine* and were almost the only reports the British public received of what their government was up to.

Legislative secrecy was considered a requirement of good government, at least for some things. (The Constitution itself had been drafted under conditions of strict secrecy; Washington himself on one occasion berated the Philadelphia delegates when one had been careless with his papers, risking a leak.) The two houses have come to hold most of their sessions in public, broadcast on television for all to see; but the Constitution does not require them ever to do so. They had to maintain a journal of their actions and votes, though they could omit "such Parts [of their proceedings] as may in their Judgment require Secrecy" and they must, if one-fifth of the members present asked, publish their individual votes in the journal.

By the terms of the text, even some votes could be kept secret, though they would have to be recorded in the journal. Some scholars have found in the Constitution a preference for openness in government. Wherever they find it, it is not in Article I.

SECTION SIX. Judges, lawyers, and ordinary people are fond of suggesting that the Constitution sets up a system of "separation of powers." That phrase appears nowhere in the Constitution and is contradicted by a number of its provisions. But the Framers did take steps to ensure that Congress was protected from other branches for its official actions. The immunities and disabilities in Section Six are far more important in maintaining our system than many other provisions often cited as key to the "separation of powers."

To begin with, members are paid by "the Treasury of the United States" (not, as the delegates to the Confederation Congress were, "kept" by their sending state governments). They are federal officials, and their pay is "ascertained by Law," thus publicly known. No legislative leader or executive official can reward or penalize members of Congress for their actions by withholding pay or adding benefits. Members of Congress vote (even if the session was held in secret, the votes would be made public) on their own salaries and are held to account for them. (The accountability requirement would much later be strengthened by the Twenty-Seventh Amendment.)

Next, they cannot be arrested for any but the most serious crimes while attending sessions or going to and fro. This immunity protects Congress from both the president and the courts. It was the upshot of centuries of battle between the English Crown and Parliament. At the outset of the English Civil War, for example, Charles I entered Parliament with the intention of arresting five dissenting Members who were thought to be planning a bill of impeachment against the queen. (Forewarned, the five hid themselves, and the king said, "I see the birds have flown.")[4] In the new republic, the birds can roost in Congress, no matter how unwelcome they might be to those outside it.

No one can drag members before a court or a grand jury and force them to account for their actions; "for any Speech or Debate in either House, they shall not be questioned in any other Place." In the English Bill of Rights, this principle of immunity was known as "freedom of speech," a right guaranteed to Parliament rather than to individuals.[5] Even if lawmakers question the actions of individuals or government actors in libelous or even quasi-treasonable terms, this "freedom of speech" confers absolute immunity on members for anything they say on the floor of either house and has been interpreted to cover also most functions directly related to lawmaking. Neither the executive, the judiciary, nor any private party can punish a member for official actions, or even force upon one the burden and expense of defending against indictment or civil suit.

But important as these immunities are, they are dwarfed in importance by the disability contained in the next part of the section. No member of Congress, according to its terms, can (1) accept a federal appointment during his term of office if the job had been created during the term, or if its salary had been increased; or (2) accept "any Office under the United States" while remaining a member.

The second disability at a stroke outlaws the parliamentary system of the British Constitution. Every member of the British government is also a member of Parliament, representing some constituency in the kingdom. Parliament itself thus forms the government and controls its function and existence. A majority in Parliament may dismiss any minister, including the prime minister, at any time by majority vote; a majority in Parliament may control the government's actions from day to day.

In the new United States government, this is impossible. Officials must be flesh or fowl, legislative or executive, and never both at once. A member of Congress appointed to the Cabinet must leave Congress at once, and vice versa. And beyond that, executive officers need not be members and cannot be removed from office by defeat in a local election. This is a wide structural gulf between the two branches, matching the structural protection for the judiciary erected in Article III by life tenure and senatorial confirmation. (Another provision of Article I also takes aim at the parliamentary system. Members of both House and Senate must be "inhabitants" of the states they represent. In Britain, then and now, parliamentarians need not ever have set foot in their constituencies, and the party leaders dole out the "safe seats" to their favorites. In Article I, the representatives must at least come from the places they represent.)

The first part of the disability was only slightly less important to an eighteenth-century American. To us, the word "corruption" has a wide variety of meanings, including private bribery and embezzlement of public funds. To British subjects at that time, however, one primary meaning of the word concerned the means by which the king and his ministers in Whitehall controlled Parliament. The Crown had an inexhaustible supply of lucrative offices and pensions to be distributed to members of Parliament who complied with the royal wishes. Parliament could also create well-paid new offices, to which members might then be appointed. "How potent the influence of royal patronage was, may be gauged from the fact that in the first Parliament of George I, no less than 271 members held offices or pensions," one historian notes.[6]

In the new Republic, the lure of lucrative office was to be diminished. A member offered a patronage plum must leave office to take it, and could not do so if he had voted to create it or enrich its holder. Although in making and administering the laws Congress and the executive might clash or cooperate, each tub of the new system would have to rest on its own bottom.

SECTION SEVEN. A generation of viewers has grown up with the "Schoolhouse Rock" version of Section Seven, which describes how a bill becomes a law. Once again, the branches are not separated; in fact, the legislative process entangles them in an intricate dance.

To begin with, there is a rather half-hearted gesture toward the House as "the people's house," giving it the sole power of originating bills authorizing the spending of money. Since the fifteenth century, the British Commons had asserted the sole right to originate taxation and spending measures, which could be disapproved but not amended by the House of Lords. The House of Representatives receives a pale shadow of this right: since "the Senate may propose or concur with Amendments as on other Bills," it thus is a coequal in the budgeting process.

After this, there is the familiar process by which bills become law. Both houses must pass a bill, which must then be "presented" to the president for his approval. He may sign it, in which case it is entered into law. But the president may "return" the bill (what we call "veto" it) for any reason whatsoever. He must, however, explain why he is doing so. The explanation goes in a message to the house that passed it. After consideration of his message (they must "enter the Objections at large on their Journal") that house may re-pass it by a two-thirds margin. This vote must be recorded. If it passes again, they send it on to the other house. If both houses re-pass by two-thirds, the bill becomes law without any presidential action; if not, the bill fails. Congress may not finesse the president's veto by calling a measure something other than a bill, for the requirement of "presentment" applies to "Every Order, Resolution, or Vote to which the concurrence of the Senate and House of Representatives may be necessary except on a question of Adjournment."

The presentment clause would not permit a president to veto his own impeachment or that of one of his appointees—matters of impeachment, involving the adoption of Articles by the House (without Senate concurrence) and trial by the Senate (without House concurrence) do not involve any legislative measure "to which the Concurrence of the Senate and House of Representatives may be necessary."

The presidential veto is at once weaker and more powerful than the king's asserted "negative" on parliamentary bills. The king's veto was absolute—but that made it such a potent weapon that kings had been forced to stop using it. Because Congress could theoretically override a presidential veto, however, it seemed less drastic an action than an absolute veto. Nonetheless, the requirements of re-passage are strict—so much so that, by most estimates, no presidential veto of a substantive bill was overridden until 1866, when Congress re-passed the Civil Rights Act over Andrew Johnson's veto.

The presidential veto provision is justly hailed as one of the Constitution's "checks and balances" (another phrase that appears nowhere in the Constitution). "Checks and balances" are the antithesis of "separation of powers." To political theorists, "separation of powers" means each branch must remain utterly independent of the other—the legislature passing laws without any participation by the executive, the executive enforcing laws without participation of legislators, the courts adjudicating cases without reviewing the validity of laws. To the eye of a theorist, our system would not seem to embody "separation" at all, but something closer to the untidy British concept of "mixed government."

The Constitution nowhere speaks of three separate "branches" of the federal government. Branches—separate stalks diverging wholly from a common root or place—is a metaphor about government. Like all metaphors, it may mislead us as we make a functional analysis of what the text actually says. Is the federal government divided neatly into three and only three branches, into one of which every part must fit?

The Constitution does mention the word "branch" once, but in a different context. Voters for the House are voters for "the most numerous Branch" of a state legislature. That's a slightly different use of the word—both houses of a state legislature are legislative in nature, and so their division into branches says nothing about the division between legislative, executive, and judicial. When speaking of the latter functions of the federal government, they are identified as "powers"—"all legislative powers" (Article I), "the executive power" (Article II), and "the judicial power of the United States" (Article III). In some places, the Constitution imposes separation of these powers; in others, it commands intermixing. If we were to begin discussing them as "the web of powers," that metaphor might free us from some old misconceptions.

The diction of this section is quite lawyerlike and fussy—more statutory than poetic. (When we come to Article V and the question of whether a president can veto a proposed constitutional amendment, however, we will see that the lawyer's reading does not always trump a broader interpretation, in keeping with the document's nature as a people's constitution, not a statute.) The veto's intricacies seem designed to level the playing field so that neither Congress nor the president can outflank the other. The president can't hold onto a bill until Congress adjourns. He has ten days to sign it or "return" it with "objections"; if he does neither, it becomes law. Congress can't finesse the president by sending over a bill and adjourning. In that case, the president has what has come to be called a "pocket veto"—he simply refuses to sign, and the bill lapses. Finally, Congress can't get around the "presentment" clause by calling a bill something else—a "joint resolution," for example. If a measure requires "the Concurrence of the Senate and House of Representatives," it must be "presented." The sole exception is a joint measure to adjourn Congress, in which the president takes no part. If a president could veto a decision to adjourn, he could simply keep Congress in session until it did his bidding.

SECTION EIGHT. Important though the structural provisions are, the heart of Article I lies in Section Eight. Article I is the longest article in the Constitution; Section Eight is the longest section. Lawyers, and judges adjudicating cases, parse Section Eight clause by clause, like pathologists dissecting a corpse—does a given assertion of congressional power fit under the "interstate commerce" clause, the "intellectual property" clause, the bankruptcy clause, or some other? Such an inquiry is necessary if we are to understand Section Eight as law, which must of necessity contain limitations as well as extensions. But it is poetry as well as law, and before dismembering the cadaver we should read it once and appreciate it as a living whole.

Its language is not disjunctive but inclusive; it is a list but also a catalogue. The Constitution by and large cloaks its epic ambitions in sparse language; but Section Eight, which lists Congress's textual powers, has a cadence and scope that make it in the reading something more than a list of specific functions. Whitman, three-quarters of a century after the writing of the Constitution, limned the society that had grown up under its protective aegis:

I HEAR America singing, the varied carols I hear,
Those of mechanics, each one singing his, as it should be, blithe and
      strong,
The carpenter singing his, as he measures his plank or beam,
The mason singing his, as he makes ready for work, or leaves off work,
The boatman singing what belongs to him in his boat, the deckhand
      singing on the steamboat deck,
The shoemaker singing as he sits on his bench, the hatter singing as he
      stands;

The wood-cutter's song, the ploughboy's, on his way in the morning, or at
the noon intermission, or at sundown,
The delicious singing of the mother, or of the young wife at work, or of
the girl sewing or washing,
Each singing what belongs to her, and to none else,
The day what belongs to the day—at night, the party of young fellows,
robust, friendly,
Singing with open mouths their strong melodious songs.[7]

In the taciturn context of the Constitution, Section Eight's 430 words loom
like the entire 1855 edition of *Leaves of Grass*, which in nearly 100 pages tried
to both capture and reconstitute the American nation in all its aspects, from the
commercial to the military to the sexual. *Leaves of Grass* drew its inspiration
from one of the most powerful lyric poems ever produced, the section in Book
18 of *The Iliad* that describes the miraculous armor forged by the fabricator-god
Hephaestus for the great warrior Achilles.

In 140 lines, Homer describes this shield as containing "a world of gorgeous
immortal work," which depicts not only heaven and earth but the entire civilization
of Ancient Greece. There are two cities. One, the city of peace, contains peaceful
scenes from "weddings and wedding feasts" to meetings of law courts, from farmers
tilling "broad rich plowland" to young girls "crowned with a bloom of fresh gar-
lands." The other city, the city of war, is replete with scenes of combat and devasta-
tion, "a divided army gleaming in battle-gear" in a struggle where "Strife and Havoc
plunged in the fight, and violent Death." Together, these two cities encompass all of
human life, and they are surrounded by "the Ocean River's mighty power."[8]

As the shining silver shield reflected the Greek world, Section Eight reflects
the Framers' ideal commonwealth. Like Achilles's shield, it depicts two cities—
in this case, we might call them the city of trade and the city of war. Trade governs the first half of the powers: to borrow money, regulate commerce, establish
uniform rules for bankruptcies, coin and regulate money and punish counterfeiting; warfare governs the second half—the powers to declare war, commission privateers, capture and punish pirates, establish and maintain an army and a
navy, and to call and regulate the militia.

There are a few powers that do not fit easily into either city. The clause permitting "an uniform rule of naturalization" gave Congress only partial control over
the entry of immigrants. Is that economic or military regulation? Interestingly
enough, during the nineteenth century the federal courts annexed this limited
power to the city of war; without much textual support, the "naturalization
clause" was construed to confer "plenary power" on Congress to admit, include,
or expel any noncitizens it chooses—the reason being that foreign civilians, like
foreign troops, were potentially invading and conquering forces.

Also midway between the two cities, Congress is given the power to govern federal territory. This is in part a military power—it extends to military property within the states—but it is also the power to create a city, which is called "such District (not exceeding Ten miles square) as may, by cession of particular States, and the Acceptance of Congress, become the Seat of Government of the United States." This power extends in both cases only to land within a state that is sold or ceded by the state to Congress.

Under this provision, Congress governs an empire of military installations around the country; but the "seat of government" power gave rise, in time, to the thriving city of Washington, DC, which is not a fort or stockade but a complete civilian city-state. It exists uneasily within the Union as a federal enclave, as completely under congressional control as is Elmendorf Air Force Base or the island of Guam, with no rights of congressional representation.

America since 1787 has acquired a vast continental empire that was not part of the United States when the Constitution was framed. Nothing in Article I, Section 8 applies directly to this territory. The power to govern forts and the seat of government specifically refers to the territory it covers as being ceded to the Union by individual states. A later provision in Article IV obliquely confers a power to "make all needful Rules and Regulations respecting Territory or other Property belonging to the United States." But it does not make clear that Congress can *acquire* such territory from other countries rather than from states, or govern it once acquired. This was a constitutional problem for President Thomas Jefferson, as we will see.

Having divided the powers into these three piles, let us look carefully at the two largest ones. First, the city of trade. Congress can borrow money to buy and sell; it can create a currency by which commerce can be carried on, issuing both coin and "securities," and punishing counterfeiting of both. It can regulate the weights and measures by which items are bought and sold, and it can maintain the road and postal network by which they are shipped; and, finally and most important, it can "regulate Commerce with foreign Nations, and among the Several States, and with the Indian Tribes."

It's customary for lawyers and judges to pull these powers apart, speaking of, say, "the Indian commerce power," or "the borrowing power." Again, this sort of taxonomic aggressiveness is part of what we pay them for. But the economic powers granted in Section Eight can also be read to form a seamless whole. This might be called *the power to create an economic system*, complete with money, credit, transport, and communications; to operate within the states to create "post offices and post roads" as a means of knitting the country into one economy; and to prescribe rules for commerce between any of the actors, inside the country or outside. Congress seems to be not only the arbiter but the creator of the new economic unit, not only the center but the spinner of the web.

That central agency is augmented by what has come to be misleadingly called "the intellectual property clause," which is worth quoting in full: "To promote the Progress of Science and Useful Arts, by securing for limited Times to Authors and Inventors the exclusive Right to their respective Writings and Discoveries." This is the only clause in Section Eight to have an explanatory preamble; that language seems to refer to a kind of general interest in knowledge and progress as much as to the money that was to be made from patents and copyrights. And there is no suggestion that these limited rights are *property*, as we now assume copyright and patent rights to be.

In the absence of this clause, Congress might have had *more* power in this area than it does with the clause. Monopolies are certainly regulations of commerce, and nothing anywhere else in the Constitution *forbids* the new government to grant monopolies and copyrights, of indefinite term if it chose. Under the clause and its preamble, however, Congress seems to be required to grant them only for "limited times"; to grant them not to its favorites, but to the "authors and inventors" themselves; and perhaps to grant them not as a means of enriching favored private parties but only if such a grant will "promote . . . progress."

Thus the city of trade, which seems to be one nation rather than a complex of quasi-independent republics. The map of Congress's city of war is more detailed and complex. It centers around the power to "declare war." It is customary to call it the "war power," but it is not the power to "make war," which would take in the power to initiate, direct, and conclude armed conflict. Declarations of war are now obsolete, thanks to the United Nations Charter—but in their time they were a formal legal declaration that a "state of war" existed between two powers, triggering certain rights and obligations on both sides. Congress had that legal authority; but it is not precisely the same as having the exclusive authority to decide on, plan, and carry out military operations. The Constitution nowhere bestows or withholds the power to "make war," which has given rise to long and bitter infighting between the president and Congress.

The king of England, by contrast, was generally understood to have the authority to "make war," from the decision to attack to the power to conclude peace, without the concurrence of Parliament. Even today, the prime minister of Britain can take the United Kingdom to war without a parliamentary vote; it is considered the government's "prerogative" to decide on war and peace. Parliament participates only by voting or withholding funds to carry on military operations. Only part of that prerogative power was given to Congress.

Probably more central than the power to "declare war" is the power "to raise and support Armies" and "to provide and maintain a Navy." Of all the Constitution's provisions, in 1789 this one was probably the most radical and shocking. There was no limitation of this power; Congress can (as we now take for granted) maintain an army and a navy in time of peace as well as of war. That was a drastic change from the Articles, which took for granted that all military forces would be raised by states, not the Confederation—and which strictly forbade even states to maintain "any body of forces . . . in time of peace" except for a citizen militia.

Standing armies were anathema to eighteenth-century republicans, seen as agents of the Crown against the people. Under the Constitution, however, Congress could raise, maintain, and govern an army in peacetime, so long as its appropriation of funds to do so did not extend for more than two years at a time. Equally startling was the power to transfer into federal hands command of the state militias "to execute the Laws of the Union, suppress Insurrections and repel Invasions." This sweeping grant of power meant that federalized militia could be used to subdue not only invaders and lawbreakers but also recalcitrant state governments—even in time of peace. (In 1957, Arkansas governor Orval Faubus sent the Arkansas National Guard into Little Rock to block court-ordered desegregation of Central High School. President Eisenhower, with the stroke of a pen, transferred the Guard to federal control and commanded it to protect the black students rather than block them.) The Constitution put a sword into the hands of the federal government, and gave Congress the power to fund and govern its use.

Even when the state militia was not directly placed under federal authority, it remained at least partially under congressional authority. Congress has the power to govern its organization, its armament, and its discipline by national rules. The states, however, have two subordinate powers into which the federal authority cannot reach: first, the power to appoint the officers of the militia and, second, the power to carry out the discipline ordered by Congress when the militia is not directly under federal authority. The first power, "the Appointment of the Officers" of the militia, is notable for another reason—it is the only power mentioned anywhere in the Constitution expressly given to states and expressly barred to the federal government. Many people over the years have interpreted the Constitution to oust federal authority over wide areas of government; it seems worth mentioning that the text itself ousts it only in this one small area.

All in all, both in the city of war and in the city of trade, Congress is given what might be seen as a tapestry of powers; they are legislative because they permit Congress to make rules for carrying on war and commerce, not to carry out either directly. But they indicate a legislative body with comprehensive authority in these two areas.

This interpretation is given strength by two clauses of Section Eight that we have not yet considered, but that form a frame around the enumerated powers (as "the Ocean River's mighty power" ran around the rim of Achilles's "indestructible shield") and seem to underline not their limitation but their extent.

At the beginning of the catalogue of congressional powers comes this oracular phrase: "The Congress shall have Power To lay and collect Taxes, Duties,

Imposts and Excises, to pay the Debts and provide for the common Defence and general Welfare of the United States; but all Duties, Imposts and Excises shall be uniform throughout the United States." This can be read two ways, depending on the meaning given to the comma after the word "excises." Either reading gives Congress wide discretion in the type and amount of taxes it imposes, as long as they are "uniform." The first reading would be that the power to tax is a separate power from three subsequent powers, the powers to "pay the debts," to "provide for the common defence," and to "promote the general welfare." If these are in fact separate powers, then they dwarf the specific grants in the rest of Section Eight. Virtually any domestic measure may "promote the general welfare." The specific powers thus would be simply examples to show the kinds of actions Congress could take—in the city of war, to "provide for the common defence" and in the city of trade "to promote the general welfare."

That interpretation is far-fetched. The entire clause seems more like a grant of *taxing* power coupled with a limitation requiring that Congress tax only for genuinely public purposes—paying the nation's debts rather than private ones; defending the entire community; and benefiting all, not just a few.

Even in this limited reading, the "tax and spend" clause is a sweeping endorsement of congressional discretion. It seems to endorse any kind of tax or fee, as long as it is "uniform throughout the United States"—meaning, most plausibly, uniform in every section, not uniform for every citizen. The only requirement is that Congress decree that it is acting for the public good—hardly an onerous requirement.

More sweeping still is the auxiliary power enumerated in the last clause of Section Eight: "To make all Laws which shall be necessary and proper for carrying into Execution the foregoing Powers, and all other Powers vested by this Constitution in the Government of the United States, or in any Department or Officer thereof." This is a broad grant in two ways. First, even if a power is not granted to Congress in Article I, Congress may still further it by legislation if the Constitution entrusts it to any branch of the federal government. (The most obvious example of such a power is "the judicial power of the United States," granted to the judiciary by Article III. Congress can clearly, under the "necessary and proper" clause, pass legislation to further the jurisdiction of the federal courts and enforce their judgments, even though Article I makes no mention of such a power. A clear example is 28 U.S.C. Section One, which creates the Supreme Court. Nothing in Article I, Section Eight gives Congress the power to set up a Supreme Court, but the power has to exist if there is to a be a Court into which "the judicial power" can be vested.)

Second, it amplifies the enumerated powers by use of expansive language. Necessity and propriety are, by and large, in the eye of the legislator. Debate over the meaning of this clause broke out within the new government almost immediately and persists to this day; but it is more often read as an endorsement of implied powers than as a limitation of the enumerated ones. The first and in some ways still most famous example was the power of chartering a bank, which Chief Justice Marshall found warranted under the "necessary and proper" clause as a means of furthering the power to regulate commerce.[9]

But though the "necessary and proper" clause is expansive, there are still powers Section Eight does not include. Unlike the shield in Homer, Congress's shield does not explicitly comprise all of human life: most conspicuously missing is any reference to "The delicious singing of the mother—or of the young wife at work—or of the girl sewing or washing"; any reference, that is, to the private realm of family, child-rearing, and sexuality that the eighteenth century identified as the realm of women. But other subjects are missing too: education, health, morality, and all the realm of what we today call "the quality of life" or "the tone of society." What does this silence mean? Is it a silent instruction that Congress is to confine itself to specified matters and leave those not mentioned to the states exclusively? Here our mode of reading may matter quite a bit. "Affirmatio unio exclusio alterius est" (*to affirm one thing is to exclude all others*) is a common maxim of statutory construction. Fundamentalist biblicism often finds prohibition in silence. Broader forms of reading might consider the entire context of Article I, noting that there are actual specific prohibitions elsewhere in the document, and conclude from the language of the "general welfare" and "necessary and proper" clauses that Congress's powers are not to cabined by silence. The answer a reader reaches will often depend on that reader's underlying view of America—on the picture that reader sees in Achilles's shield.

SECTION NINE. Section Eight and Section Nine are both poetic; but their poetics are quite different. In its inviting anaphora, Section Eight echoes the Sermon on the Mount; Section Nine by contrast is stern and forbidding, remotely echoing the prohibitory tone of the Ten Commandments. Here are things Congress is absolutely not to do. The prohibitions of Section Nine are not, however, areas of life or law that are declared off limits; nothing in this section takes any area of life or law away from Congress and explicitly reserves it to the states. The prohibitions do not relate to forbidden ends. Instead, Section Nine forbids to Congress certain specific means of achieving its ends.

The first prohibition is now obsolete but was important at the time. Before 1808, Congress may not prohibit "The Migration or Importation of such Persons as any of the States now existing shall think proper to admit." As always when the 1787 Constitution speaks of "persons," it is an evasive euphemism. These "persons" are slaves, and the trade in human beings could not be forbidden for the first twenty years of the new republic. "Migration" and "importation" may simply reflect lawyers' tendencies to double language; but they can also be construed to refer to the *international* slave trade ("importation" being the locution for the forcible kidnapping and sale of Africans from their home countries) and the *domestic* slave trade ("migration" delicately referring to the transfer by force of humans already in the United States to new masters).

There is a curious feature to this prohibition, one that appears nowhere else in the document: it makes a distinction in power among states. States that have already been formed ("now existing") retain the privilege of importing slaves; but Congress could apparently bar the movement of slaves into or out of *new* states created by Congress after the formation of the Union. (The Confederation Congress had already barred the entry of slaves into the Northwest Territory.)

All in all, the "migration or importation" clause has a double quality. On the one hand, as was noted at the time, it represented a generous concession to the deep South states, which feared that their interests would lose any fair political battle after ratification; on the other, it is phrased in a narrow, circuitous, and grudging way, as if passively (and inadequately) to express the Constitution's disapproval of the vile institution it was protecting here and elsewhere.

The next prohibition isn't explicitly directed at Congress—it says that "the Privilege of the Writ of Habeas Corpus *shall not be suspended*" (presumably by any governmental actor) unless required by the public safety in "Cases of Rebellion or Invasion." The naming of these two conditions has given rise to a controversy about whether habeas corpus could be suspended in the absence of either. What if no invasion has occurred, but one might? What if small groups of domestic terrorists are threatening attacks that don't amount to "rebellion"? But the larger and more enduring controversy arises out of the impersonal prohibition. The clause does not *create* an individual right to habeas corpus or *give* the government the power to suspend that right; both right and power seem to be taken for granted.

Assuming the constitutional predicates are met, who is entitled to suspend? The most obvious reading would be that the power lies in Congress (note that if so, it is a legislative power not "herein granted," one preexisting or arising out of the very nature of a national legislative body). As history has unfolded, however, the asserted demands of "rebellion or invasion" and of other domestic emergency have led the president to claim the power for himself. In the most famous cases in American history, Abraham Lincoln (who was dealing with open rebellion) repeatedly suspended the writ on his own authority and even defied a writ issued by the chief justice. Lincoln then asked Congress at its next meeting to ratify his actions, which it did. In the most recent case, by contrast, George W. Bush asserted the power to suspend without need for Congress; he agreed to seek legislative consent only after the Supreme Court rejected his claim of sole power.

In any case, there seems little doubt that the Framers understood a legislature to have the power to suspend (as Parliament had done) and sought to restrict but not eliminate it.

The next prohibition addresses two other legislative means of oppression. Unlike the suspension clause, it is textually aimed at Congress, because it forbids passage of one kind of bill and another kind of law. A "bill of attainder" was a parliamentary device by which an individual was named, adjudged guilty, and punished by the legislature itself in a statute. Often attainder brought with it the death penalty and "corruption of blood," which barred the attainted person from passing on his estate by inheritance or bequest.

Attainder was a tempting and elegant tool for parliamentary majorities to use against their opponents. But the new Congress was not to have this power, and the state legislatures are barred from attainder by Section Ten.

Matching the prohibition on attainder is the ban on "ex post facto" laws, meaning laws that make conduct illegal after the fact that had been legal when done. The bare words don't clearly limit this ban to criminal statutes; but they do appear in a provision aimed at limiting the severity of criminal statutes, and courts have limited the prohibition to criminal matters. (States are also barred in Section Ten from passing ex post facto laws.)

The mysterious phrase "direct tax" reappears here, in a context that makes its meaning even less clear than it was in Section Two. "No Capitation, or other direct Tax" is to be imposed by Congress unless it is in proportion to the census. Remember that Section Eight was extraordinarily permissive about the kinds of taxation the new Congress could assess. If they are "direct taxes," however, they must be in proportion to population.

Under the Articles, Congress had no taxing power. It was limited to sending bills to each individual state for that state's share of "the charges of war, and all other expenses that shall be incurred for the common defence or general welfare." Each state's bill was to vary according to "the value of all land within each state" that was in private hands, as estimated by Congress. These bills, which were called "requisitions," were not taxes on the states, because there was no mechanism to force states to pay them. They weren't taxes on individuals, because the Articles did not say they had to be *collected* by the states from the owners of the land; the states were only obligated to furnish an amount of money in proportion to the value of the land, however they chose to raise it.

So "direct taxes" could mean taxes directly on the states—converting an Articles-style "requisition" into a demand on the state. Or it could mean a tax laid on property owners in proportion to the property they owned. That is a plausible meaning, considering that the phrase differentiates between "direct" taxes and "capitation tax." The latter is a "head tax," an equal tax to be paid by every adult regardless of wealth or property (what came to be known in the segregated South as a "poll tax"). Would an income tax, which falls directly on individuals, be a "direct tax"?

The Supreme Court was later to hold that the Constitution did not grant Congress the power to tax individual incomes unless the tax was proportioned by state population, which would make the tax inequitable and unworkable; that was changed in 1913 by the Sixteenth Amendment, which granted Congress the power "to lay and collect taxes on incomes, from whatever source derived, without apportionment among the several States, and without regard to any census or enumeration."

No mystery surrounds the next prohibition, against laying any tax or duty on exports. "Duties, Imposts, and Excises" on imports were textually permitted; indeed, until the outbreak of the Civil War, those protective taxes on foreign goods funded almost all of the federal budget. But even in 1787 the United States was dividing on economic lines, with some states, chiefly in the slave South, producing agricultural crops for the world market and others, chiefly in the North, aspiring to manufacture for domestic sale goods that the colonies had been required by the British mercantile system to import from the mother country. Congress could encourage manufacture by making imported goods more costly; but it could not tax the exports of the commodity-producing states. This provision had little economic theory behind it; it represented a straightforward political concession to the plantation South, an outright bribe to secure its delegates' support at the Convention and its citizens' acquiescence to ratification.

The next prohibition also arose out of the United States' position as essentially a colony of the world market. Both imports and exports traveled by water, and control of sea and river ports gave some states a means of extorting money out of other states. Under what is called the "no preference" clause, the states can't charge duties on goods in ships and boats passing through their territory; and Congress cannot make interstate discriminations between ports. This did not mean that Congress can't encourage or subsidize some ports and not others; it can. It can't, however, decree that ports in Pennsylvania as a whole would be subject to different regulations from ports in, say, New York.

The next prohibition forbids Congress from in essence giving itself or anyone else the keys to the treasury. All government expenditures must be made by "Appropriations made by law," which shall be "published" at regular intervals.

Finally, the new government could not create a nobility—the Duchess of Carbondale,[10] and others—nor can its officials accept titles, or anything else, from a foreign government without congressional consent.

The eight prohibitions in Section Nine are (with the exception of the "suspension" clause) relatively qualified. But it should also be noted that there are relatively few of them, and that most of them concern matters at the margin of Congress's authority. Again, they do not oust Congress from areas of regulation, and they leave a wide variety of tools at the new government's disposal. The relative narrowness of these prohibitions becomes clearer when compared with the broad list of "thou shalt nots" that the Constitution's next section proclaims against the *state* governments.

SECTION TEN. Section Ten begins with a list of things the states may not do under any circumstances, then moves on to list things that Congress may permit them to do. In the realm of foreign affairs, states are absolutely barred from making treaties with other countries or from creating their own forces of privateers by letters of marque and reprisal. Financially, states cannot issue their own currency, either in coin or in "bills of credit" (paper money). In addition, they have no power to declare anything but gold or silver "legal tender"; this provision was aimed at the practice of some state governments after the Revolution, which had sided with debtors and mortgagees by issuing inflated state banknotes and requiring creditors, who had made loans in silver or gold, to accept the less valuable paper as repayment.

A persistent strain of constitutional thinking argues that the document prohibits the federal government also from issuing paper money; the clearest way to discuss this is to note that, well, it doesn't. Only states are barred from emitting paper money or from making it "legal tender." There is a kind of biblical aspect to the idea that, having forbidden paper money for one kind of government, the Constitution *must* be saying that it is sin for all levels. In that reading, paper money is sin, regardless of who prints it. A statutory reading would pay more attention to the specifics—the provision clearly addresses states and not the federal government. Other readers might note that it appears in a section aimed exclusively at the states, and might further note that the plenary power over the house of trade given in Section Eight (including the power to "emit bills of credit") makes it a strained reading to suggest that the framers were sneaking in a very important prohibition on the federal government here. At any rate, the power of Congress to create paper money has been sustained for more than a century.

In addition, states could not "impair the Obligation of Contracts"; it's easy to read this provision as protecting a right to enter into contracts (indeed, even the Supreme Court, for a time, fell into this error). But what the provision forbids is "impairing" existing contracts. State law in most areas, now as then, governs the formation of contracts, and states are under no obligation to allow parties to enter into any specific kind of contract.

But once parties have made a valid contract, states cannot change their laws to relieve one party or the other of its obligations. Thus, laws requiring mortgage holders to "forgive" their debtors would be forbidden to the states. (Note, however, that as with the paper money provisions, nothing in the Constitution's text forbids *Congress* from changing or invalidating contracts after the fact.)

States are, like Congress, forbidden to pass bills of attainder or ex post facto laws; and they may not create their own local nobility any more than Congress can create a national one.

Congress may tax imports but not exports. States may not tax imports or exports, without Congress's consent—with one exception. States then as now often required items in commerce to be inspected for health reasons; they may, without congressional consent, continue to do this and to charge a fee for doing so—but the fee may only be as much as is "absolutely necessary" to fund the inspection program; to prevent states from getting greedy, any surplus funds generated by state inspection fees must be forfeited to the federal treasury.

Here's a textual paradox: the language implies that there may be state "duties and imposts laid . . . on imports *or exports*" if Congress gives its consent. A literal reading would thus suggest that Congress cannot tax exports but that it can do the same thing by licensing states to do it and then collecting the proceeds. Such a reading makes sense only if we make the fundamentalist assumption that the Constitution contains no mistakes; if we read it as a human document, it is easy to conclude that this apparent paradox is simply a slip.

Congress can also consent to state "duties of tonnage" on shipments from outside the country. It could also allow states to enter into "any agreement or compact" with a foreign country, even though a state may never enter into any "treaty, alliance, or confederation." That prohibition extends not only to such pacts with foreign countries but also with other states, in fact; states may not negotiate interstate agreements with each other, according to Section Ten, without congressional permission.

Finally, states are not to go to war with anyone, unless they have been invaded or armies are massing on their shores. Like foreign policy and foreign trade, war belongs to the new union.

All in all, Section Ten seems to set out a distinctly subordinate role for the states in the new union—especially when contrasted with the Articles of Confederation, in which the states retained primary responsibility for the armed forces. The prohibition is most stern within the walls of the city of war. Within the city of trade, Article I generally is more relaxed. Congress is granted authority over the field of interstate commerce; but the states are not barred from commercial and trade regulation as they are from foreign policy matters. States can't discriminate against each other, close their borders, or tax interstate shipments. But aside from that, the economic sphere is tacitly set out as an area of concurrent authority. As is so often the case, what the Constitution does not forbid is in some ways as important as what it does.

Overall, though, what emerges from Article I is the vision of unity, of a strong central government protecting the states, limiting their interaction with each other and the world, and controlling tightly any military power that might threaten its supreme authority. The states are a part of Achilles's two cities, but they seem more to be contained within it than to be constraints on its scope. As Walt Whitman heard *America* singing, not different states with disparate voices, so Article I sets out a vision of one country in everything that really matters to the cities of peace and of war.

Article II

Under the Bramble Bush

In the Book of Judges, Gideon's son Jotham tells the people of Judah the Parable of the Bramble, a warning against the kind of man who aspires to sit on a throne. In Jotham's story, the trees of the field seek a king. The olive, and the fig, and the grapevine, useful trees, refuse to turn away from bearing fruit; but the bramble, a worthless weed, gladly accepts, and warns them that if the trees disobey, "let fire come out of the bramble and devour the cedars of Lebanon."[1]

From as far back as biblical times, Western culture has been of two minds about powerful rulers. We crave the king's strong protective arm, but we fear his heavy hand. Samuel the prophet warned the children of Israel that kings were an offense to God; the ancient Greeks chafed at the caprices of their kingly warriors. The noble Romans overthrew the Tarquins and instituted the Republic, only to fall under the yoke of the Caesars. And the colonies groaned under George III.

And yet, like the children of Israel, early Americans also sometimes yearned for a king. The years between 1776 and 1787 in many ways were years in the wilderness, and the thirteen tribes of America were beginning to fall apart. Like people everywhere, they feared a king and needed one. Like Americans today, they lived with what the scholar Harvey Mansfield called "the ambivalence of executive power,"[2] and that ambivalence seems to be reflected in a cryptic, incomplete text. Supreme Court Justice Robert Jackson, facing a conundrum of presidential authority, once lamented that the materials concerning this part of the Constitution are "almost as enigmatic as the dreams Joseph was called upon to interpret for Pharaoh."[3] If this is unfair, it is unfair to the Bible, not the Framers.

Article II creates an office, President of the United States, that remains a kind of inkblot onto which generations of Americans have projected their hopes and fears. There is no Homeric catalogue of presidential powers; at the same time, there is no Levitical set of prohibitions.

Article I names (and thus demands the existence of) officials from other branches—the vice president to preside, the chief justice to oversee presidential impeachment trials. Article I also dictates some officers and internal organization of the Houses of Congress—there will be a speaker for the House, a president pro tempore for the Senate.

By contrast, Article II has nothing to say about the internal organization of the "executive branch"; it does not mention a Cabinet or any specific official below the president. Article I sets out a list of things that Congress may do and the states may not. Article II tells us nothing about the president's relationship to the states; it is as if they are to be acquainted only through Congress. Article I tells us in detail what Congress may not do; Article II says almost nothing about what the president may not do.

Article II tells us there will be a president, and it tells us (quite ineptly) how the president will be picked. But what exactly this president will do—and must not do—is left almost completely to the readers' imagination.

SECTION ONE. The very first words of Article II plunge us into one of the most vexing and enduring debates in all of constitutional law and history. *"The executive Power,"* the Article begins, "shall be vested in a President of the United States of America." Article I began "all legislative Powers *herein granted.*" Legislative powers are granted or withheld one by one; "the executive power" seems to be one thing, complete in itself, given to the new leader as a unit. What does the phrase mean? At least two interpretations seem most plausible.

First, "the executive power" could mean only the power to execute the powers expressly granted to the president by the Constitution, the provisions of the Constitution itself, laws passed by Congress, and treaties binding the nation. That's a logical reading, since an executive must have something to execute; it seems nonsensical to imagine execution in a vacuum. But this reading has one thing working against it—it almost certainly can't be right. That's because, as we'll see shortly, the explicit powers granted in the text are few and even those few are incomplete. A president could not use even his express powers without making use of powers not explicitly granted. Further, Congress might expressly not grant adequate powers to execute the statutes it passes, preferring to keep authority under its own control. A president confined to specifically granted powers might be end up as a kind of congressional butler. Both the political wishes of Americans and the demands of international relations and national security have demanded a potent prince, not a tiptoeing minion, to lead the republic.

The alternative interpretation is that "the executive power" exists without relation to the succeeding text; it is a power that belongs of right to any head of state, who must be able to do certain things if a nation is to retain its nationhood. Many theorists of the executive branch embrace this view heartily. They argue that the listed powers in Article II are irrelevant to constructions of "the executive power"—that the people's king exists, in effect, outside the Constitution.

If "the executive power" existed before and outside the Constitution, there is another word for it with which the Framers would have been intimately familiar: *prerogative*. The king of England (by the eighteenth century, this would have meant in effect the king and his chosen ministers) held certain powers that existed before the growth of Parliament and that Parliament could not share or limit.

British scholars then as now disagree about their number and extent, but they included the power to veto any law passed by Parliament for any reason; the power to call Parliament into session, to adjourn a session in progress, to bar Parliament from meeting, and to dissolve Parliament and call for new elections; the power to charter corporations and grant economic monopolies; the power to pardon any criminal defendant, except one impeached by Parliament; the power to raise and maintain an army (subject only to the requirement of obtaining funding from Parliament), including commissioning its officers and commanding its activities at home and abroad; the power to conclude binding treaties and conduct foreign relations; and the power—the sole power—to declare war, wage war, and make peace.

On none of these crucial matters was the assent of the people's representatives required. (Most of these powers remain prerogatives of the British Crown—meaning now the current prime minister and Cabinet—to this day.)[4] As we chart the shape of the office created by Article II, it's well to keep that list of powers in mind. The Framers seem to be at pains to make clear that in the new Republic, most of them are not prerogatives, but shared powers. Some of them are lodged in the president, however; and some are not mentioned, and thus might be up in the air.

Section One does not elucidate the meaning of its first three words, because it is primarily concerned with the election of the president and of the vice president, both of whom "shall hold his Office during the Term of four Years." (The text does not give Congress the power to extend or curtail the presidential term by as much as a day; this is probably wise, as it would open a back door for presidential removal, but it did create difficulties when the realities of launching the new government met the timetable set up by Article I's requirement of a December session of Congress each year.) Though the vice president shares the president's term, and his mode of election, the text does not give him any share of the executive power, any more than it does to any of the Cabinet.

The term "executive power" may have been obscure, but it was hardly unfamiliar in 1787—Americans had been modeling executives in their state constitutions since Independence, when they had to devise substitutes for the royal governors who ran most of the colonies. The person in whom the power was vested, however, had a somewhat surprising name—"president."

In our time, when republics from France to Uzbekistan take for granted that their head of state will be a president, that word glides by easily. But in 1787, the word did not have the meaning of "head of state." It had two meanings—one, the most obvious, being the presiding officer of a meeting or assembly; the other being "the appointed governor or lieutenant of a province, or other division of a country, as a colony, city"—the appointing authority presumably being a monarch.[5]

Founders such as Adams and Hamilton had proposed the title "Governor," which to their ears sounded grander. Most states in 1787 had governors, while three, including Pennsylvania—as noted by Akhil Reed Amar in his magisterial book, *America's Constitution: A Biography*—had "presidents."[6] In fact, Benjamin Franklin, the oldest and most venerated member of the Philadelphia Convention, was serving as "President of Pennsylvania" even while he was a delegate to the Convention.

"President" is a curious term for the American head of state, because "presiding" in any meaningful sense is the one thing the president of the United States does *not* do. The Constitution gives him the power to request written opinions from "principal officers," but makes no mention of a Cabinet, or of Cabinet meetings. The president never presides over Congress; indeed, by custom, he cannot enter either house without standing outside and asking permission. The *vice president*, in fact, does preside (we see the vice president behind the president during televised addresses to Congress)—he is, strangely enough, "president" of the Senate, which, even more strangely, has a "president pro tempore," to be president when the vice president cannot be president. (The Speaker presides over the House; no terminological confusion there.)

The Confederation Congress also had a president, but that figure had no executive power, simply presiding over congressional sessions. Akhil Amar believes that "the Philadelphia delegates . . . were consciously or subconsciously influenced by the fact that George Washington was the presiding officer—the unanimously chosen 'president'—of the Philadelphia Convention itself."[7] If so, that is just another small example of the ways in which Washington, by his example, changed the way that people around the world talk and think about government.

Presidential election summoned forth what is without doubt the Framers' worst work, the system of presidential electors. We speak today of "the electoral college." The National Archives, keepers of the Constitution and its text, use this term on their website, and the codifiers of the US Code use it for the title of the section of statutes governing presidential election. But the term does not appear in the Constitution; I suspect that it would have horrified most of the Framers. They would have been most familiar with two "electoral colleges," neither of them an object of reverence.

First was the College of Electors of the Holy Roman Empire. This body still existed in 1787; George III was a member. It last conducted an election five years after the convention, designating Francis of Bavaria as the last Holy Roman Emperor. The second was the College of Cardinals, which met in secret conclave at the death of a pope to select his successor. Both Colleges were Catholic institutions, with, to American eyes, unsavory histories of secrecy, bribery, and assassination as instruments of state. Of the delegates to Philadelphia, only two were Catholic; by and large, the United States was a nation of rock-ribbed Protestants—Anglican, Lutheran, Congregational, Quaker, Baptist, and others—with a horror of Roman authority and "Popish" pageantry.

The second reason the words "electoral college" might have sounded sour in their ears was that there is nothing "collegial" about the electors. They never meet as a body; they never debate; they are not to deliberate or to join together to choose a president. They do not come from the nation's political leadership—they can't be members of Congress or hold any other "Office of Trust or Profit under the United States." To make it impossible that the electors as a body could conspire to make a favorite president, Congress is empowered to require that the electors meet only once, on the same day, in different places. Thus, there is never an assembly of the electoral "college" itself, and the members cannot know how the other electors have voted. They can only vote once. After that vote, they play no further role. If no candidate gets a majority, the Congress, not the electors, picks the president.

The system by which electors pick the president has been altered twice since 1787 (see the Twelfth and Twenty-Fifth Amendments). But interestingly, the language governing how electors themselves are selected has never been changed: electors are "appoint[ed], in such Manner as the [state] Legislature . . . may direct." In some states, the legislatures from the beginning directed popular voting for electors (either at large or by district) from the state; in others, however, the legislature retained the appointment power itself, disdaining to consult the voters.

(Even today, any state legislature willing to endure the political fallout could do the same—just call off the presidential election within the state's borders and pick its own team of electors. In the year 2000, the Florida legislature was preparing to void the contested election for the state's twenty-nine electoral votes and simply designate a set of Republican electors. This ploy might have fallen victim to another little-known aspect of the text, which we will look at shortly.)

The electors are apportioned in a manner that overrepresented the slave states, and that also to this day overrepresents the small states. A state's electoral total is equal to "the whole Number of Senators and Representatives" granted to the state. Thus, the slave states, with smaller free populations than the northern states, got excess influence in presidential selection equal to the advantage they received from the three-fifths ratio in the House; the small states got (and still get) more influence than their populations would entitle them to in a popular vote because they got two electoral votes for their senators.

The electoral votes do not represent the people in numbers, and the electoral system has no commitment to popular selection of the president. This already seems like a bad idea, but at this point, the original electoral-vote system went truly haywire. When the electors met in their state capitals, each elector was to vote for two names. The elector could vote for one name from his state if he chose; but he had to vote for two, and one could not be an "inhabitant" of his state. Here's the exploding cap in the cigar: there was no way to indicate which name the elector favored for president and which for vice president.

Under the current system as well as the old one, the state's votes are counted and listed, and the list is sent under seal to the president of the Senate (normally the sitting vice president, but remember that the office of vice president might be vacant). A joint session of Congress gathers to watch as the votes are opened and counted.

Under the original system, the count produced a winner only if one and only one candidate got a majority of the electors. If that happened, then the one getting the most became president, his number two becoming vice president. In a contested two-party election (which the Framers apparently did not foresee) this would make one candidate president and his opponent vice president. That happened in 1796, when Thomas Jefferson ran against John Adams; Jefferson lost and found himself vice president, an uncomfortable situation for both men, especially as the vice president was scheming to unseat the president at the next election.

But that is mild compared to the next possibility: since each elector voted for two, two candidates could tie, and each could have a majority. Or no candidate could get a majority. If either of those things happened, a bizarre Rube Goldberg–style process of selection kicks in (one that remains largely in place, waiting to cause almost certain disaster, today).

First, the House of Representatives becomes the body to choose the new president. If there are two tied majority winners, the House must pick one of the two. If there is no majority winner, the House must pick from among the top five vote getters. (The Twelfth Amendment changed this to the top three.) The choice is by written ballot.

In either case, though, the House votes by states—that is, all the members from one state will vote among themselves; the winner of that process will then receive the state's one vote. Two-thirds of the states must have at least one member present; the winning candidate must gain the vote of a majority of the states present.

These convolutions make a certain demented sense given the presuppositions of the Constitution. The natural body to select the president would be the Senate, in which each state is equally represented. But there would be two drawbacks to that approach. First, the Senate later in Article II is given a number of powers shared with the president (once again undercutting the notion of a neat "separation of powers"). If the Senate also had the potential to grant election or reelection to a president, that might destroy the independence of the president and make the Senate a ruling cabal. (This would have seemed more possible in 1787, when the maximum number of senators would be twenty-six, than it does today.)

Second, a sitting vice president, as president of the Senate, might have the inside track if the Senate picked the new president, once again threatening the independence of the office. This is no problem if the House elects; but then what becomes of equal representation? The vote by states is the answer. In practice, though, this is quite different from vote by the Senate. If the senators picked the president, each state would have an equal number of votes. The two senators might disagree; if so, they would just split their votes. In the House system, each state must cast a unified single vote or none at all; if a House delegation could not agree, the state's vote would not be cast—and if enough state delegations were deadlocked, a majority of the states present would not vote, the ballot would fail, and another vote would have to be taken.

The election has been thrown into the House only twice. The first time, it took thirty-six ballots and six days for the House to choose Thomas Jefferson over Aaron Burr, who, though they were running mates, had tied Jefferson in the electoral vote. The ordeal was made more nerve-wracking because the House that met to decide the issue was the House that had been elected more than two years before; under the December meeting provision of Article One, this House convened after a new House had been chosen but before it took office. The new House was strongly Jeffersonian, but it would not take office until the same day as the new president, so the voting had to be carried out by the old House, which was Federalist. Many supporters of the loser, John Adams, flirted with voting for Burr because they thought Burr would be less "Jeffersonian."

(In the only other time the House has made the choice, the members picked John Quincy Adams on the first ballot, even though Andrew Jackson had more electoral and popular votes than any other candidate. By that time, the candidates ran by ticket, and both candidates had selected the same running mate, John C. Calhoun.)

Meanwhile, after the House picked a new president, the new vice president would be the candidate with the most votes. (This system had been changed by the time Adams was selected in 1824.) In the case of a tied majority electoral vote, this would be the other member of the tie; in the case of a choice among the top five, it would mean the remaining front runner. This could easily be a candidate who had received more electoral votes than the president-elect who had defeated him in the House. What if no candidate had a majority, the House picked a new president from the top five, and the two top remaining candidates were tied? Then the Senate would get involved, and would pick between those two the new vice president.

Every time I read this section, I ask myself whether any of these smart people really thought this system would work smoothly. That's an especially good question when you consider that there's some evidence that most of the Framers expected the House to choose the president much of the time. Washington would serve of course; but after him, the assumption was that no single figure would be known to the people of the country, and the electoral vote would scatter. The rickety House-voting system arose out of the electoral-vote system; the electoral-vote system arose because many states, especially those with large slave populations, would lose influence under a popular-vote system. This way, the system's equivocal popular legitimacy was hastily camouflaged. As we will see later, it didn't work well, and it is still rickety even after it has been changed.

As a final element of the process of presidential selection, Congress is given the power, if it chooses to do so, to SET "the Time of choosing the Electors, and the Day on which they shall give their Votes; which Day shall be the same throughout the United States." Under this language, Congress could, if it chose, permit the presidential election—the fifty-one state elections in which voters choose electors—to last more than one day, or to take place on different days in different states, though it has not done so. By 1845, Congress designated the first Tuesday after the first Monday in November, where it remains today.

The Florida Legislature's plan to award the state's electors to George W. Bush would have sparked a constitutional dispute under this clause. Such a subsequent choice would not be unconstitutional because it set aside a vote of the people; the vote of the people still counts for nothing in the selection of a president. ("The individual citizen has no federal constitutional right to vote for electors for the President of the United States," the Supreme Court matter-of-factly reminded the nation in its decision in *Bush v. Gore*).[8] The Florida Legislature's scheme might have failed because the choice of electors (by their legislative vote) would have taken place after election day, "the Time of choosing the Electors." The real choice of electors, under the Constitution, would have been the one made on Election Day.

Let's leave presidential selection for a while—we will have to come back to it repeatedly as we study the amendments to the Constitution. Who can be president? He must be a "natural born Citizen, or a Citizen of the United States, at the Adoption of this Constitution." This language raises two important points. One is simply a historical oddity: many lawyers and lay people alike believe unshakably that the "natural born" citizen provision was inserted into the Constitution by political enemies of Alexander Hamilton, who was born in the British colony of Nevis. But the second clause shows that that is wrong: Hamilton was a citizen "at the time of the adoption," and he had papers from the New York Legislature to prove it. In 1787, only those aged eleven and under were "natural born" citizens of something called "the United States of America." All potential presidents, including George Washington, had been born as subjects of the British Crown. (Martin Van Buren, who took office in 1837, was the first American president to be born after Independence.) Hamilton failed to run for president first because the political stars were not aligned, and eventually because Aaron Burr killed him in 1803.[9]

The second point is textually more consequential. Though Article II requires "natural born" citizenship, the Constitution does not explain what the phrase means. There was no constitutional definition of American citizenship until 1868, when the Fourteenth Amendment was adopted. Nor was there any existing body of American immigration law to explain it. The phrase had been used in a fourteenth-century British statute, which specified that the children of British subjects born abroad were "natural born" subjects of the Crown.[10] Congress defined "natural born" citizen in 1790 to include children of Americans born abroad;[11] but the words were dropped five years later.[12]

The "natural born" language renders ineligible any naturalized citizen. But beyond that, did it count as "natural born" anyone born in any of the states? Only those born to citizen parents in any of the states? Anyone born to one or two citizen parents in a foreign country? Anyone born in the present states and the territories to the West? What about an "Indian not taxed" born within the United States? What about "other persons," African slaves? What about "free blacks," who occupied a subordinate status to free whites in many states?

These questions may seem theoretical, but they gave rise to a scalding debate around the time of the Civil War about whether slaves were citizens by birth. This cryptic clause in Article II is the only discussion of birth citizenship in the Constitution. The issue was not whether a freed slave could be president—that wasn't going to happen—but whether Chief Justice Roger B. Taney and the extreme pro-slavery view he represented were correct that black people were not and never could be citizens of the United States. Anti-slavery thinkers had for thirty years pointed to the "natural born citizen" language to argue that this meant any person born in the United States. The Constitution does not say "white natural-born citizen," they said, and thus citizenship has no racial component.

The president must also be thirty-five years old, and must have lived in the country for fourteen or more years. (The text isn't clear about whether a citizen who had lived in the United States for fourteen years and then moved abroad would be ineligible; is it the fourteen years immediately before the election or just a total of fourteen years in life? In practice, it is the latter. Herbert Hoover, for example, left the United States at twenty-two and lived abroad most of the time until 1917, but was inaugurated as president only twelve years later.)[13]

Next comes the clause governing presidential succession, which is almost as poorly drafted as the provisions on presidential selection. What happens in case of the president's "Removal . . . Death . . . or Inability to discharge [his] Powers and Duties?" Well, the vice president takes over—we all know that. But does the vice president become *president*? That's not as clear. The text says that if for any reason the president can't discharge his powers and duties, "the Same shall devolve on the Vice President." That's not quite the same thing as saying that he "becomes" president; it might mean that the vice president would fill the presidential function—as "acting President," say—until a new president could be elected at the next regular election. The ambiguity is deepened by the language we saw in Article I introducing the vice president, who was to preside over the Senate except when "he shall exercise the office of President." The original Constitution contained no provision for replacing a vice president called to take over for the president.

In 1841, Vice President John Tyler was required to step in after President William Henry Harrison died one month into his term—and no one knew for sure whether he was "President" or "Acting President." Tyler took the presidential oath and insisted that Tyler was in fact president, and in time this was accepted, so much so that the question did not arise during later successions. But the textual ambiguity was annoying, and the framers of the Twenty-Fifth Amendment, 180 years after the Philadelphia Convention, finally cleared up the sloppy draftsmanship of the original Framers, providing that "in case of the removal of the President from office or of his death or resignation, the Vice President shall become President," and setting up a different procedure if the president becomes "unable to discharge the powers and duties of his office."

The entire office of the vice president is created in stilted and sullen language. The Framers seem as ambivalent about the office as have been most of its holders. The first vice president, John Adams, once wrote that "my country has in its wisdom contrived for me the most insignificant office that ever the invention of man contrived or his imagination conceived."[14] A later and less distinguished holder of the office, John N. ("Cactus Jack") Garner, expressed the same thing more succinctly: the office, he said, was "not worth a bucket of warm piss."[15] That's a bit harsh—but only a bit.

Like a huge but helpless whale, the vice presidency is strangely stranded in the midst of the Constitution. The vice president is the only other officer besides the president to be chosen nationwide. He is elected by the electors. On the other hand, he does not take a constitutionally prescribed oath, like the president (his oath is prescribed by statute, the same oath taken by "any individual, except the President, elected or appointed to an office of honor or profit in the civil service or uniformed services").[16] His salary is not protected from being raised or lowered during his term, as the president's is. Though the vice president is the second in succession to the president, he is not functionally subordinate to the president: the office has no constitutionally assigned executive duties or powers and the president cannot fire the vice president or, indeed, make the vice president do anything. The vice president's sole duty is a legislative one—presiding over the Senate; and he doesn't need the president's permission to do it. Small wonder that for much of American history, presidents and vice presidents often did not meet for months at a time.

This strange draftsmanship gave rise to the tortured arguments advance by Vice President Dick Cheney that he was not a member of the "executive branch" (at least when it was inconvenient for him to be). Those arguments begin to seem plausible—if we allow our awareness of what the Constitutional actually says to be obscured by what we have been taught it says. The very question of what "branch" the vice president belongs to is not a textual question, because, as we noted earlier, the Constitution doesn't set up "branches" of government. Instead, it lays out "powers," designates officers to exercise them, and places limits on their exercise.

Legislative and executive power mix promiscuously in the appointments process, treaty-making, the war powers, and the presidential veto. No serious person has argued that this somehow makes the president a member of "the legislative branch"; and for the same reason, the vice president should by the logic of the whole document be regarded, however awkwardly, as part of the executive establishment. The Framers' ambivalence and hastiness took an office that must in the best of circumstances be a little awkward and exaggerated its flaws; it might be excessive to compare it to a warm pitcher of anything, but it is true that, except in the moment of succession, the vice president is at best nearly useless and (as we have recently learned) at worst dangerous, a kind of pretender president lurking in the shadows.

Many Americans devoutly believe another myth: that the Constitution sets up an order of succession for the event that both president and vice president are unable to serve. In 1981, when President Ronald Reagan was hovering between life and death after an assassination attempt, Secretary of State Alexander Haig strode into the White House briefing room to reassure the nation: "Constitutionally, gentlemen, you have the President, the Vice President and the Secretary of State in that order. . . . As of now, I am in control here, in the White House, pending return of the Vice President and in close touch with him."[17]

His attempt at reassurance was a failure. Perhaps only a small part of the failure stems from the fact that he had claimed a place in the line of succession that

the secretary of state actually doesn't hold. The Constitution specifies the ambiguous succession of the vice president, then leaves to Congress the decision
"what Officer shall then act as President." Congress has used this authority to
set up a different line of succession from time to time. Currently (and at the
time Haig made his proclamation that "I am in control"), the order is vice
president; Speaker of the House; president pro tempore of the Senate; and
only then, the members of the Cabinet, beginning with secretary of state and
continuing in descending order of the creation of their departments until
it reaches the secretary of homeland security. Congress could change this
tomorrow, of course, as it did in 1947, when it moved the secretary of state
from second to fifth.

The president (though not the vice president) must be paid a salary, which
can't be raised by a grateful Congress or reduced by a vindictive one; the office is
to be financially independent. He can't accept any other income from the federal
government or from any states.

Finally, the president's oath is the only oath of office prescribed by the
Constitution. The Constitution provides that those who object to swearing
may "affirm" its provisions, a measure aimed at accommodating Quakers, who
regarded oaths as blasphemous. (Franklin Pierce, an Episcopalian, is the only
American president to "affirm"; America's two Quaker presidents, Herbert
Hoover and Richard Nixon, both chose to "swear.")[18] The oath-taker commits
only to two acts: first, faithful execution of the office and second, best efforts
to "preserve, protect and defend" the Constitution. There is no mention of
the people. The president's only named superior is the document we are
reading.

That should be a reminder that the holder of this office is not a king in the
mold of the biblical bramble bush, but a minister, responsible to a written and
binding law. Over the years, this has not stopped would-be kings from sending
forth fire to burn the hillsides; what is remarkable is how often a shared allegiance
to the Constitution has foiled their plans.

SECTION TWO. Considering the power and mystique that has accumulated
around the American presidency, a reader can be forgiven for wondering
whether a page has been dropped out of the text of Article II. The president's
listed powers are not very impressive.

The president has two kinds of powers—those he may exercise by himself
and those he can only exercise in relation to Congress. Most of his sole powers
are in Section Two. There are strikingly few of them. He is given command of the
armed forces in war or peace. (He is not "commander in chief" of the United
States, as presidents sometimes like to imply—only of the military.)

The president may require the head of each "executive department" to give
his or her opinion in writing—for the record, so to speak—on "any Subject

relating to the Duties of their respective Offices." This seems odd, doesn't it? What it doesn't say is that the president can then tell these "heads" what to do. Yet if he couldn't, wouldn't they have some of the "executive power" that is supposed to belong to the president?

In the same breathless sentence, the president is given the power to pardon "offenses against the United States"—except when Congress has impeached and removed an executive official. Since impeachment was mostly seen as a weapon against incompetent executive cronies, it would hardly make sense to allow the president who originally appointed them to undo the conviction by granting a pardon and returning the defendant to office.

Next come two important parts of the Crown prerogative the president shares with the Senate: the president can "make Treaties," but only "by and with the Advice and Consent of the Senate." That phrase is hard to interpret; at one point, George Washington believed that it required him to go to the Senate and ask its advice before conducting treaty negotiations. The "by and with" language can certainly be ready to suggest that a president should not negotiate a treaty without prior authorization of the Senate ("by [its] advice") or conclude it without its subsequent approval ("with [its] consent"). But Washington's first attempt at prior consultation proved farcical; after an inconclusive discussion, the Senate referred his question to a committee and ask him to come back later. The old lion stumped angrily off, muttering between his wooden teeth that he would never enter the Senate again.[19] Since then, the "advice and consent" power has been exercised only after a treaty has been negotiated.

The section also portions out the prerogative of appointment to office. When it comes to ambassadors, ministers, and consuls (diplomatic titles all), "judges" of the Supreme Court (now called "Justices" by statute), and "all other Officers of the United States," the president can only "nominate." Senate approval is required for such appointments to take effect. What we call today the Cabinet is covered by the third category, as is the officer corps of the military. This language would require presidential nomination and Senate confirmation for every janitor in every federal office; but the section goes on to say that Congress "may by law vest the appointment of such inferior officers, as they think proper, in the President alone, in the courts of law, or in the heads of departments."

The language sets out two important limitations. First, the offices must be "inferior" ones—this would bar Congress from delegating, say, the commanding general of the army or the "heads of the executive departments" to the president's sole nomination. And second, Congress may not vest the appointment of any officer, inferior or not, in *itself*—presidents, department heads, and judges may appoint, but Congress may not. This is an important provision relating to "separation of powers," but like the ban on members of Congress holding executive office, it appears in meek guise.

The president has a limited power to staff the government if the Senate is adjourned. If a vacancy "may happen" during a Senate recess, the president may fill that vacancy with a temporary commission. The appointment will last only until the end of the next Senate session; if by that time the Senate has not approved the nomination, the office will become vacant again. The "may happen" language could be read to mean that the office must *become* vacant *after* the Senate has recessed; if a vacancy occurs during a session, the president thus would be expected to submit a nomination before the session goes into recess. What would happen, then, if the Senate should refuse to consider the nomination, and instead went into recess? The nomination may have "happened" during a Senate recess; but, as presidents read the language, it continues to "happen" after a recess has begun; thus presidents have made recess appointments to counter Senate intransigence.

Recent legal developments illustrate that matters of pure text still, after more than two centuries, have practical importance. Since at least the early twentieth century, presidents and their lawyers have read the clause to permit the president to make a recess appointment at any time the Senate is in recess, whether that is a brief break in the midst of a full two-year Senate term or instead the formal gap that occurs every two years between one term of the Senate and the first meeting at the beginning of a new Congress.

In the twenty-first century, partisanship in Washington has reached near paralysis, and the practice of the filibuster (a Senate tactic of delaying debate unless one side can get a 60-vote supermajority to end it) has made it harder and harder for presidents to gain Senate confirmations for their nominees. By late 2011, Republican filibusters had blocked all of President Obama's nominees for the National Labor Relations Board, and the board no longer had enough members to take any legal action. In January 2012, the Senate took a 20-day holiday break. However, because of a maneuver by the Republican House, the Senate was required to hold "pro forma" sessions, which consisted of one Senator driving in from the Washington suburbs, "convening" the one-member body, and immediately adjourning again.

Relying on advice from his lawyers, Obama declared that he considered the Senate in "recess" despite the "pro forma" sessions. Relying on the recess power, he named three members to the Board. A year later, when the Board proceeded in court against an employer, the D.C. Circuit Court of Appeals held the appointments illegal. Its opinion orbited most strongly around the meaning of the word "the." The opinion consulted Samuel Johnson's *Dictionary of the English Language*, published in London in 1755, and found this short definition: "an article denoting a particular thing." Therefore, it concluded, the "original public meaning" of "the recess" meant one and only recess, the recess that comes every two years at the end of each Congress.[20] In vain did critics wonder whether the phrase "the dark of night" was supposed to mean "the one darkest hour of the one darkest night of the year"; one of the glories of being a federal judge is that one can consult whatever sources one chooses and read them how one thinks best, and Obama's NLRB was struck down by authority of six words written nearly a quarter-millennium ago by Dr. Johnson.

Whenever "the recess" occurs, the recess power includes, at the president's option, the power of appointing Supreme Court justices who have not yet been confirmed; this option was used as recently as the 1950s, when President Eisenhower named both Chief Justice Earl Warren and Associate Justice William J. Brennan as recess appointees to the Court. Both men were later confirmed to their positions permanently.

The section thus gives careful attention to the appointment and confirmation of federal officials. But it strikingly omits any discussion of their removal. Once appointed, do "officers" serve for life? May they be dismissed by the president? If so, why, if their appointment is jointly vested in the president and the Senate? Must a president obtain senatorial consent to remove a member of the Cabinet, or a general? Could the Senate on its own hook withdraw its "advice and consent" from the appointment of a serving official, thus forcing his resignation even over the president's objections?

Try as one might, it's hard to discern any plausible explanation for this failure other than oversight. It certainly didn't reflect any generally shared view of the executive's removal power. We know that because the First Congress in 1789, which included a number of Framers among its members, found itself frankly flummoxed by the silence over removal and had to conduct a tedious debate over what it meant. President John Adams did not appoint a Cabinet loyal to himself when he took over, in part because he was not sure that he had the power to remove George Washington's incumbent Cabinet.

In 1868, a congressional majority locked in a death struggle with President Andrew Johnson passed an act requiring senatorial consent to dismiss a Cabinet official, then impeached Johnson for firing his war secretary without permission. The president was acquitted by one vote in the Senate, and the act was repealed in 1887. The general interpretation has grown up that Congress may create an office with a fixed term; that it may create an office for which someone other than the president holds the removal power; but that it may not vest the removal power in itself, and that when Congress is silent on the question of removal, the official serves "at the President's pleasure." But the issue is still unclear, and questions about the never-mentioned "removal power" continue to pop up in front of the Supreme Court.

Section Three. Section Two set out powers; Section Three sets out duties. The first is that the president "from time to time give to the Congress information of the state of the union." This doesn't require an annual prime time address to Congress, televised and attended by Supreme Court justices, Cabinet members, military leaders, and real-life American heroes. Indeed, it does not require an address at all—many presidents have simply sent over written messages—nor a transmittal of information every year. "From time to time" suggests that the president may choose his own intervals for giving the "information," or that he may choose to give it at no fixed interval, but simply when it seems to him useful to do so. But it would also seem to forbid the president to refuse to give information at all. The "state of the union" is to be reported as a regular feature of government.

The president also has the duty to recommend to Congress "such Measures as he shall judge necessary and expedient"—that being a more consequential grant than it may seem, because even with his broad prerogative, the king of England was barred from proposing legislation.

The king summoned and dismissed Parliament, but the Constitution fixes a date for the session of Congress, one the president cannot block. The president can summon Congress into session—but only on "extraordinary occasions," a term for which no definition is supplied. At a minimum, it seems to suggest that the president should not assume the power of summoning Congress as simply part of his day-to-day authority; if he calls them in, he'd better be ready to explain why.

The king could dismiss Parliament, but the president may not adjourn Congress. If the two houses can't agree between themselves on when to go home, however, the president may decide the issue, sparing the nation the painful spectacle of a never-ending Congress.

The president "shall receive Ambassadors and other public Ministers." The Senate doesn't "receive." From this skimpy grant of ministerial power arises the fixed notion, enunciated by the Supreme Court and by many commentators, that the president is "the sole organ of the nation in foreign affairs." The Constitution doesn't really designate a "sole organ" in the diplomatic arena; the phrase was first used in 1800 by John Marshall, who at that time was not a justice but simply a member of the House.[21] Its provenance is thus suspect, but the necessities of international relations (and perhaps the collective memory of the king's prerogative) have conjured sweeping authority out of Article II's taciturn text.

The president shall "take Care that the Laws be faithfully executed." Is this a duty—or a power? It seems straightforwardly like a duty. The president is an "executive"; he looks up the law—which is defined in Article VI, Section Two, as "this Constitution, laws made pursuant to it, and treaties made or which shall be made under the authority of the United States"—then he carries out its positive commands to him and enforces its negative commands to others.

But of course it's not quite so simple. What if the law is confusing or vague? What if two sources of law conflict? What if Congress passes a law that is flatly unconstitutional? What if the president interprets the law differently from those who wrote it (Congress) or those who interpret and apply it (the courts)? What if the president thinks the country needs him to do something the Constitution doesn't say he can do?

In 1952, the government attorneys representing the Truman administration told the Supreme Court that President Truman had the power to seize and operate the entire American steel industry during a strike that threatened to curb steel production during the Korean War. This claim was made even though no congressional statute gave the president this power, and even though Congress had never "declared war" in Korea or even given the president the authority to engage in the conflict.

Truman had claimed a unilateral power to carry on the war, which he said was required by the United Nations Charter, a "treaty made . . . under the authority of the United States"; then to carry out the unilateral war, he claimed the domestic power to take over a huge chunk of the economy and run it to his own specifications. One basis of his power, his lawyer argued to the Supreme Court, was the "take care" clause. Without steel he couldn't prosecute the war that the treaty authorized him to engage in, so to "take care" that the treaty was enforced he had to take over the steel mills.[22] The Court repelled this claim, with some asperity (it was in his concurrence in this case that Justice Jackson referred to Article II as resembling Pharaoh's dreams); but the mystery remains of how far the president may go in bootstrapping his "take care" power.

Presidents have claimed the power to act without any authorization at all, under the bare "executive power"; they have claimed the right to proclaim their own interpretation of statutes without reference to the intentions of Congress; and they have claimed the power simply to suspend statutes during anything they call an emergency. Both sides of these disputes point to the "take care" language, and both sides have a point. This conundrum will never go away.

Finally, the president "shall Commission all the Officers of the United States." These officers, remember, are nominated by the president and confirmed by the Senate. After this process is complete, however, they may not begin their work until the president delivers a signed commission. On a number of occasions, presidents have withheld the commissions, and appointees who had fulfilled all the legal requirements of office never were able to serve. Commissioning could be viewed (as Chief Justice Marshall viewed it in *Marbury v. Madison*, the case that set forth for the first time the Supreme Court's power to strike down congressional statutes) as a "ministerial" act, required of the president once Senate approval is complete. However, later presidents have interpreted it as part of the president's "executive" power, to be exercised only if he believes it to be legal and appropriate.

SECTION FOUR. Finally, "the President, Vice President and all civil officers of the United States" may be impeached and removed for "Treason, Briberty, and other high Crimes and Misdemeanors." Impeachment is thus not limited to the president. It has most often been used against judges, who remain on the bench despite accusations or even convictions of corrupt activity. Both the vice president and "all civil officers" are liable to impeachment as well.

The inclusion by title of the vice president should dampen the claim that he is a member of the legislative branch. The "civil officers" clause is perfectly ambiguous but was interpreted by the Senate, very early in our national history, not to apply to senators and representatives.[23] There is a constitutional method for their removal—expulsion by two-thirds vote—involving only their respective houses; it would have been anomalous to give both houses a voice in a different means of removing a member of one house.

The grounds for impeachment are "Treason, Briberty, and other high Crimes and Misdemeanors." "Treason" is defined in the Constitution itself; "bribery" had a clear meaning even in 1789; but there is nowhere to look up a meaning for "high crimes and misdemeanors." Would it be restricted to offenses roughly as bad as treason or bribery? In statutory matters, lawyers call this a construction *ejusdem generis*, meaning that a series should not be interpreted to include disparate items. "For God, for country, and for Yale," for example, is a clear violation of that principle; similarly, to read the clause as "treason, bribery, or jaywalking" would outrage common sense.

But that doesn't end the enquiry, because reasonable people may disagree about how "high" an accusation is. Some impeachable offenses may not even be crimes according to the statutes; some statutory crimes might be tangential to a president's fitness for office.

Former president Gerald Ford, while still a member of the House, once remarked that "an impeachable offense is whatever a majority of the House of Representatives considers it to be at a given moment in history."[24] Certainly as a descriptive matter that would be true, as no authority could step in and bar the House from impeaching a judge, or a president, whether for illicit sex, jaywalking, or drinking Pinot Noir with fish. But the practice of the Senate, beginning early in the Republic, has been to decline to convict officials impeached by the House on purely partisan or political grounds.

When Ford made his remark, he was vainly seeking to impeach Justice William O. Douglas essentially for being too liberal and kind of a sleazy guy. Thus, his statement might be regarded as exemplifying precisely the wrong view of the House's responsibility. Historical tempers have cooled only slightly after the impeachment of Bill Clinton for lying under oath about a sexual relationship. Many Americans still believe his actions were a threat to the very rule of law; others insist that the "offense" was more low farce than high crime, and that the zeal of Clinton's foes was partisan hypocrisy rather than constitutional passion.

Finally, note that nothing in the text explicitly limits impeachment to present holders of the offices in question. Why would Congress impeach and "convict" someone who was no longer in office? Well, note that in Article I, Section Three, the maximum penalty is defined as "removal from Office, and disqualification to hold and enjoy any Office of honor, Trust or Profit under the United States." Thus an out-of-office miscreant could be impeached and barred from holding office again.

Even after Bill Clinton had left the White House, some commentators suggested bringing yet more articles of impeachment against the former president.[25] It was silly talk, and soon abandoned. But textually, it was far from nonsense.

So ends Article II, oddly truncated. Article I was precise, verbose, Homeric. Article II is more like a modern poem, suggestive and imprecise. Rather than the catalogs of Whitman, it calls to mind the sparseness of a modern American poet like Wallace Stevens. In "Thirteen Ways of Looking at a Blackbird," Stevens was torn between the expressive power of song ("the beauty of inflections") and the very different impact of silence ("the beauty of innuendoes"), unsure whether to prefer "The blackbird whistling/ Or just after."[26]

In those terms, the beauty of Article I is largely in inflection, what is said. The power of Article II arises from innuendo. The president in the text is less a portrait than a set of dots to be connected as need and imagination dictate. Few powers are explicitly given; that has led many readers to imagine one kind of leader, a kind of chaste republican first magistrate. No power is explicitly forbidden; that has led others to imagine quite another kind of leader, an elected Caesar whose job it is to dominate the people and the other branches.

That the article ends with procedures for deposing this ambiguous king may seem anticlimactic. But in fact, it may reflect the only unambiguous triumph of this aspect of the Framing: out of a history in which supreme power could usually only be ended by its holder's death, they imagined a new kind of king, who would rule as he was permitted and as he dared, and who would then peaceably pack his bags and leave. That we take this latter fact for granted is a triumph of our system that few in 1787 could have confidently foreseen.

Article III

Solomon's Sword

Of all the figures of this earthly life, there is only one we fear to meet beyond the grave: the judge.

In the Hebrew Bible, Israel's greatest king is not a warrior or a lawgiver, but a judge. Solomon, David's son, asked God not for victory or power but for wisdom: "Give therefore thy servant an understanding heart to judge thy people," he prayed, "that I may discern between good and bad: for who is able to judge this thy so great a people?"[1]

Solomon's greatest judgment was rendered in a dispute over a newborn child; one woman's child had died in the night, and both claimed the surviving baby. "And the king said, 'Bring me a sword.' And they brought a sword before the king. . . . And the king said, 'Divide the living child in two, and give half to the one, and half to the other.'" The true mother yields her claim, while the impostor is willing to accept half a corpse as her share. When the people heard the story, they "saw that the wisdom of God was in him, to do judgment."[2]

Wisdom? Perhaps. But it was Solomon, not the quarreling women, who brought the sword into the room.

Frightening though they may be, judges are an indispensable part of any system. Americans today take pride in our strong and independent system of courts—when, that is, they are not cursing activist judges, villainous lawyers, and soft-headed juries. Americans love the law and fear it. This ambivalence about courts was present even at the creation. Under Article III, we are allowed to have a system of federal courts. But we don't have to.

Article III first specifies that there must be at least one federal court, the Supreme Court. It allows Congress to create others if it wishes. The Constitution says nothing about which courts Congress should create. But any courts Congress does "ordain and establish" are to be staffed by a fearsome, powerful new kind of judge, empowered to split babies without fear of the people's wrath or the legislature's retaliation.

So "the judicial Power of the United States" may reside in one court or many. Article III is more precise in listing the kinds of cases federal judicial power may decide. This it does two ways: by listing two *kinds of cases* to which the power extends, and by naming some *kinds of parties* whose cases, of whatever kind, must have at least a chance at a federal forum. This detailed catalogue suggests federal jurisdiction is the exception, not the rule. Most ordinary disputes must remain in state courts.

Article III next carefully protects the vaguely sketched Supreme Court, listing a small set of cases that such a Court must be able to hear no matter whether the Congress, the states, or the parties want it to or not. The sketch of a court system is never completed, though. As if even the outline so far developed has become almost too scary, the Article finally turns to listing a few vital things the nonexistent federal courts can't do.

SECTION ONE. We begin with another ambiguous vesting clause: "the judicial Power of the United States" is to be vested—we'll consider in a minute in whom. But first note the different wording among the three Articles. "All legislative Powers herein granted" refers us to the Constitution's text for its interpretation; "the executive Power" is free-floating, something that seems to exist apart from text, place, and time; "the judicial Power of the United States" refers to a specific set of powers, but one for which there is no previous definition.

It cannot mean the then-existing power of United States courts, for there were no US courts in the Confederation years. Only state courts existed, and when their decisions clashed, or when states found themselves at legal odds, the Articles of Confederation had set up a cumbersome ad hoc procedure by which Congress would appoint arbitrators to settle the dispute.

Now there would be a federal judicial power and a place for it. But while Articles I and II created institutions where their vested powers would live—a Senate, a House, a president—the judicial power was to be vested in "one supreme Court, *and* in such inferior Courts as the Congress may from time to time ordain and establish."

Unlike the House, which has a set initial number of members outlined in the text, or the Senate, which will have exactly two members per state, or the executive, which consists of a president, the Supreme Court has no prescribed number of members. Unlike the Congress, which has detailed procedures, the Supreme Court has no constitutional rules. Its very size is left up to the Congress, which has at various points in history reduced (it has been as low as six) and enlarged it (to as many as ten). The current number of nine justices was set in 1869.

The text does not even say explicitly that Congress is to create the Supreme Court and to set the number of justices at its discretion. Where does this power come from? It is not textual. Article III allows Congress to "ordain and establish" *inferior* courts, but is silent as to who will do the same for the "one supreme court." The power can't come from Article I, Section Eight, Clause Nine, which gives Congress only the power to "to constitute tribunals *inferior to the supreme Court.*"

Yet a court cannot create itself, and where else could the power lie? The president might have greedily claimed the power to create the Court (on the theory, beloved of presidents and their lawyers, of "what's not clearly Congress's is mine"). But he would not be able to appoint "judges of the supreme Court" by himself—Article II, Section Two, specifically provides that is to be done "by and with the advice and consent of the Senate." Congress, if empowered to create "inferior courts," surely must be able to do the same for the "one supreme Court." Creating a court is a "legislative power."

But consider the paradox: the Constitution requires the existence of one Supreme Court, both reposing power in it and defining (as we'll see) its irreducible minimum jurisdiction. But what if Congress, meeting in 1789, had refused to set one up? Or what if a future Congress, vexed by Supreme Court decisions to which its members object, were to *abolish* the current Court and try to vest the judicial power in another, or return it to the state courts, or just forgo a judiciary altogether?

I once attended a meeting of Northwest mountain people who believe that virtually all of modern life is unconstitutional. The speaker explained to the listeners that they, as "sovereign citizens," were the "one Supreme Court" of Article III. The nine-headed hydra in Washington was as fraudulent as the IRS or the Federal Reserve, he said, because the Constitution said nothing about such a multimember body.

Like a lot of crazy ideas, that argument has a certain internal logic. It illustrates something important about how to read a Constitution. In this clause, the Constitution apparently neglects to grant the authority for creating an institution whose existence it demands. If, like some biblical interpreters, we assume that the Constitution is inspired, infallible, and complete, then the "one supreme Court" thus must *already exist*, independent of the will of Congress. If we read the Constitution as a statute, we use the old maxim of statutory construction, *expressio unius exclusio alterius est* ("to express one thing is to exclude all others"), and the textual grant of power to set up "inferior" courts would mean that Congress had no power to set up a Supreme Court. But if we read the document as a human instrument, necessarily incomplete and ambiguous, intended to outline a system of government and leave the details to future decision, then it makes sense to conclude that its authors assumed that Congress would create a Court and either forgot to explain exactly how to do so, or (more likely) assumed we are smart enough to figure it out. What that Court would look like is left to the imagination. The very term "Supreme Court" in 1787 was something of a novelty. In Britain, the two high courts were the House of Lords, which heard final appeals at law, and the Privy Council, which heard appeals in equity. The term had been used before: Virginia's highest court, established in 1779, was the Supreme Court of Appeals. But there was no ready-made idea of what a "supreme court" was. The name at the time had a kind of poetic suggestiveness, which, over time, has acquired a retroactive air of precision. It could, for example, have been made up of the judges of other courts (as was the Virginia model), who would sit occasionally as a supreme tribunal. There could thus really have been only a chief justice, presiding over judges borrowed from elsewhere.

In any case, the First Congress set up a Supreme Court, and other Congresses have created the rest of the court system. The president and the Senate staff the federal courts. After that, however, the executive and legislative branches lose most of their control of the judicial power. That's because Article III requires that all federal judges, "both of the supreme and inferior Courts," hold their offices for "good Behaviour."

That's a curious phrase to modern ears—in contemporary law, "good behavior" is largely the concern of prison inmates, who earn reduced sentences for following prison regulations. One legal scholar has commented that this clause "could well be the most mysterious provision in the United States Constitution—and that, of course, is really saying something."[3]

The phrase comes from English common law. The king couldn't fire a judge just because he didn't like his decisions; the judge had to be found guilty by a court of some offense. How does that fit into the Constitution? It could mean that any judge found guilty of a crime could be removed. By whom? The Constitution mentions only one method of getting rid of any federal official: impeachment by Congress. But impeachment is not mentioned in Article III; in fact, the Constitution never says that *judges* are subject to impeachment at all. Article II specifies that "the President, Vice President and all civil Officers of the United States" are subject to impeachment and removal. But the president and vice president are *executive* officials, who serve for fixed terms, not for "good behavior," and thus might need more protection in office. We could read "civil officers" as being only executive officials as well. That could mean that the strictly limited grounds for impeachment—"treason, high crimes and misdemeanors"—don't apply to judges. Could "good behavior" be a separate requirement for judges—that is, requiring them not only to avoid treason and crimes of state but any other crime? Or any "behavior" Congress disapproves of? Could Congress by statute render judges liable to removal by other judges, or by Congress, or even by the president, if any of them determined that a judge's "behavior" was no longer "good"? Some scholars and politicians have seriously suggested that Congress should have the power to remove judges for offenses that would not be impeachable—for example, giving opinions the majority does not like—and by procedures that do not require the two-thirds majority needed for a Senate conviction in impeachment.

Never in American history, however, has that reading been adopted. Most serious interpreters read this text as meaning that a judge holds office for life, or until resignation or impeachment. It certainly reads like a measure that protects judges, rather than one that empowers the other branches. It's coupled with language that requires that judges receive a regular salary that cannot be cut no matter how much their decisions may displease the president or Congress. It would be odd indeed if their salaries were guaranteed while their jobs were not.

The compensation clause, like the provision barring members of Congress from executive positions, is an important "separation of powers" provision. Missing, however, is a mechanism used to separate the judicial power from the other two. While members of Congress may not hold "any Office under the United States" during their terms, neither judges nor executive officials are so barred; thus one person might apparently hold judicial and executive office at the same time. It seems outlandish to imagine that a judge today might also be, say a member of the Cabinet. America's first chief justice, John Jay, however, was sent while on the bench by President Washington to negotiate a treaty with England; John Marshall, our greatest chief justice, continued in office as secretary of state for more than a month after taking office on the Court. More recently, Associate Justice Robert Jackson was the nation's chief counsel at the Nuremberg war trials; and Chief Justice Earl Warren chaired the "Warren Commission," a body created by the president to investigate the Kennedy assassination. At least theoretically, a sitting justice might enter the Cabinet, or even run for national office; the Constitution does not forbid it, whatever judicial ethics might suggest.

Note too that the chief justice is mentioned only in Article I. Article III does not name that position as something separate from the "one supreme Court," or give instructions about where he will come from. The president has always appointed the chief justice, not because Article III says he shall, but because Article II gives the president, with Senate approval, the power to appoint "Judges of the supreme Court."

So there has to be a chief justice. But since the Article does not specify a number of "judges" of the Supreme Court, Congress could in theory comply with its requirements by creating a one-member Court, made up of a single chief justice. Mercifully, Congress never has. The Supreme Court, as we shall see, is granted jurisdiction over appeals; thus it makes sense to organize it as appeals courts have always been organized—as multimember tribunals, not the province of a single judge. The current Court numbers nine justices and hears each case en banc, meaning that all nine justices sit and deliberate. The Constitution doesn't require that. In theory, Congress could, if it chose, split it into (say) three three-judge panels to render final judgment, subject only to special review by all nine judges in exceptional cases.

SECTION TWO. Article III then goes on to specify the extent of "the judicial power." Before looking at its scope, we should be alert to two different legal attributes of courts, which are not the same. Courts cannot *exist* without power; they cannot *function* without jurisdiction. Power means that a court system as a whole has the ability to decide cases and render judgments; jurisdiction is the authority of a specific court to exercise that power over specific parties and disputes. It's a distinction only lawyers could love, but it is a consequential one. As we'll see, Article III gives some details of both, but leaves a great deal to work out about how the two interrelate.

First, the power: it encompasses both "law" and "equity," two complete systems that existed at that time in British jurisprudence, each with its own set of rules and court structure. Common-law courts were the king's courts. Their job was to resolve disputes that threatened the king's peace. They could issue verdicts in criminal matters, and they could award money damages in civil cases. If a losing party declined to pay the judgment, the court would order the sheriff to seize the loser's property and give the proceeds to the winner.

This not infrequently resulted in absurd or unjust results and sometimes made it impossible for a prevailing party to get relief. Over the centuries a parallel chancery system evolved under the supervision of the lord chancellor. When a common-law court had rendered an absurd or unfair judgment, the chancellor (or in time officials acting in his name) could step in and "enjoin" the result, fashioning different, more freestyle remedies. These could include orders to individuals to perform specific actions, enforced by imprisonment for contempt of court if a party refused to obey.

At law, final appeal ran to the House of Lords; the Court of Chancery could be reversed only by the king's Privy Council. The Constitution's text makes plain that in the new nation, the one Supreme Court was to have power to determine the final result in either system.

Next, the grant of judicial power is specified in two *kinds* of cases. The first variety consists of cases "arising under this Constitution, the Laws of the United States, and Treaties." This is called "federal question" jurisdiction. Even if I am suing my next-door neighbor, if the suit depends specifically on federal law, the federal judicial power can reach it.

The second kind of case consists of those arising in admiralty. These cases involved private civil disputes over international shipping and passengers. For a nation heavily dependent on the sea trade with Europe and the Caribbean, it would have made sense to have one set of courts dealing with these important matters.

The admiralty clause marks the second reference in the text to what we would call "international law." Courts of Admiralty enforced a system of laws common to all nations using the high seas and used a very specialized set of procedures.

Most prominently, these courts did not provide for trial by jury; this fact had made them unpopular during the years before the Revolution.

Thus the judicial power always reaches two kinds of cases, federal and admiralty. But the judicial power can *sometimes* extend to ordinary garden-variety cases—contract disputes, tort suits, property claims, and any of the other ordinary business of court. That would happen when the parties were from different states, or when their claims reached across state lines. Those cases were disputes (1) involving foreign diplomats; (2) between any party and the federal government; (3) between two state governments; (4) between a state government and citizens from another state; (5) between foreign citizens and state governments; (6) between parties from different states; and (7) between parties from the same state if they claimed title to land under two different land grants from two state governments. The last one seems a bit puzzling today—it would be unthinkable today for Idaho to grant title to land in Montana. But at the time of the Framing, everyone knew that the current thirteen states would soon be allowing new states to be formed in the West out of their present western lands. The situation could easily arise in which a new government of, say, Kentucky could grant title to land that was already covered by a grant dating from the days when Kentucky was part of Virginia.

The idea seems to be that federal power must reach any dispute in which one side would have an unfair home-field advantage in the state courts. Local judges and juries are notoriously partial to local parties, and their bias might infect the court system, or lead to disputes between state court systems.

The grant of power over disputes "between a state and citizens of another state" slides smoothly by the eye in this context. If a national referee was needed for disputes between states themselves, and disputes between citizens of different states, then the same underlying logic of fairness would suggest that it should cover a dispute between ordinary people in one state who had legal disputes with the government of another state. This clause, however, was to prove intensely controversial in practice, and to spark, in 1795, the first amendment to the new Constitution after the Bill of Rights.

The foregoing list covered the cases to which the judicial power extended; but power, as we noted earlier, is not the same as jurisdiction. Jurisdiction is needed to bring a case within the walls of a particular court. Consider, for example, a dispute between two neighbors over the boundary between their yards. The state judicial system will have power to resolve the disputes. But if one party storms into traffic court and demands relief, he will be shown the door. By statute, the traffic court has *jurisdiction* only over traffic offenses; jurisdiction over land disputes lies in other courts.

Bear in mind that there need be only one federal court, the Supreme Court, if Congress chooses not to create "inferior" courts. Where, in that case, would a party go to seek a trial on a dispute covered by federal judicial power?

First, the clearest answer: in a small class of cases, an actual trial may be held in the Supreme Court itself. This "original" jurisdiction extends to (1) cases against diplomats and (2) cases against states themselves. That means the Supreme Court could sit as a trial court in those cases. By its terms, though, it's not a grant of *exclusive* jurisdiction. It was not clear that there would ever be any federal court other than the Supreme Court. If Congress hadn't created "inferior courts," then even most federal cases would start in the state courts and come to the Supreme Court only on appeal. The original-jurisdiction clause suggests that there was a small class of cases so clearly federal that no state court could be trusted to hear them at any level. Only a federal court could hear these cases, even if the Supreme Court was the only federal court in existence.

Congress, however, elected at once to set up lower federal courts. Over the years, Congress has granted original jurisdiction in most of these "original juris-diction" cases to the lower federal courts as well, with appeal flowing from them to the Supreme Court. It is logical and efficient—the Supreme Court has no trial mechanism (many of the justices have never even seen the inside of a trial courtroom). Findings of fact will be better made by trial judges or juries, with the Supreme Court exercising its now-traditional function of reviewing the judgment only for errors of law.

However, the Supreme Court by statute retains *exclusive* original jurisdiction in one specific class of cases—those between two state governments where one state seeks to force the other to do something such as give up disputed territory. In those infrequent cases, the Supreme Court will hold a "trial" by appointing a "special master" with the skills and time to determine these factual issues; the master's conclusions may then be approved or rejected by the Court itself, which considers them much like an appeal from a trial court.

In all other federal cases, the Supreme Court "shall have appellate jurisdic-tion." What this means is that if a case, because of its subject or its parties, is one to which the judicial power extends, then the Court may hear appeals of the judgment regardless of whether a state or federal court delivers that judgment. The appellate jurisdiction implies the ability to set aside the judgment and either enter a new judgment or send the case back to the original court with instruc-tions on how to decide it.

This revision power extends both to the lower courts' conclusions of law and to their findings of fact. The inclusion of law and fact was controversial at the time and to some extent remains so today, because it implies that a federal court might have power to ignore a state jury's verdict. Common law judges decided questions of law and so instructed the jury—*You may find Stagger Lee guilty of murdering Billy Lyons only if Stagger Lee was not acting in self-defense or upon rea-sonable provocation, intended to cause Billy's death, and did in fact cause it;* the jury "found" the facts—*Stagger Lee was not provoked beforehand and was not defending himself when he fired the pistol; he intended to kill Billy, and he did in fact cause the injuries that killed him; we find him guilty.*

In many court systems then and in some today the higher courts are almost completely barred from disturbing a jury's determination of fact. If the Supreme Court can set aside jury verdicts, then in theory it could impose a federal solution on civil disputes despite the will of the people expressed by a jury of citizens. And even worse, it might use this jurisdiction to set aside a jury's verdict of "not guilty" in a criminal case and clap disfavored defendants into prison despite a verdict of acquittal. (This possibility was foreclosed by the Fifth Amendment.)

But in this sweeping grant we see the ambiguous relationship between power and jurisdiction—because the Supreme Court's appellate jurisdiction does not extend of its own force to these cases. The grant of original jurisdiction was unqualified, and it seems unlikely that Congress could prevent the Court from exercising it. However, the appellate jurisdiction is granted "with such Exceptions, and under such Regulations as the Congress shall make." Thus Congress need not grant the Supreme Court actual jurisdiction over all appeals to which the judicial power extends. It has allowed the Court some discretion about which of certain kinds of cases it will hear, and it has chosen to allow state courts to make final decisions in some classes of cases. It has done so over the years in various uncontroversial ways. For example, the mere fact that a case *might* involve a question of federal law is not enough to give rise to appellate jurisdiction over a state court judgment. Appeals in a small class of cases *must* be heard by the Court: cases where state courts invalidate federal laws or uphold state laws against a claim that they violate the US Constitution. Other state cases that decide federal issues may come before the Supreme Court only if the Court considers them worthy of its time. And if a case involves federal law but is decided also on state law grounds, the Supreme Court will usually not hear it.

But lurking behind the words "exceptions" and "regulations" is a more serious question. Could Congress simply determine that a certain kind of federal case will be a complete "exception" to the Supreme Court's jurisdiction, or to any federal jurisdiction whatever? Over the past half-century, members of Congress have tried repeatedly to circumvent Supreme Court decisions they disliked— such as those requiring school desegregation, or banning mandatory school prayer, or protecting criminal suspects in certain ways—by proposing statutes barring the Court from hearing appeals from state courts on these issues. The statutes to date have not passed, and so the power has not been tested. Previous decisions of the Court suggest that Congress's power to create "exceptions" is quite broad; for years, scholars have debated whether it is complete. Many suggest that there is an irreducible "core" of jurisdiction needed to make the constitutional scheme work. Congress has, perhaps wisely, never pushed the issue; it seems unlikely that a modern Court would sustain a congressional statute that attempted to neuter it on any important issue.

Having defined the federal power and outlined the potential shape of its jurisdiction, Section Two next turns to a very short list of "thou shalt nots" directed at the federal courts. Neither Congress nor the federal courts can abolish trial by jury in criminal cases. Nor may they seize local defendants and carry them off to distant places to stand trial: criminal trials must take place in the state where the crime allegedly took place. A crime committed in the federal territories, or on foreign soil ("not committed in any state"), however, may be tried wherever Congress chooses.

This part of Section Two applies, as noted, only to criminal trials. By guaranteeing trial by jury in those cases, the drafters raised alarms that they were silently abolishing juries in civil cases. (The objectors were reading the Constitution like a statute, again by the principle that to say one thing is to deny all others.) Whether that was a valid objection or not, a guarantee of jury trial in civil cases was added in the Seventh Amendment.

SECTION THREE. Section Three, the most detailed and rigid prohibition in Article III, is one of the most important protections of civil liberty in the entire Constitution, including the Bill of Rights. It binds both the federal courts and the Congress that would create them. Simply put, the law and the courts could not become an instrument of political oppression by defining political dissent as treason.

Treason was the mega-crime of English history; the very word still chills the blood. At common law, the penalty was drawing and quartering—being pulled apart by horses and then hacked apart by swords—and then disembowelment. Traitors entered the Tower by a special "Traitor's Gate"; a traitor's head often decorated a pike for the crows to feast on; a traitor's estate was forfeit to the Crown.

Kings loved treason. Why not? They got rid of potential enemies, and they got rich off their wealth. Until the dawn of the eighteenth century, those accused of treason got no real trial. They were dragged before judges who doubled as prosecutors. Sometimes Parliament took onto itself the power of trying accused traitors through a "bill of attainder," a simple legislative determination that a named person was a traitor and was to be executed.

The offense of treason was broad: it included "compassing the death of the King"—that is, saying or imagining that the king might die. Adultery by the queen was treason—Anne Boleyn was beheaded on charges that she had lain with other men. Common-law judges, loyal arms of the Crown, used the doctrine of "constructive treason" to extend the offense further, until politicians simply accused of opposing royal policies could find themselves marched to the block, leaving their families penniless and disgraced. Indeed, by the late seventeenth century, treason charges could even be brought against the king himself if the political winds blew against him—Charles I was executed as a traitor in 1649.

The Framers in Section Two placed a limit on Congress and the courts— treason against the United States, it says, "shall consist only in levying War against them, or in adhering to their Enemies, giving them Aid and Comfort." Under this language, presidents cannot drag their defeated political opponents to the gallows. And the courts, says Article III, cannot adopt the inquisitorial ways of British treason prosecution: no conviction can be had, except "on the Testimony of two Witnesses to the same overt Act" or by a public confession of the accused, made in court, where the public would see whether a torturer was standing by to refresh his memory.

Section Two then restricts the penalties Congress may enact for any "Attainder of Treason." That may be confusing, because Article I already flatly outlawed "bills of attainder." But the word "attainder" by itself simply means verdict or judgment of criminal liability. A "bill of attainder" was a device by which a legislative body bypassed the requirement of a trial by passing an act declaring a certain person a traitor. A defendant convicted by a duly constituted Article III court after a trial by jury would nevertheless be "attainted" by the court's judgment. Even after a proper trial, however, treason could not carry the penalty of "corruption of blood"—a penalty that barred a convicted traitor's heirs from inheriting any of his property; forfeiture for treason may be enforced only "during the Life of the Person attainted."

All in all, treason was to be defined narrowly, and treason statutes were to be enforced with caution. In 1803, President Jefferson tried to stretch the definition in his prosecution of his own vice president, Aaron Burr. Jefferson's cousin, Chief Justice John Marshall, enforced Section III to the letter, whether out of textual fidelity or merely for the pleasure of galling a Virginia cousin whom he detested. The result ever since has been a very narrow reading of the meaning of treason.

Ironically, the largest group that ever "levied war" against the United States— the leadership of the Confederacy during the Civil War—never faced treason trials. President Andrew Johnson made liberal use of the pardon power to forestall any prosecution. Johnson was no Solomon.

Article IV

All God's Children

The first three articles create a federal father who is three persons in one—Congress the lawgiver, president the enforcer, and Supreme Court the judge. Article IV turns to the Union's children: the states. It makes rules for how they must treat each other, and pledges the federal father's protection and discipline. Article IV shows remarkably little concern for the "sovereignty," or "rights," of the children. Instead of empowering, it admonishes. States are to behave properly toward each other; do nothing that might infringe the father's realm; seek the father's blessing upon their very governments; seek shelter under the paternal wing.

SECTION ONE. Most of incidents of our legal lives involve relations with our state governments. States register our births, our marriages, our deaths. They grant divorces and decide child custody. They give or withhold driving permits, business charters, and professional licenses. They recognize our title to property, and they decide how and to whom that property will go after we die. Remarkably enough, nothing in the Constitution *explicitly* bars the federal government from taking over these roles, but it will never happen. Most Americans prefer them to be carried out close to home. (As we saw in the discussion of Article I, a reading of Section Eight's "two cities" might suggest that matters of home, heart, and hearth "belong" to the states; but there is no explicit statement of that principle anywhere in the document.)

But what if a citizen of one state sues a citizen of another in state court? Or what if a litigant, having lost in one state, were to flee to another and refuse to accept the judgment? Chaos would lurk if the courts of one state could refuse to follow the judgments of another—a disappointed litigant could relocate and claim the benefit of more favorable law.

A second question is the portability of a state's public "acts." Must Americans be born again or marry again if they move from one state to another? Section One sets out two principles for limiting this kind of legal disorder. First, each state was expected to respect "the public Acts, Records, and judicial Proceedings of every other State." Second, Congress could have the final say on how those "Acts, Records, and judicial Proceedings" were to be documented by the states, on what individuals would have to do to prove that they existed, and finally, on "the Effect thereof."

The Full Faith and Credit Clause has been uncontroversial when applied to court judgments. One state's courts, in a proper case, would decide issues between two litigants, and those judgments are not to be reopened because another state's courts might have decided them a different way. Other "public acts"—specifically the act of recognizing a valid marriage—raise a more complex question.

Since 2004, some states have begun allowing same-sex couples within their borders to marry, while others have enacted statutes or state constitutional amendments forbidding same-sex couples to marry. If two men or two women marry in, say, Maryland (whose legislature voted to allow gay marriage, and whose people voted in 2012 to approve that law), does Alabama have to recognize their union? In 1934, long before this question had been dreamt of, the Supreme Court had enunciated this rule: "Marriages not polygamous or incestuous, or otherwise declared void by statute, will, if valid by the law of the state where entered into, be recognized as valid in every other jurisdiction."[1] The Court in the 1934 case held that the "public policy" exception did not permit the District of Columbia to refuse to recognize the remarriage of a woman whose first husband had divorced her for adultery. In the District, the adulterous partner in a divorce was not permitted to remarry. The woman, however, had remarried in Florida, which had no such rule. The Court carefully read the DC statutes and found that they did not explicitly declare all such marriages void; they simply prohibited performance of such marriages in DC.

This decision embodies what is called the "public policy" exception to "full faith and credit": again, states must recognize other states' marriages unless they are "polygamous or incestuous, or otherwise declared void by statute." That exception is now relevant to the question of same-sex marriage. Congress has enacted a number of provisions under its power to regulate the "Acts, Records, and judicial Proceedings" and "the Effect thereof." Mostly they have to do with the formalities of proving a state record or judgment in another state—seals and certifications. But in recent years a very unusual provision was added to this part of the United States Code:

> No State, territory, or possession of the United States, or Indian tribe, shall be required to give effect to any public act, record, or judicial proceeding of any other State, territory, possession, or tribe respecting a relationship between persons of the same sex that is treated as a marriage under the laws of such other State, territory, possession, or tribe, or a right or claim arising from such relationship.[2]

This provision is one part of the Defense of Marriage Act (DOMA), passed by Congress in September 1996 and signed by President Bill Clinton shortly afterward. Another part of the act, Section Three, proclaims as federal policy that in construing federal law, "the word 'marriage' means only a legal union between one man and one woman as husband and wife, and the word 'spouse' refers only to a person of the opposite sex who is a husband or a wife."[3]

Whatever one thinks of these provisions as social policy (not to hide the ball, I dislike them intensely), there is a kind of constitutional disjuncture in their bases. The language about construing federal law seems, as a matter of constitutional law, relatively straightforward: Congress is specifying rules of construction for *federal* law.

Section 1738C, which was Section Two of DOMA, however, is more anomalous. It squats uneasily amid other sections of the US Code that are designed to govern procedure and evidence, not underlying policy. Pegged to the constitutional language of the clause that says "Congress may by general Laws prescribe . . . the Effect thereof," it licenses states, at their option, to *ignore* one set of legal acts by other states. And that language raises a question that is, in moral terms, inconsequential but in constitutional terms quite important. It is this: whether or not Congress acted wisely in enacting Section 1738C, has it acted beyond its Constitutional powers? While states may have a limited power to ignore marriages that violate their "public policy," does Congress have a role to play in encouraging or authorizing specific exceptions? Behind that is another question: is a same-sex union like a polygamous or incestuous language— shameful, taboo virtually everywhere in our civilization—or is it an expression of a basic right of two adults to order their lives without pernicious discrimination by the state? If it is the latter, then no constitutional "public policy" can justify a bar on same-sex unions.

At this writing, the issue of DOMA's constitutionality is pending before the Supreme Court in a case called *United States v. Windsor*. But that case concerns only Section Three of DOMA—the provision stating how federal law applies to same-sex marriages valid under state law. The question of how one state must treat another state's marriages is not directly implicated by the case. A federal district court in Florida in 2005 rejected a same-sex couple's claim that the state must recognize their Massachusetts marriage, stating that "Florida is not required to recognize or apply Massachusetts' same-sex marriage law because it clearly conflicts with Florida's legitimate public policy of opposing same-sex marriage."[4]

But the way the Court decides *Windsor* could have serious implications for the "public policy" exception. States may have their own "public policy"—but that public policy can't violate the U.S. Constitution. Consider the case of Mildred and Richard Loving. Residents of Virginia, they married in 1958—but the wedding was held in the District of Columbia, because Virginia at that time barred any marriage between a white person (Richard) and a person having any drop of non-white blood (Mildred). Later that year the Lovings were arrested in Virginia and banished from the state on pain of prison. In 1967, the Supreme Court held the Virginia statute unconstitutional because "under our Constitution, the freedom to marry, or not marry, a person of another race resides with the individual and cannot be infringed by the State."[5] The problem was one of "the equal protection of the laws," which usually forbids racial distinctions.

The opportunity exists for this Court to hold that that principle extends to same-sex marriage too. If it voids Section Three of DOMA by saying that distinctions of sexual orientation by the federal government offend the principle of equal protection, then it seems unlikely that similar state distinctions could survive.

However it resolves that issue, the Court's decision will create new reasons to argue over the text and history of both the Equal Protection Clause and the Full Faith and Credit Clause. For the moment, however, we can take note that the opaque technical language of Article IV, and the way we read it, can also take on overwhelming importance in our most intimate decisions.

SECTION TWO. Article One, in setting out provisions for congressional apportionment, had created a human hierarchy: free citizens, those not yet free or bound for freedom, "Indians not taxed, and "other persons"—slaves. Traces of that hierarchy now appear in Section Two, which sets out what is to happen when people from one state travel to another.

First, citizens "of each State shall be entitled to all Privileges and Immunities of Citizens in the several States." This provision is marvelously ambiguous in many ways. To begin with there was a troublesome ambiguity in the original Constitution about who was a "citizen of the United States." The president must be a "natural born" citizen; members of the House and Senate must have been citizens for a certain number of years. Congress had the power to set up a system by which foreign-born persons acquire citizenship by naturalization. But there was no general definition of United States citizenship in the 1787 document.

State citizenship at that time was the defining characteristic of Americans, with national citizenship depending on it; the first part of Section Two, which we call the "comity clause," apparently guarantees that an individual who has citizenship in one state did not lose it by crossing a state line.

But what are these "Privileges and Immunities of Citizens in the several States"? Critics over the years have proposed at least two possible meanings. First, the clause might mean that every American citizen had some unspecified set of rights guaranteed nationally and that did not change from state to state. But what has prevailed is the second meaning: once a state citizen enters another state, the citizen must be treated in the new state *no worse than* the new state treats its own citizens. The clause requires "comity," or equal respect, from the state legal systems when it comes to citizens' rights.

This is an important guarantee—no impulse is more widely shared in political systems than the impulse to treat outsiders badly, and states are disallowed from yielding to it. But the scope of the guarantee made clear how limited was the protection of national citizenship. Both in the original Constitution, and even in the Constitution as amended by the Bill of Rights, national citizenship in itself provided almost no individual rights that state governments were bound to respect.

States in the new union could restrict the vote by race, sex, and wealth; they could limit officeholders to members of one or another religious sect; they could deny their citizens freedom of speech and the press; they could establish a church and require citizens to fund it; they could create and enforce fine gradations of civil status without even a formal nod toward equality. The only restriction imposed by their membership in the Union was that citizens of other states could be treated no worse than a state's own citizens. That baseline of equality, however, kicks in textually only once the out-of-state citizen has *entered*; could a state entirely bar entry of out-of-state citizens? The text nowhere forbids this; and note that the text does explicitly spell out the right of states to *permit* "migration or importation" of outsiders. Would permission to permit imply permission to exclude?

The Comity Clause is derived from a much clearer if equally troubling provision of the Articles of Confederation, which guaranteed equality of treatment to "free inhabitants" (thus eliding the entire vexed question of citizenship, and making no mention of race, but making sure that slaves were not included) of the states, "paupers, vagabonds, and fugitives from Justice excepted." The Articles went on to guarantee that "the people of each state shall have free ingress and regress to and from any other State."[6] The Framers omitted this; but it seems to have been taken for granted almost from the beginning that "comity" included the right of free entry as well as equal treatment once inside.

So much for ordinary citizens traveling interstate. One step down the hierarchy come persons "charged in any State with Treason, Felony, or other Crime." Remember that the Articles of Confederation had exempted from the right of "free ingress and regress" all "fugitives from justice." While suggesting that states could prevent fugitives from entering, the Articles were silent about what if any rights fugitives would have if they succeeded in entering another state. The Framers omitted language about the right of entry and exit; but they decided to be far more specific than the Articles about fugitives.

In so doing, they again incorporated by reference a concept from international law, that of extradition. Extradition was not a common-law concept—indeed, in 1857 one English writer called it "a foreign and un-English word to express an un-English thing."[7] It was a transaction between sovereign states. Under an extradition treaty, a fugitive from one country would be arrested in a second country and returned to his country of origin. Section Two does not use the term (un-English, you know), but provides an automatic mechanism to carry it out.

Before considering the mechanism, however, note the definition of those subject to it—a person "charged in any State with Treason, Felony, or other Crime." Why is "treason" there? Surely an accused traitor could be arrested by federal authorities anywhere in the United States. That certainly is correct when it pertains to the federal treason statute. But treason is not restricted to treason against the national government. Recall that the Treason Clause of Article III referred to "treason *against the United States.*" In English legal history, subjects could commit treason not only against the king or the nation as a whole—"high treason"—but also against their feudal lords or lawful masters under articles of indenture or apprenticeship—"petty treason."

In the new nation, states asserted their rights to punish their own citizens for treason not against the nation but against themselves. Prosecutions for treason against state governments continued long after the Constitution was ratified. Probably the most famous treason execution in American history—the hanging of John Brown in 1859 for his leadership of a raid on a federal arsenal at Harper's Ferry, Virginia—was for treason against the Commonwealth of Virginia, not the United States. Even though his crimes took place on a federal reservation, Virginia insisted on trying Brown for state treason. (Had he been prosecuted in federal court, Brown would have had an arsenal of constitutional arguments, and northern opinion might have even demanded an eventual presidential pardon.)

At his trial, Brown argued that, not being a citizen of Virginia, he owed the state no duty of allegiance; but a defendant who had tried to incite a slave revolt received little legal solicitude from a judge and jury committed to slavery.

The crime of treason against a state still exists, at least in theory. As recently as 2005, Governor Jennifer Granholm of Michigan, stung by criticism of her tax policy by a Michigander writing in the *Wall Street Journal*, said that the column had been "treasonous to the state of Michigan." Another writer pointed out that the Michigan state constitution contained the same definition of treason as does Article III of the US Constitution. The critic had hardly "levied war" against the government in Lansing.[8]

But the main work of the extradition clause was not to retrieve state traitors, but to provide what should be done with those accused of "felony or other crime." Here the clause was clear: such a person "shall on Demand of the executive Authority of the State from which he fled, be delivered up, to be removed to the State having Jurisdiction of the Crime." The "executive authority" of the state of refuge has no discretion; extradition, once requested, is to be automatic. The one limit on the obligation is that a state that has custody of a fugitive can insist that he or she fulfil any criminal sentence pronounced in the state having custody before being returned to the state seeking extradition.

The clause does not provide an enforcement mechanism. Unlike the Full Faith and Credit Clause, which does explicitly give Congress power to prescribe rules for proof and effect, the Extradition Clause grants no power to Congress. But Congress quickly adopted statutes to require states to comply with extradition requests. The power to enforce the Extradition Clause is yet another example of a "legislative power herein granted" that is neither contained in Article I nor indeed created by text. A state-oriented reader could argue that Congress has no extradition-enforcement power, and that extradition requests between states are to be negotiated between them as equal "sovereigns," just as independent nations, joined in an extradition treaty, must still often negotiate the actual transfer of fugitives. A pro-federal reader could argue that the mandatory language of necessity creates enforcement authority in Congress.

The implied power over extradition is not seriously questioned today, and federal rules govern interstate extradition. Many citizens still believe that states have the discretion to refuse to grant extradition if they believe a fugitive is being unfairly treated by the state from which he fled. But the Constitution gives no such power. Some of the misunderstanding may arise from the use in news reports of the phrase "waived extradition." Waiver of extradition does not refer to a discretionary act by the state, but to a concession by the defendant—that is, a fugitive may choose not to insist on the time-consuming formalities of extradition but simply to return voluntarily to the original state.

During the antebellum era, Kentucky sought extradition from Ohio of Willis Lago, a "free man of color," on charges that he "did seduce and entice Charlotte, a slave, the property of C. W. Nuckols, to leave her owner and possessor" and flee with him to free territory. This was not a crime in free Ohio, and the governor of the state refused to give him up. In a classic constitutional bait-and-switch, the Supreme Court sternly held that the governor had no power to resist extradition for any crime under the laws of the first state; having made that clear, the Court then held that the governor was *obligated* to render the fugitive, but that federal courts could not *order* him to do so.[9] The fugitive remained free until the outbreak of the Civil War mooted the case; and the principle that federal courts could not order compliance was abandoned a century later. Today, if a state refuses to extradite a fugitive, the state seeking extradition may go to court to get an order requiring it.

Now Section Two descends to the bottom rung of the Constitution's ladder of personhood. The final provision is known as the Fugitive Slave Clause; it is perhaps the most notorious single clause of the original Constitution, and probably contributed more than any other to the catastrophic failure of that Constitution in 1861.

Of course, the Fugitive Slave Clause does not announce itself as such. The word "person" appears, and with it the silent specter of slavery is back in the room: "No Person held to Service or Labour in one State, under the Laws thereof, escaping into another, shall, in Consequence of any Law or Regulation therein, be discharged from such Service or Labour."

Note the delicacy of the language—not a slave, but a person somehow required to render "service or labor"; not a person required to provide service or labor "by law," which might imply *federal* recognition of slavery, but a person *held*, without saying legitimately, "under the laws" of a state; not even a person who clearly owes service to anyone—a slave's owner is described as "the Party to whom such Service or Labour *may* be due."

But this rhetorical concession to anti-slavery sensibilities is more than canceled by the harshness of the provision as a whole. Section Two creates something almost shockingly anomalous—a *private* constitutional right, the power to demand that government use public power to act in a citizen's purely private interest. It is the only such individual right of action created by the original document. A "person held to service or labor" was to be returned. The demand for the return would not come, as in the case of extradition, from the original state from which the fugitive escaped; instead, it could come directly from "the Party to whom such Service or Labour may be due."

Such a "person" is to be "delivered up on claim" of the person to whom the labor "may be due." It did not say "upon proof," or "demonstration," or "upon a finding by due process of law." Read literally—and slave states had some very good lawyers ready to argue this literal meaning—it meant that a person alleged to be a fugitive slave must be surrendered without any due process upon the naked allegation by a white person to be the alleged fugitive's owner. A putative owner would make a "claim" of ownership, and that claim would end the matter.

Congress enacted the first fugitive slave law in 1793.[10] The determination of slaves to escape, and the growing popular revulsion against slavery in the free states, however, made it harder and harder for slave owners to reclaim their slaves on free soil; in response, the federal Fugitive Slave Act of 1850 removed considerations of state law or procedure from the rendition of slaves. An entire new federal bureaucracy was erected, independent of the Article III courts, to render allegedly escaped slaves without delay. Instead of state or federal judges, claims by ostensible slave owners were brought before a federal commissioner; the master's allegation was to prevail absent contrary evidence—and the alleged slave was not permitted to testify in his or her own behalf. Commissioners were paid by the case. For each "slave" returned, they received $10—about two weeks' pay for an unskilled laborer; for each alleged slave they released, they got only $5.[11]

Nowhere in the original Constitution was the stark contradiction between the "blessings of liberty" and the need to protect slavery more corrosively expressed. Successive attempts to enforce the Fugitive Slave Clause did more and more damage to the overall framework of the Union; and the Fugitive Slave Act of 1850 did as much as any other southern aggression to bring on the cataclysm that destroyed the original Constitution in 1861.

SECTION THREE. The language of "state's rights," as we've seen, is never used in the Constitution. But under Section Three, states do have a right to life as binding as their right to "equal suffrage" in the Senate. Congress may admit new states into the Union by simple majority vote, without consulting the states—no amendment is needed. (Under the Articles of Confederation, no new "colony" could be admitted to the Union without the consent of at least nine state governments—the sole exception being carte blanche for Canada to join at any time without congressional or state consent.)

But "new states" cannot be construed to mean states "formed or erected within the jurisdiction of any other state." Thus, a state that found itself outvoted by a congressional majority could not be filleted into less troublesome parts by the congressional knife. But what if the state were to consent to its partition into two or more states? Here is where the effort at textual exegesis becomes maddeningly pernickety.

Here is the language: "but no new State shall be formed or erected within the Jurisdiction of any other State; nor any State be formed by the Junction of two or more States, or Parts of States, without the Consent of the Legislatures of the States concerned as well as of the Congress." There are two ways to read this. The first is that everything after the initial "but" is modified by "without the consent . . ." In that case, a state legislature could consent to the creation of a new state entirely made up of territory inside the existing state. But there is that semicolon, which seems to make the first limiting clause grammatically complete, and to apply the "without the consent" language only to the second clause. On this reading, a new state may *not* in *any* case be created entirely within the jurisdiction of one state; but a new state *may* be created by splitting off chunks from two or more states and jamming them together by act of Congress, as long as the legislatures of all of the states in question assent to this creation.

Grammatically the question is nearly in equipoise. On the one hand, contemporary grammarians assert, semicolons serve principally "to separate two or more independent clauses that are placed next to each other within a sentence"; and this is true even if the two clauses are "co-ordinated . . . syndetically (with a coordinator)."[12] This would suggest that the two clauses be read as if they were separate sentences:

> No new State shall be formed or erected within the Jurisdiction of any other State.

Nor [shall] any State be formed by the Junction of two or more
States, or Parts of States, without the Consent of the Legislatures of the
States concerned as well as of the Congress.

On the other hand, the same grammarian advises a somewhat less reductive
use of the semicolon: "When co-ordinators are present" (as in the "nor" in Section Three) "commas can be used instead of semicolons, but semicolons are
required to mark the units if the clauses have internal commas that might obscure
the structure of the sentence."[13] Under this analysis, the entire sentence could
consist of two prohibitions limited by a common final clause:

No new State shall be formed or erected within the Jurisdiction of any
other State,
        nor any State be formed by the Junction of two or more States, or
Parts of States,
        [but either of the above may be done with the] Consent of the Leg-
islatures of the [State or] States concerned as well as of the Congress.

Before dismissing this disjunction as a grammarian's version of Voltaire's
dancing angels, consider that (1) on the one occasion in which a new state has
been created from another, the issue was literally one of life and death and (2)
one's answer will be shaped by and reveal a good deal about the political predi-
lection with which one is reading the Constitution.

First, as to history. The Commonwealth of Virginia, by far the largest and richest of the states at the time of the Framing, voluntarily ceded what are now Kentucky and parts of Ohio to the Union. But until the Civil War, Virginia still included
the mountainous region now known as the state of West Virginia. When the pro-
slavery forces decreed that Virginia would follow the lower South into rebellion in
1861, the people of the western part of the state were outraged. Meeting in a second convention, they announced that the state government in Richmond was
illegal; they created a new Virginia General Assembly and elected a new governor.
The new "state government" then gave its consent to the creation of the state of
West Virginia, and Congress approved its entry into the Union in 1863.

Virginians have ever since grumbled that the state had been sliced in half uncon-
stitutionally. The question reveals layers of legal quibbling. Was the "General Assembly" that gave its consent a legal body? Confederate and post-bellum legal
thinkers have attempted to have their cake and eat it too—Virginia's secession was
legal, they argued; but even after it had withdrawn from the Union, the General
Assembly remained the lawful state government for constitutional purposes. Thus,
in effect, the national government, faced with an armed rebellion, would have had
to ask the leaders of the rebels for permission to retain the loyal portion of the state.

That bring us to the second question, which is not historical but philosophical: could *any* power under the Constitution consent to the dismemberment of a state? Here is where constitutional interpretation becomes almost theological. Can it be possible that neither Congress, nor the state legislature, nor the two together can constitutionally consent to the dismemberment of a state? What kind of political union would be implied by such an irreducible minimum of sovereignty? It resembles the perennial paradox posed by generations of smart-alecks in Confirmation Class: could God make a rock so heavy he can't pick it up? Could the people of the United States have intended to create a Union whose form and content even they cannot alter?

The most interesting thing about this patently absurd interpretation is that, by the standards of constitutional discourse, it makes a kind of strange sense. "The Constitution, in all its provisions, looks to an indestructible Union, composed of indestructible States," Chief Justice Salmon P. Chase wrote in 1869.[14] "Indestructible" is nowhere in the text. It is a constitutional principle by virtue of its vindication in battle. The indestructibility of the states, by contrast, has at least a hint of textual basis.

One school of interpretation regards the Constitution as primarily concerned with the states. In this account, the states existed prior to the Union; they created the Union by a compact among themselves; they erected a structure that protects their own prerogatives as prior and superior to either the rights of individuals or the powers of the Union. They are not creatures but creators and cannot unmake themselves any more than human beings, in Christian theology, could divest themselves of their souls. The vision has the seductiveness of so many fundamentalist propositions. There is no need for qualification or explanation. The Union proceeds from the states and may not extinguish them.

The problems with this reading are at least twofold. The first is philosophical. The idea of any indestructible human institution makes no sense within a political philosophy that is not based on religious revelation. God can bind humanity in ties it does not choose and cannot break; but other humans cannot. No body of people can create a political system that future generations cannot alter.

The second relates more directly to the reading of text. If the Framers intended to make the states indestructible, surely they would not have used the vagaries of the semicolon to signal their audacity. Only if we regard the principle as so clear from the very nature of the Union itself could this oblique evocation of it count as evidence. And history suggests that no one has ever found it so clear. I say that not solely because the nationalist forces of the Union threw it aside when it became inconvenient, but because southern constitutional thinkers, the very authors of the "compact theory" of the Constitution, themselves chose to ignore it when it suited their political purposes.

In 1845, the pro-slavery forces in Congress engineered the admission of Texas as a state, thereby bringing another slave state into existence to augment the slave power in Congress and the electoral college. And because they had the votes to cement their victory, they wrote into the resolution admitting Texas the following provision: "New States, of convenient size, not exceeding four in number . . . may hereafter by the consent of said state, be formed out of the territory thereof, which shall be entitled to admission under the provisions of the federal constitution."[15] The purpose of this proviso, historians agree, was to place additional contingent Senate and electoral votes in the pocket of slavery, to be deployed in the remote chance that the free states amassed enough power to limit slavery or amend the Constitution to ban it. And the language of the statute can be read to empower the Texas legislature to create the new states without any further permission from Congress. ("[C]onsent of said state" is required, but the text makes no mention of "consent of Congress," and it suggests that states formed with the state's consent "shall be entitled to admission.")

States that may be created in such suspect circumstances, it seems, could hardly claim indestructibility from the possibly sloppy application of a semicolon.

In addition to admitting new states, Congress may under Section Three "dispose of and make all needful Rules and Regulations respecting the Territory or other Property belonging to the United States." Once again we have a legislative power not contained in Article I, Section Eight—in fact, we have two. Under this language, Congress may regulate federal property of any kind, and may also govern and regulate "territory" belonging to the Union. "Territory" was hardly a mysterious term to the Framers—the leading public issue of the summer of 1787 was the organization of the massive Northwest Territory, 260,000 square miles bounded by the Ohio, the Mississippi, and the Great Lakes, which had been ceded to the Confederation by Virginia, Massachusetts, New York, and Connecticut. The "Act to Provide for the Government of the Territory Northwest of the River Ohio" (which we remember as the "Northwest Ordinance of 1787") was probably the most important piece of legislation enacted by the Confederation Congress. It was passed on July 13, 1787, in New York, while the delegates in Philadelphia were struggling in secrecy.

The Northwest Ordinance could actually be viewed as a kind of lost American Constitution; it remains one of the most comprehensive and progressive pieces of social legislation ever enacted by Congress.[16] It outlawed slavery in the territory, provided for a system of inheritance designed to break up entrenched wealth, proclaimed a policy of nurturing "Religion, morality, and knowledge" through public education; guaranteed the Native peoples of the region protection against unauthorized seizure of land; and included an extensive list of rights, including freedom of religion. Remarkably, it foreshadowed by more than a century and a half the doctrine of "one person one vote" in legislative apportionment. These elements are striking by their absence in the original Constitution.

But for purposes of parsing Section Three, what is important is that the Ordinance provided for the creation of "not less than three nor more than five" new states from the territory. In this context, the word "territory" clearly contemplates the continued management of this vast territory. The second word, "other Property belonging to the United States," seems, in context, to refer to things and land owned outright by the federal government directly within the Northwest Territory. There was no need for Article IV to specify Congress's power to regulate property and land within the existing states—that power was already guaranteed, both as to the District of Columbia and to federal reservations within the states, by Article One Section Eight, which gives power "To exercise exclusive Legislation . . . over such District (not exceeding ten Miles square) as may . . . become the Seat of the Government of the United States, and to exercise like Authority over all Places purchased by the Consent of the Legislature of the State in which the Same shall be, for the Erection of Forts, Magazines, Arsenals, dock-Yards and other needful Buildings."

Having empowered the new Congress to govern the Northwest Territory, the clause then goes on to make clear that it was not intended to resolve the ongoing negotiations between the states that had ceded the territory and the federal government as to the boundaries of the ceded land, the conditions under which it would be ceded, and any compensation therefore: "nothing in this Constitution shall be so construed as to Prejudice any Claims of the United States, or of any particular State."

This part of Section Three seems a fairly comprehensive grant of power over territory not part of the states; but considering that comprehensive wording, one power is conspicuously omitted—nothing in Section Three gives Congress the power to *acquire* new territory not belonging to the United States as of 1787. Section Three by its precise terms seems to refer only to existing territory.

This omission would bedevil President Jefferson when, in 1803, he, acting on his sole authority, bought from Napoleon an area of 828,800 square miles— more than three times the size of the Northwest Territory. Jefferson at first intended to ask Congress to propose a constitutional amendment authorizing acquisition of new territory. "The constitution has made no provision for our holding foreign territory, still less for incorporating foreign nations into our Union," he wrote to Senator John C. Breckinridge of Kentucky.[17] His reasons, he wrote to Virginia Senator Wilson Cary Nicholas, a month later, were purely textual: the limits of the United States in 1787 were "precisely fixed" by a treaty with Britain, and the Constitution "expressly declares itself to be made for the U.S." Because of that language, "I cannot help believing the intention was to permit Congress to admit into the Union new States, which should be formed out of the territory for which, & under whose authority, they were then acting."[18] To claim the authority under the existing Constitution, Jefferson said would make the Constitution "a blank paper by construction."[19]

The "blank paper" language is often quoted by constitutional interpreters who favor a "strict," or anti-federal, construction of the constitution. Rarely do they note that the words appear in a letter in which Jefferson explains, without a great deal of regret, that he's willing to stretch the Constitution, just this once, far beyond what he thought it really said: "I confess, then, I think it important, in the present case, to set an example against broad construction, by appealing for new power to the people. If, however, our friends shall think differently, certainly I shall acquiesce with satisfaction, confiding, that the good sense of our country will correct the evil of construction when it shall produce ill effects."[20] Louisiana would be admitted by statute, not because doing so was constitutional but because it was really, really important.

Oh, well.

SECTION FOUR. Article IV overall is stern and parental. Section Four commits the federal Zeus to protect its children—not at their request or desire but for their own good.

First, the federal government must "guarantee to every State . . . a Republican Form of Government." This clause receives little attention from constitutional lawyers and scholars, because the Supreme Court in 1849 held that the Court had no role to play in its operation.[21] Deciding whether a state had a "republican form of government," the Court said, was up to Congress, not to the courts.

Because of that decision, very few cases have been litigated under what is called the Guaranty Clause. And even legal scholars have a tendency to confuse "justiciability"—applicability in court—for significance. In fact, the clause remains of intense interest for anyone trying to understand the theory of government embodied in the Constitution.

As we have noted before, one way to read the Constitution is as a state-centered document, concerned with protecting the state governments and their people against potentially overweening federal power. We've also noted that the textual traces of such an intention are relatively few when balanced against the number of provisions that seem designed to empower and energize the new national government. Of all those powers granted to the federal government, though, it is difficult to think of one more breathtaking than this—the power to decide (apparently by ordinary legislation) whenever a state government falls short of a national standard of republicanism. Though the Guaranty Clause does not specify what the federal government can do in pursuit of this obligation, it seems hardly extreme to conclude that a state government failing such a federal test could be dissolved by law and, if necessary, broken up by force.

There is a strand of constitutional thinking that dwells on the idea of "state sovereignty." Despite having been proclaimed dead as early as 1865 by, among others, President Andrew Johnson, the idea arises over and over in American discourse. Its persistence is even more striking because the Constitution nowhere uses any such term—even though the language guaranteeing state sovereignty was readily available in Article I of the Articles of Confederation. Advocates of "state sovereignty" derive it from their overall reading of the Constitution and from the structure of the Union it created.

But surely the Guaranty Clause is powerful contrary evidence. If the federal government may, at its sole discretion, displace the existing government of a state and replace it with a new one, can it make sense to speak of the state as "sovereign" in any meaningful sense? The breadth of federal political power under the Guaranty Clause seems more sweeping when we consider the inherent subjectivity of the words "republican form of government." Neither in 1787 nor now is there a general agreement on any precise meaning for this term. Most people would probably agree that a state could not make its chief executive a hereditary monarch, or institute totalitarian rule by a single all-powerful party. Beyond that, however, republicanism is largely in the eye of the beholder.

Many, for example, consider representative government, expressed in deliberative assemblies, the hallmark of true republicanism. Consider devices like initiative and referendum, which substitute direct democracy for the considered judgment of representatives. Could Congress outlaw the initiative by statute, acting on the Guaranty Clause? If not, why not? If so, how much further could it go? Nebraska maintains a legislature with only one chamber, even though both the federal government and the other forty-nine states have two.[22] Could Congress make a judgment that bicameralism is essential to republican government, void Nebraska's constitution, and order the state to produce a new one? Some states, like North Carolina and Oregon, sharply restrict the powers of their governors; others, like Virginia, make the governor the most powerful part of state government. Could Congress order the "strong governor" states to adopt weak governorships, or vice versa?

As a matter of practical politics, nothing like this is likely to occur. The states are able to protect their political prerogatives through the rough and tumble of the legislative process. But the text of the Guaranty Clause complicates any simple vision of the states as invulnerable constituent elements of the Republic; it treats them rather at least potentially as wayward children to be disciplined at the federal will.

Counterbalancing the breathtaking sweep of the Guaranty Clause, however, the rest of the first part of Section Four imposes obligations on the federal government. It must "protect" the states "against invasion"; by the text, Congress has no discretion to cede territory to an invader without at least an effort at protection;

but this is surely a minimal limitation on federal power, as any conceivable government not staffed by traitors would do so.

More dramatic, however, is the obligation to protect each state against "domestic violence." This obligation is not discretionary with Congress. It is triggered by "Application of the Legislature, or of the Executive (when the Legislature cannot be convened)." Again, to contemporary readers, this seems as unexceptionable as the obligation to defend against invasion. But the wording reflects a fear that Congress might choose not to intervene in certain domestic revolts. To eighteenth-century eyes the clause screamed the two most terrifying words in the southern vocabulary could hear: *slave revolt*. The figures from the 1790 census show why—three years after the Convention, five of the original thirteen states had slave populations amounting to one-quarter or more of their total populations. South Carolina, which for much of its colonial history had a black majority, was 43 percent black; Virginia was 39 percent.[23] The slave system would collapse if slaves could not be intimidated into submission; had they united in revolt, the states would have been uninhabitable. Serious slave revolts were few; but the specter of black rebellion haunted southern dreams, especially as during their waking hours the slave masters knew that many of their fellow American whites disapproved of slavery and would balk at being asked to die for its preservation. The language of the Domestic Violence Clause took the choice away from the political process; protection against the slaves was mandatory. Sinful though the federal government's children might be, the federal father was committed to preserve and protect their sin.

Article V

Alter or Abolish

The people's right to alter or abolish their form of government was, to the American revolutionaries, supposedly absolute. Yet, strangely, neither the people nor the states may even begin the process of amending the Constitution until Congress permits. That body "whenever two thirds of both Houses shall deem it necessary," may propose an amendment or amendments and send them to the states for ratification.

Congress's role is even more powerful because since the beginning, Article V has been interpreted to give the president no role to play. He does not sign, and may not veto, a proposed amendment. A litigant objecting to the Eleventh Amendment argued before the Supreme Court that the proposed amendment had not been "presented" to President Washington for his assent or veto; the Court in 1798 responded with more clarity than analysis that "[t]here can, surely, be no necessity to answer that argument. The negative of the President applies only to the ordinary cases of legislation: He has nothing to do with the proposition, or adoption, of amendments to the Constitution."[1]

As a matter of constitutional text, though, that's far from clear. Article I, Section Seven, provides that "[e]very Bill which shall have passed the House of Representatives and the Senate, shall, before it become a Law, be presented to the President of the United States" for his assent or veto. True, a proposed amendment might not be called a bill, but Congress can't finesse the president's veto by labeling it something other than a bill. This possibility is forestalled in the same section: "Every order, resolution, or vote to which the concurrence of the Senate and House of Representatives may be necessary (except on a question of adjournment) shall be presented to the President of the United States" for veto just as if it were called a bill. Proposed constitutional amendments must pass "both Houses" by a two-thirds vote, and they are called "Joint Resolutions." Why, then, do they not need to be presented to the president?

It is true that a proposed amendment has already gotten enough votes to overcome a presidential veto. But that has no constitutional significance. Even a bill passed unanimously must still be presented to the president. In one and only one case—a resolution having to do with "adjournment"—the Presentment Clause makes an exception. Logically, presentment of bills, regardless of their margin, makes sense because presentment allows the president to register not only his opposition but his reasons for opposition: his veto must contain his "objections" to the bill, and the houses of Congress must take heed of them at least by "enter[ing] the objections at large on their Journal, and proceed[ing] to *reconsider* it," a wording that implies at least the formality of thinking again.

The real answer to this puzzle is that in 1789, when the first ten amendments were proposed, neither George Washington nor any member of Congress raised the issue. There's no clear evidence why. Those involved might simply not have thought of it; or they might have thought that, since Congress had proposed the amendments (as the text of Article V prescribes), the president had no role to play. Washington—like every president before Andrew Jackson—conceived of the presidential veto as applicable only to measures that the president considered unconstitutional. A constitutional amendment by definition can't be unconstitutional.

At any rate, David P. Currie, who devoted his long scholarly career to tracing the ways in which members of Congress have interpreted the Constitution, found no discussion of the question in the First Congress in the Annals of Congress, the best record we have of early congressional debates: they "reveal no discussion of this important question," he writes. "Yet the action of the First Congress was cited to the Supreme Court as a precedent when it upheld the eleventh amendment against the contention that it should have been submitted to the President for approval, and the precedent has been followed with rare exceptions ever since."[2]

Had Washington thought differently, his example would probably have molded our understanding of the language forever after. Unlike Washington, most presidents don't like yielding the limelight to Congress (or anyone else) and would welcome a role to play in amending the Constitution. From time to time, they have hovered awkwardly around the Article V process, like party crashers trying to appear at ease. Abraham Lincoln issued a statement signing the resolution proposing the Thirteenth Amendment, which abolished slavery (the Senate immediately passed a resolution noting that the signature was not required);[3] this precedent caused some embarrassment three years later, when his successor, Andrew Johnson, refused to do the same with the proposed Fourteenth Amendment. (He apparently considered ordering his secretary of state not to transmit the proposal to the states for ratification.)[4] Lyndon Johnson indulged in a resplendent though useless ceremonial signing of the proposed

Twenty-Fifth Amendment, which changed the procedures for presidential disability and succession.[5] But no president has ever asserted a serious power to veto a proposed amendment.

Once Congress has acted, three-quarters of the states must ratify. But even in the ratification process, Congress has a surprising level of control: it has the discretion to choose how the states' assent or refusal of an amendment may be expressed. The text says that ratification may also be entrusted either to the state legislatures or to *conventions* within each state "as the one or the other Mode of Ratification may be proposed by the Congress."

The device of the convention was a centerpiece of eighteenth-century political theory. Unlike the legislature, conventions were thought to embody the people themselves. The Framers required that the proposed Constitution be ratified by conventions of the people.

Even today, when considering a proposed amendment, Congress at its sole option may specify the same mode for ratifying a proposed amendment. Article V is silent on what would happen if the legislature of a state refused to call such a convention. It is an open question whether, in the event of defiance by a legislature, Congress could simply pass a statute calling a convention in that state.

The convention route has been used only once, to approve the Twenty-First Amendment repealing the prohibition on alcoholic beverages enacted by the Eighteenth Amendment. When we look at those two amendments we will see some of the reasons that Congress chose the convention route in that case. What's more intriguing is why Congress has not done so before or since. If a proposed amendment is popular, convention ratification would make its approval more likely; state legislatures, by design, often allow minorities to block action.

Why wouldn't Congress just bypass them? Simply as a matter of legislative shoe-making, two-thirds votes in both Houses may be hard enough to cobble together; adding in a seemingly novel approval procedure might mean the difference between success and failure. In addition, members of Congress are politicians with important relationships with legislators in their home states. Those state lawmakers might react with disfavor to being cut out of the approval loop.

Congress does not have a *complete* stranglehold on the proposal of amendments. Article V states that "on the Application of the Legislatures of two thirds of the several States, [Congress] shall call a Convention for proposing Amendments." This language strikes terror into the hearts of politicians and has done so from the very dawn of the Constitution. During the debate over ratification, many opponents of the proposed Constitution wanted to call a second convention and rewrite it; others wanted to condition their ratification on the summoning of a new convention. The Federalists were dead set against either—in part because they understood how thoroughly the first convention had exceeded its authority. The Philadelphia convention's charter was limited to "revising the Articles of Confederation," but instead it had proposed entirely replacing them. Who knew what another convention might do?

The same question lingers over the possibility of another convention. On several occasions, a movement to call such a convention has fallen only a few state legislatures short of the required number. In those cases, the call of such a convention was explicitly intended to propose specific amendments that had been bottled up in Congress—one that eventually passed, requiring popular election of senators; two others that failed, one voiding the Supreme Court's requirement of state legislative apportionment by the rule of "one person, one vote" and a second requiring a balanced federal budget.

What if the legislatures pulled the trigger and Congress ducked? The Constitution doesn't say what would happen if Congress simply refused to call a convention. Perhaps the only guarantee against it would be the members' unwillingness to defy public opinion. The more realistic question is whether an Article V convention, once called, could be limited in its authority. That is, assume that three-quarters of the state legislatures pass resolutions making "application" for a convention "for proposing amendments" in order to achieve some specific goal, such as a balanced-budget amendment. Could Congress call such a convention *limited* to considering that one question? If so, why? The text provides for a "convention for proposing amendments," not "an amendment," and the mandatory language includes no provision permitting Congress to set or limit the subject matter of such amendments.

Once convened, an Article V convention would have a claim to direct authority from the people. What would prevent it from ignoring any legislative limitation and proposing any amendments it chose? Or, for that matter, from doing what the Philadelphia Framers did and simply writing an entirely new Constitution? Any proposed amendments or new Constitution would, of course, require approval by three-quarters of the states. By a strict reading of the text, it would be Congress, not the convention, that would specify whether those proposed changes would require approval by legislatures or states. But that seems like a fragile dam to contain the massive deluge of public involvement an Article V convention might trigger.

An Article V convention might include state-convention ratification in its proposal, daring Congress to defy the people's will. We can imagine a scenario in which a new set of Framers could sweep away the Constitution and produce a revolution.

Also unnervingly, the text gives us no description of how such a convention would work. Congress presumably could decide on the number of representatives for each state—and that battle alone would probably paralyze debate for months. In the Philadelphia Convention, each state—giant Virginia or tiny

Delaware—could have as many delegates as it wished, but had one and only one vote. Would a convention in the twenty-first century be called on the basis of state equality?

The undemocratic implications of this are if anything more profound than were those of the Philadelphia meeting. Disparities in population between the most populous and the least populous states are far larger than they were in 1787. The most populous (California) has more than seventy times the population of the least (Wyoming). A small minority of the population could block a proposal backed by states representing the overwhelming majority of the people.

One final part of the language of Article V has been less than scrupulously observed: amendments approved and ratified are to be considered "valid to all Intents and Purposes, as Part of this Constitution."

The very existence of Article V suggests that the Framers knew they might have made mistakes. As generations have passed, however, Americans have come to regard them as almost inhumanly wise. As a result, amendments tend to be construed narrowly. Judges tend to assume that the original Constitution is so perfect that the framers of an amendment can't really have meant to make much of a change. This peculiar style of interpretation led one constitutional scholar to speak of "the irrelevance of constitutional amendments."[6] Historian Michael Vorenberg notes that the intervention of courts into constitutional interpretation "made almost irrelevant the precise phrasing of the Reconstruction amendments."[7]

Courts find amendments easiest to apply when the amendments are narrow and technical. It's more daunting to apply amendments that actually change fundamentals in the Philadelphia document. The 1787 Constitution has a hold on the imagination that survives its amendment, much the way the fading traces of an image burned in the eyes may make it difficult to see what is actually in front of an observer's nose.

Article VI

The Supreme Law of the Land

The theme of Article VI is the Constitution itself and its relationship to the nation that enacted it and the people it governs. Section One makes clear that when the Constitution came into effect, the "United States" remained legally the same country as "the United States, in Congress Assembled" that had borrowed money during and after the Revolution. "All Debts contracted and Engagements entered into, before the Adoption of this Constitution, shall be as valid against the United States under this Constitution, as under the Confederation."

Securing the money to repay foreign debt had been a serious problem under the Articles: the Confederation Congress was empowered only to beg for funds from the states. The states felt little urgency about repaying the French government, an ally. When the United States agreed to repay Britain for British property seized during the Revolution, repayment became even less popular. Failure to repay foreign debts would provide a prime excuse for ambitious European powers to meddle in American affairs. (In fact, the British were refusing to remove their troops from the Ohio Valley until British creditors were paid.)

Section Two, which has come to be called "the Supremacy Clause," is among the most important clauses in the entire 1787 document. Judicial review—the authority of judges to invalidate unconstitutional law—is the most radical single innovation in constitutional theory the United States has ever produced. Article VI, Section Two, is the source of authority for judicial review. It's striking then that this section doesn't actually refer to it.

First, Section Two validates the Constitution: "This Constitution, and the Laws of the United States which shall be made in Pursuance thereof; and all Treaties made, or which shall be made, under the Authority of the United States, shall be the supreme Law of the Land notwithstanding." This has a comforting sound: good old Constitution, the supreme law of the land. But the Constitution is not "supreme" by itself; it is one of three sources of supreme law. First in the clause is the

Constitution; next come laws "made in pursuance of" the Constitution; and third come treaties "made or which shall be made under the authority" of the United States.

These three are "supreme," but the text doesn't say which is "supremest." By its terms, the Constitution is as valid as a federal statute or binding treaty—but no more so. In fact, one way to read this clause is simply as a declaration that *federal* laws are supreme over *state* laws. By the clause's text, "the supreme law of the land" is binding on *state* judges "any Thing in the Constitution or Laws of any State to the Contrary notwithstanding." So it could be that the Constitution, laws, and treaties are being designated simply as "supreme" over *state* law, with no implication of hierarchy among themselves.

Thus, the clause wouldn't cover conflict among the three sources of federal law. A federal statute at variance with the Constitution—say, a statute preferring the ports of one state over those of another, in clear violation of Article I, Section Nine—is not necessarily rendered invalid as a result of that conflict. One or the other must prevail; but the clause doesn't say which.

True, it does say that to be supreme, laws must be "made in pursuance of" the Constitution. But that's not the same as saying "in conformity" with the Constitution. "Pursuance" has at least two meanings. One refers to time; it could simply mean "after," meaning that all statutes passed after ratification of the Constitution will be "the supreme law of the land." The other is legal or procedural; it could mean "in compliance with." That would mean that the Constitution is by its very existence "the supreme law of the land," while laws are "supreme" only if they conform to the Constitution's requirements.

But which requirements? It could simply mean the *procedural* requirements of the Constitution—that is, that no federal "law" shall be supreme unless it has been adopted by both houses of Congress and either signed by the president or reenacted by two-thirds of both houses after his veto. If that is the meaning, then a court presented with a conflict between the Constitution and a federal statute could not invalidate the statute. It would arguably be required to treat the two conflicting provisions the way it would treat two statutes that seemed to conflict with each other.

Judges facing that kind of conflict try first to "harmonize" the two statutes, meaning to read them in such a way that there is no conflict. If that's not possible, then courts often conclude that the later enactment controls the earlier one, even implicitly repealing it if necessary.

That has a strange sound to contemporary American ears, but would not have seemed quite as odd in the eighteenth century. A statute of Parliament was binding, even if it violated the principles of the British Constitution; the only test of its constitutionality, in the long run, would be whether the people sustained the Parliament by supporting the government at elections. If the

Constitution and "laws made in pursuance" of it are truly on an equal footing, then American statutes would be tested for constitutionality in the same way—by the political process. That's not as wacky as it sounds; one of the first great constitutional crises in American life, the fight over the Sedition Act of 1798, was resolved when the voters dumped the party that wrote the act.

But "pursuance" could also mean in conformity with the *substantive* requirements of the Constitution—in which case our imaginary port-preference law would not be "supreme" even though properly enacted, because it conflicts with Article I, Section Nine, which says "[n]o preference shall be given by any regulation of commerce or revenue to the ports of one state over those of another."

So a court could strike the statute down. Or could it? If Article Six, Section Two, empowers federal courts to invalidate federal statutes, the drafters certainly picked a strange way of saying it. Judicial review of federal statutes has over time become a central feature of our system; but it doesn't flow straight out of the text.

The third source of "supreme law" is described in different words. To be "supreme," treaties need not be made "in pursuance" of the Constitution; they qualify if they are "made" or "shall be made under the authority of the United States." This language is confusing. The language makes sense when referring to "treaties made . . . under the authority of the United States," because by 1787 the United States was bound by a number of treaties agreed to by the Confederation Congress and ratified, in accordance with Article IX of the Articles of Confederation, by nine state legislatures. Those treaties would be valid, and enforceable in court if need be, under the new language of Article VI even though not made "in pursuance" of the 1787 Constitution. But why then add "which shall be made"? That language could simply be read to mean "treaties made validly under the Articles before the entry into force of this Constitution and treaties made validly under this Constitution after its entry into force." That seems like the most logical reading—but some eminent legal authorities have read it to mean that the United States government has authority to make treaties in ways other than by the terms of Articles I and II.

Thus in certain circumstances, a treaty of the United States has been held to trump state law on natural resources—even though it wasn't clear that Congress had the power under the Constitution to pass a similar law.[1] And many agreements between the United States and other countries are made under our national "authority"—by agreement of the president—even though they aren't approved by the provisions of Article II. These are usually binding, and indeed are the supreme law of the land.

The next clause of Section Two singles out state judges as bound by "the supreme Law of the Land . . . any Thin in the Constitution or Laws of any State to the Contrary notwithstanding." This language implies a judicial duty to ignore certain state laws. This is a very limited kind of judicial review, however:

state-court judicial review *of state law* to ensure that it conforms to *all federal law*. What if a state judge concludes that a *federal* statute is not valid under the *federal* constitution? Would a *state* official (the judge) have the power to set aside a federal law whenever he or she believes it not to be in "pursuance" of the Constitution?

Read as a whole, the clause seems most logically designed to prevent state judges from ignoring federal laws and giving effect to state laws. In this reading, it is a provision designed to guarantee *federal* supremacy over the states, not *judicial* supremacy over the Congress.

Yet from this slender textual basis, federal courts have spun almost the entire web of what we call "constitutional law," meaning judicial enforcement of specific interpretations of the Constitution.

Section Two was quite intrusive on state courts' prerogatives, instructing state courts in what sources of law to use, and placing the states' laws at the bottom of the list. Section Three is even more intrusive: it provides that members of both the United States Congress and the *state* legislatures, "and all executive and judicial Officers, both of the United States *and of the several States*, shall be bound by Oath or Affirmation, to support this Constitution."

An "oath" is a religious act. Those who violated their oaths were destined for hell. English law required oaths, and further required that all witnesses express a belief in the Christian afterlife. If people believed there was no heaven and no hell, why would they hesitate to lie?

Some groups refused to swear oaths—not necessarily because they did not believe in the Christian God but because they took His word more seriously than others. Quakers and other smaller Protestant sects considered themselves bound by the words of Jesus, who in the Gospel of Matthew told his disciples, "Swear not at all; neither by heaven; for it is God's throne: Nor by the earth; for it is his footstool: neither by Jerusalem; for it is the city of the great King. Neither shalt thou swear by thy head, because thou canst not make one hair white or black. But let your communication be, Yea, yea; Nay, nay: for whatsoever is more than these cometh of evil."[2] Such scrupulous Christians, and others who objected to swearing to God, were permitted by the text to serve by "affirming"—declaring under penalty of perjury—their support for the Constitution.

Citizens and scholars alike enjoy arguing about whether the Constitution contains "the separation of church and state." At the most basic level, those words never appear in the document. Analysts then spend a good deal of time analyzing the First Amendment to see whether its religious guarantees together create a separation principle. But even before the First Amendment was added, the Constitution contained a very basic separation: "no religious Test shall ever be required as a Qualification to any Office or public Trust under the United States."

Anyone—Christian or Jew, Catholic or Protestant, believer or freethinker—was eligible for federal office.

In England, office was open to Anglicans and a few other favored Christian groups; in Catholic countries, to Catholics. In the United States, no church could have a hand, however indirect, in selecting secular rulers, at least at the federal level. In eighteenth-century terms, this was a radical proposition.

Although it may seem like the musty constitutional attic, then, Article VI holds some important treasures, which, when dusted off, seem to be closely related. The Constitution embodies and replaces the old confederation government, reaffirming its acts and obligations; it governs all those holding political authority within the United States; and it requires some forms of acknowledging its authority while barring others.

The constitutional system is supreme; we know it is supreme because it says it is supreme; we believe it is so because we must swear to it.

Article VII

Bloodless and Successful

Imagine today that a "blue-ribbon commission," established by Congress to propose solutions for economic problems, were to produce a new Constitution and announce that the old country would be dissolved when enough states agreed to join the new one. The new country would be "the United States of America." States that didn't join could do whatever they wanted, but they couldn't use the name United States of America any more.

Would that be legal?

Until we get to Article VII, the Constitution is just a document—a proposal by a rump group (like our "blue-ribbon commission") acting without any clear authority.

What would make this proposal into an agreement by "we the people" to be governed by its terms? The Articles of Confederation could be amended only one way: unanimous approval by the state legislatures. The Articles' formal title, in fact, was "Articles of Confederation and Perpetual Union." Article XIII provided that "the Articles of this Confederation shall be inviolably observed by every State, and the Union shall be perpetual; nor shall any alteration at any time hereafter be made in any of them; unless such alteration be agreed to in a Congress of the United States, and be afterwards confirmed by the legislatures of every State."

This was a problem. The chance that all thirteen state legislatures would agree to a new Constitution, one that radically diminished their own authority, was probably a bit less than zero.

The Framers therefore decided to finesse the problem by creating their own method of ratification. "The Ratification of the Conventions of nine States, shall be sufficient for the Establishment of this Constitution between the States so ratifying the Same." Very few sentences in the original Constitution did as much work as this one. It deprives Congress, the state legislatures, and even the state conventions of any power to amend the new Constitution—the only issue any of them could consider was ratification of "this Constitution," not some other version.

Even more radically, though, it offered the prospect of a shattering of the "perpetual union" and the creation of a new nation consisting of more than eight but fewer than thirteen states. All the states had agreed that the union would be "inviolab[le]," "perpetual," and not subject to "any alteration at any time" without unanimous agreement. But now states in which conventions ratified the new Constitution would be absolved of their duties—and shorn of their rights—under the Articles. States refusing ratification would be left—without their consent—to shift for themselves as independent republics, or as members of an ungainly rump Confederation, less populous than the new one and shorn even of the name "United States of America." It was a daring act of arrogation, done without a hint of permission or explicit authority.

It could be argued that, under the definition then in force, an attempt to break up the Confederation without authority constituted an act of treason. But, "Treason doth never prosper—What's the reason?" the seventeenth-century poet Sir John Harrington explains: "For if it prosper none dare call it treason."[1] Because the people—after an exhausting ratification debate—came to believe that the old Articles were unworkable and the new Constitution offered the best and perhaps only hope for survival of the "perpetual union," the Framers today are patriots rather than traitors. The proclamation of the Constitution, if it was a coup d'état, had the two essential characteristics of a good one—it was bloodless and successful.

Last Things

"Done in Convention by the Unanimous Consent of the States present," the final paragraph of the document begins. The wording slides by gracefully, but should be jarring—the Framers have not been willing to speak of the Constitution or the people as acting through states before. The Convention by its rules did vote by states. But why are the states memorialized in the text as "consent[ing]" to its proposal?

The reason lies in the word "unanimous." This introduced the new Constitution to a potentially skeptical public in the most favorable possible light. It suggests that this gathering of eminent leaders had agreed as one to recommend ratification of this new Constitution. This was in fact not so. The delegates to the Convention were deeply divided about the new Constitution. Several, including Massachusetts governor Elbridge Gerry, Virginia governor Edmund Randolph (who had been the introducer of the original "Virginia plan" on which the Convention's work began), and Colonel George Mason of Virginia, were in outright opposition. But the Convention voted by states rather than individuals, and on the final vote for recommendation, all the *states* had voted aye.

The impression of unanimity was consciously fostered as well by the final words of the document: "In witness whereof We have subscribed our names." All the members of the Convention except Gerry, Mason, and Randolph signed, including some who had not voted for the Constitution. The text said simply that they were "witness[ing]" its adoption, not that they were endorsing the document as individuals.

The document is dated "the Seventeenth Day of September in the Year of our Lord one thousand seven hundred and Eighty seven." Here is the only reference to Christianity in the entire 1787 Constitution—if it even is truly a religious reference. "Year of Our Lord" was the standard method of reporting the date in the eighteenth century, and was used by Christian, deist, and free-thinker alike to eliminate ambiguity about dates. The thinness of this religious reference is underlined by contrast with the voluble religiosity of the Articles of Confederation, which credited their approval by Congress to "the Great Governour of the World," who had "inclined the hearts of the legislatures we respectively represent in Congress."

The Constitution's oblique reference to Christianity seems at most offhand and at least inadvertent, the words of a busy group of men who had worldly, not divine, matters on their minds.

The Bill of Rights

National Decalogue

In his 2004 book *Interpreting the Bible and the Constitution,* religious historian Jaroslav Pelikan wrote that "the Ten Amendments of the Bill of Rights now seem to provide a version of the function that used to be performed for [some Americans'] grandparents by the Ten Commandments of the Decalogue."[1] For many Americans, the Bill of Rights does have a kind of divine status. The Constitution of 1787 created an energetic government with few textual limits on its powers. The Bill of Rights sets out the limits beyond which that government cannot go in its relations with its people. One would not seem complete without the other.

Even during ratification, the original Constitution was seen as disturbingly incomplete. In state after state, delegates to the ratifying conventions professed alarm at the apparent lack of limitation on the new government's powers. Federalists smoothly explained that no bill of rights was needed because the new government contained its own limits. The proper response comes from Leonard Levy, the preeminent constitutional historian of his generation: "That the Framers of the Constitution actually believed their own arguments to justify the omission of a bill of rights is difficult to credit."[2]

Levy believed that the delegates to Philadelphia were just too tired to finish the job. Whatever the reason for the omission, Madison moved to repair it when the First Congress assembled in 1789. The amendments he introduced formed the basis for the Constitution's Ten Commandments. In Madison's original bill, there were, depending on how one counts, nineteen or twenty amendments, not ten. Many fell by the wayside (remarkably enough, one was finally added to the Constitution as the Twenty-Seventh Amendment in 1992); all were extensively rewritten. That the eventual Bill of Rights has the sacred number of commandments is either happenstance or divine parallelism.

Madison believed that the Article V process should result in alterations and insertions in the actual text of the Articles. Congress rejected this approach in favor of separate "amendments" at the end of the document. That choice has had some out-size consequences for the Constitution as a text. The Philadelphia document has a hold on the national imagination out of proportion to its current relevance or valid-ity. In constitutional folklore, the Philadelphia document and the Bill of Rights have somehow merged into an "organic Constitution," superior to subsequent amend-ments and indeed in some ways impervious to them.[3] Had the First Congress's amendments been merged into the text, they might not have assumed the powerful number of ten, and the original text might seem neither divine nor unalterable.

But we have the Bill of Rights we have, engrossed in the Constitution as it is, and its hold on the national imagination is powerful. That power makes it all the more urgent that we read the existing ten amendments carefully to make sure we can differentiate what they say from what folklore attributes to them. Each provision should be carefully parsed; but a few general points emerge from reading all ten.

First, notice what the amendments do not protect. They are overwhelmingly concerned with the relationship between government and the individual. With the exception of the Tenth Amendment (and possibly of the Second), they don't show much solicitude for the states. They list many things the federal govern-ment can't do to individuals, but do not contain a single express prohibition against federal action against state governments.

Second, many of the amendments might be read as aimed at state *and* federal governments. The First Amendment, of course, begins "Congress shall make no law . . ." But the others do *not*—they simply say that, for example, "the accused shall enjoy the right to a speedy and public trial," or that "in Suits at common law . . . the right of trial by jury shall be preserved." Using statutory arguments, we in fact could make a good case that (1) the Framers of the Philadelphia Constitution understood the differences between prohibitions on Congress and prohibitions on the states; (2) when the Framers of the amendments wanted to limit the operation of one of them to "Congress," they did; and that (3) the language of the other amendments should therefore apply to all governments in the United States.

The Supreme Court rejected this argument decisively in 1833, when a litigant challenged a state improvement to Baltimore harbor as an uncompensated "taking" of his property in a harborside wharf (which would be forbidden by the Fifth Amendment). In that case, *Barron v. Baltimore*, Chief Justice Marshall wrote that because the federal Constitution created powers that resided in the federal government, the first ten amendments "are limitations of power granted in the instrument itself; not of distinct governments, framed by different persons and for different purposes."[4] Before and after *Barron*, many constitutional thinkers reached a different conclusion. After the adoption of the Fourteenth Amend-ment, oceans of ink have been spilled about whether that amendment applies the Bill of Rights against the states. The text itself is ambiguous; the answer would seem to depend largely on the reader's own philosophy of American government.

Third, the amendments' provisions fall rhetorically into different styles. Some are absolute prohibitions: "Congress shall make *no law* . . ." in the First Amendment; "*No soldier* shall in time of peace be quartered in any house . . ." in the Third. Others are *relative*, applicable only when measured against an undefined scale of magnitude: "*unreasonable* searches," in the Fourth Amendment; "*excessive* bail" in the Eighth. Some can only be understood in relation to rules not actually in the Constitution: for example, the requirement that life, liberty, or property be taken only by "due process of law" in the Fifth Amendment; the rule that jury findings of fact may not be set aside on appeal "otherwise . . . than according to the rules of the common law" in the Seventh. One of them, the Ninth, has no specific substantive content at all—it is only a principle of interpretation. The Tenth does not prohibit anything, but only concerns itself with the distribution of government powers.

All of the amendments are relatively short. The epic mode has fallen into discourse; it reappears, if at all, only in the Fourteenth Amendment, and perhaps the Twenty-Fifth. The amendments in the bill of rights fall into either absolute mode—the Law—or relative—Wisdom. But either way, they are compact, suggestive, terse. There are traces of poetry here among the commandments.

Fourth, the rights involved are, with the exception of the First, not political rights. There is no right to vote, no right to hold office, no right to be consulted about decisions, no mechanism (other than voting for representatives) by which citizens can be involved in decisions, no requirement of what we today call government "transparency." Trials must be public, but no other disclosure is required. The amendments limit what government can do to citizens; they show little concern for what citizens can do to influence government.

Fourth, the amendments guarantee what the philosopher Isaiah Berlin called "negative liberty." Today, many constitutions and human-rights instruments enshrine "positive liberties" as well—services or protections citizens can *demand* from government. Consider Article 16 of the Constitution of Iraq, written by a US-installed provisional government in 2005:

> Equal opportunities shall be guaranteed to all Iraqis, and *the state shall ensure that the necessary measures to achieve this are taken.*[5]

Or Article 25 of the US-drafted Constitution of Japan:

> All people shall have the right to maintain the minimum standards of wholesome and cultured living. . . . In all spheres of life, *the State shall use its endeavors for the promotion and extension of social welfare and security, and of public health.*[6]

The American Bill of Rights contains no hint that government is required to do anything for the ordinary citizen except stay out of the way.

All told, the Bill of Rights is a mixed bag: some clear rules, some guidelines, some statements of principles. Ambiguous in its scope and vague in its sweep. Backward-looking, not "progressive" or visionary. Full of some rights of striking contemporary relevance, and guaranteeing others, like freedom from quartering of troops, that rarely concern us today. Explicitly incomplete.

And yet, the Bill of Rights is today an essential part of the identity of every American—our Decalogue and our sacred covenant with ourselves.

First Amendment

The First Commandment—"Thou shalt have no other gods before me"—is the foundation of all Mosaic religion. The First Amendment today is similarly foundational. Perhaps because it is the first, perhaps because it is addressed to Congress by name, perhaps because of its sweeping prohibitory language, perhaps because the rights it guarantees are easily understood, perhaps because it contains so many related but distinct rights, the First Amendment has a uniquely powerful hold on the American imagination.

This amendment was not first in Madison's list; that was an addition to the Preamble affirming that all power is vested in the people. In the list as finally proposed by Congress, this amendment came third, after a measure increasing the number of members of the House (never ratified) and a second requiring that any pay increase for members of Congress be delayed in effect until after the next election (finally approved, in one of the odder uses of Article V, more than two centuries later).

But these historical facts, while interesting, do nothing to undermine the importance of the First Amendment that emerged from the process. It may be that First Amendment rights are so important to Americans in large part because an accident of history put them at the top of the list; if so, so be it—the Constitution creates our culture and generates its meanings in present minds, whatever our guesses as to its shape in the minds of the dead.

In its forty-five words, the First Amendment covers an astonishing amount of ground. Its guarantees fall into two halves—religious guarantees first, guarantees of expressive rights next. In all, there are six separate guarantees, and one of the enduring puzzles of constitutional interpretation is whether they can or should be seen as a coherent whole.

First, what lawyers call "the religion clauses." Congress is to make no law "respecting an establishment of religion," and no law "prohibiting the free exercise thereof." Religious establishment was a concept almost every American understood. We like to believe that the early settlers braved the voyage to the New

World to create a land of religious liberty, but that is only partially true. Many of them were fleeing the state-supported religious establishments of their home countries, true; but many of those sought a new homeland where they could establish their own religion at the expense of others. A majority of states in 1789 had religious establishments. The specific language about "Congress" at the beginning suggests that there is a state-oriented aspect to the First Amendment: Congress had to keep its hands off the states' official churches. "No law *respecting* an establishment of religion" is pointed phraseology. It does more than prohibit a federally established church; it suggests that Congress was not to pass any law "respecting" any of the state establishments, abolishing them, limiting their influence, or protecting religious minorities. (In fact, Madison had proposed a separate amendment directing that "[n]o state shall violate the equal rights of conscience, or the freedom of the press, or the trial by jury in criminal cases." That one never made it out of the Senate.)[7]

The second twin in the Religion Clauses is the ban on "prohibiting the free exercise" of religion. "Exercise" of religion had a specific, technical meaning in the eighteenth century. It meant, quite simply, public worship. Temporal rulers in Europe would grant—or withhold—from religious groups the "exercise" of their faith. In this meaning, "free exercise" could mean—could be confined to—the right to hold public services. Other rights asserted under the Free Exercise Clause—the right to refuse Saturday work if forbidden to do so by one's church, the right to wear special garments and, most important, the right to an exemption from regulatory and even criminal laws for certain religious practices—seem to be at best at the edge of that limited definition.

The participles in the two clauses contrast interestingly. The federal government can make no law "respecting an establishment," but no law "prohibiting" free exercise. A "prohibition" is a total ban. Subsequent clauses, dealing with free speech, press, assembly, and petition, use the verb "abridging." "Abridge" means to lessen or curtail, even if that abridgment is far less than a total ban. The two phrases, appearing together in the same sentence, could be read to imply greater latitude for government in interfering with free exercise than with establishment or with any of the expressive rights.

Hands off establishment, the language seems to say, and don't intervene with free exercise—too much. In practice, the two clauses do function differently. If a law "establishes" a religion, it is void; no argument on behalf of the government—that an established church would help with the war effort, say—will save it.

With free exercise, the analysis is different. Sometimes the courts have read "free exercise" simply to mean "belief." Government can't forbid Americans from believing in polygamy or peyotism, but it has no obligation to allow them to act on that belief. In other cases, courts have examined laws to see whether they "burden" free exercise. If so, the law was not automatically invalid; it was instead subject to a "balancing test" in which the importance of the government's interest was "weighed" against the amount of "abridgment" of free exercise. Some "burdens" passed the test; others did not.

The two clauses separate religious-freedom advocates into two camps. Some argue that recognizing a broad right of "free exercise" brings us smack into conflict with the ban on "establishment." If an ordinary citizen cannot possess and use peyote, is it "establishing" peyotism to allow members of a peyote church to do so under government regulation?

Others argue that Establishment Clause zeal has in fact "prohibited" their free exercise. For example, many religious traditions believe that public occasions are incomplete without prayer. Banning prayer at school ceremonies, they say, restricts the free exercise rights of children from religious families with these beliefs. Others argue that this kind of prayer coerces nonbelieving children into religious exercise—an "establishment" of religion and a prohibition on *their* "free exercise" to boot.

We are only two clauses into the First Amendment and already find ourselves tangled in a dense web of ambiguity.

As many religious conservatives like to point out, the document nowhere mentions "separation of church and state." They like to trace the phrase to a letter written by President Thomas Jefferson in 1802, thirteen years after the Framing of the Bill of Rights. They suggest that Jefferson's post hoc coinage means that it cannot be embodied in religion clauses framed earlier.

But the truth is that the "separation of church and state" is an American phrase that was coined more than a century before the Bill of Rights was written. In 1644, the American theologian Roger Williams, founder of the first Baptist congregation in the British New World, wrote: "The church of the Jews under the Old Testament in the type and the church of the Christians under the New Testament in the antitype were both separate from the world; and when they have opened a gap in the hedge or wall of separation between the garden of the church and the wilderness of the world, God hath ever broke down the wall itself, removed the candlestick, and made his garden a wilderness."[8] So the idea of "separation," and the image of a wall, were present in the American mind in 1789. That the words weren't written into the document doesn't establish that the text rejects the idea. The real question is what spatial metaphor can be supported in the text we have.

The government cannot pick a favored religion and tax the citizens for its support; it cannot restrict their worship (and probably more of their religious practices), and (as we saw when considering Article VI) it can't require any religious belief or practice from its own officers. In other words, whether gazing at them across a wall or not, it is maintaining a fair distance from religious matters. Should we read these three restrictions as limited and narrow exceptions to a general assumption that government should be involved in the spiritual lives of its people, or as examples of a principle that government generally should stay clear of matters of faith? The phrase "wall of separation" probably sheds more heat than light; perhaps we should focus on the practical difficulties—faced in 1789 as today—of building a nation made up of many quarrelsome faiths, practices, and degrees of belief or unbelief.

The second part of the amendment protects four rights that relate directly to politics and self-government. They receive identical protection. Congress shall make no law "abridging" the four: (1) "the freedom of speech"; (2) "the freedom ... of the press"; (3) "the right of the people peaceably to assemble"; and (4) "the right of the people ... to petition the Government for a redress of grievances."

To modern eyes, the First Amendment seems to be an individual rights provision, designed to protect dissenters against the wrath of majorities in government. I read it that way, and throughout American history it has been interpreted that way—beginning in 1798, when Thomas Jefferson and James Madison led popular opposition to the oppressive Alien and Sedition Acts. Scholar Akhil Reed Amar, by contrast, proposes a different reading—that the right of "free speech" in particular was concerned with popular majorities who might face repression in their collective capacities from an overweening, unrepresentative government. "[T]he individual-rights vision of the speech and press clauses," he writes, "powerfully illuminates a vital part of our constitutional tradition, but only by obscuring other parts."[9] If we stop for a moment and consider the idea that the First Amendment protects the rights of groups rather than primarily of individuals, the entire provision in a twinkling changes its import. In this reading, the establishment clause protects state established churches; the guarantee of free exercise protects all church bodies from federal regulation; the speech and press clauses protect state legislatures and the institutional press, and the free-assembly and petition clauses protect popular assemblies and conventions from suppression by a suspicious central government.

"The freedom of speech," lawyers like to point out, is not quite the same thing as "freedom of speech." The latter is a concept that anyone can define. The former is a term with a legal history, even as of 1789. Some English thinkers in fact had defined "the freedom of speech" as a right that belonged to legislative bodies. As we noted earlier, after the English Bill of Rights in 1689, Parliament had "the freedom of speech" to represent the grievances of the people, even if that meant questioning the king. Thus in the American context, "the freedom of speech" would mean that Congress could question acts of the president without fear of being dissolved or punished.

One thing is clear, however—almost since its inception, Americans have read the First Amendment as primarily concerned with the individual, and as embodying a concept of freedom that protects the outspoken individual as much as, or more than, the local majority. Those arguments were honed during the battle over the Sedition Act, and since then free speech has been debated almost entirely as an individual right.

If, then, "the freedom of speech" is a personal rather than a legislative right, how far does it extend? The phrase appears next to "of the press." "The freedom of the press" also had a common-law meaning: freedom from what was called *prior restraint*—a system of licensing or censorship. "Every free man has an un-doubted right to lay what sentiments he pleases before the public," the eminent English legal theorist William Blackstone wrote in 1769; "to forbid this, is to destroy the freedom of the press: but if he publishes what is improper, mischie-vous, or illegal, he must take the consequence of his own temerity."[10] In other words, publish what you want, knowing that you can be sued, imprisoned, or even put to death for what you say.

Scholars still debate whether this was all the phrase "freedom of speech or of the press" meant in 1789. But since then American society has decided the words have to mean more than that. That consensus arose out of an attempt to apply the old restrictive meaning. Less than a decade after proposing the First Amendment, Congress passed laws forbidding criticism of itself, or of the pres-ident. Federal prosecutors and judges jailed opposition newspaper editors, members of Congress, itinerant preachers—even a drunk in a tavern who made a vulgar joke about President John ("His Rotundity") Adams's well-padded rear end.

The attempt to suppress criticism backfired. Adams was ridiculed and defeated in 1800, and the new president, Thomas Jefferson, pardoned those convicted under the act. The national revulsion was so great that future administrations have almost never tried it again. Nearly two centuries later, the Supreme Court, in *New York Times v. Sullivan*, cited the Sedition Act controversy as authority for its rule that government officials can't sue their critics for libel unless they could show that the critic had defamed them personally with "reckless disregard for truth."[11] In the United States, "the freedom of speech" and "of the press" now mean much more than no licensing; indeed, the two terms now stand for the most robust scheme of free-speech protection anywhere in the world.

Two more rights are protected against abridgment: "the right of the people peaceably to assemble, and to petition the Government for a redress of griev-ances." In England, fear of riotous assembly had given rise to the Riot Act of 1713. If a crowd of twelve or more people "unlawfully, riotously and tumultu-ously" assembled, a local official could order them arrested an hour after he had "read them the Riot Act":

> Our Sovereign Lord the King chargeth and commandeth all persons,
> being assembled, immediately to disperse themselves, and peaceably to
> depart to their habitations, or to their lawful business, upon the pains

contained in the act made in the first year of King George, for preventing tumults and riotous assemblies. God Save the King![12]

Nothing in the First Amendment explicitly takes from government the power to disperse assemblies, and in fact Congress soon after the enactment of the First Amendment passed a Militia Act, still basically in force today, that authorizes the president to order mobs to disperse and "return peaceably to their homes." But the federal authority to do this is far more carefully circumscribed than was authority under the Riot Act. It is triggered only in two circumstances. The first arises "[w]henever there is an insurrection in any State" and the president has received a request for aid from "its legislature or of its governor if the legislature cannot be convened." In the second, the president on his own authority may "suppress, in a State, any insurrection, domestic violence, unlawful combination, or conspiracy" if "the constituted authorities of that State are unable, fail, or refuse" to protect citizens' rights or the insurgency "opposes or obstructs the execution of the laws of the United States."[13]

If one of those two things has happened (and only then), the president "shall, by proclamation, immediately order the insurgents to disperse and retire peaceably to their abodes within a limited time."

The act cannot be used against mere "unlawful" assemblies, but only against "insurgen[ts]," and only the president, not just any local jack-in-office, is authorized to issue a proclamation to disperse. These provisions make clear that breaking up gatherings of citizens is a serious act. Of course, at the time the Bill of Rights was framed, the provisions relating to "peaceab[le] assembl[y]" limited only the federal government; states could and did enforce far more restrictive prohibitions. Since the passage of the Fourteenth Amendment, however, the right of peaceable assembly applies against all government in the United States.

The text, however, doesn't tell us *where* citizens can assemble. It could easily have said "peaceably to assemble on public or private property," but it didn't. It took the country and its courts many years to recognize that freedom of assembly requires a place to assemble. For many years the courts took as gospel an idea expressed by Oliver Wendell Holmes Jr., as a judge on Massachusetts's highest court, when he wrote that the city of Boston could forbid anyone to speak on Boston Common for any reasons it chose: "For the legislature absolutely or conditionally to forbid public speaking in a highway or public park is no more an infringement of the rights of a member of the public than for the owner of a private house to forbid it in his house."[14] Not until 1939 did the Supreme Court reject the idea that the government "owned" the parks and streets and could open or close them just as it chose.[15] Now, by and large, public meetings can only be regulated, not prohibited—states may limit where, when, and how they take place, as long as the regulations don't discriminate among speakers and do allow reasonable venues where they can take place.

Finally, the First Amendment guarantees the right "to petition the government for redress of grievances." The right of petition had been guaranteed to British subjects since the English Bill of Rights in 1689. Does it also include the right to submit the petitions? In other words, can government stop its ears to petitioners like Billy Crystal in *The Princess Bride*, shouting "I'm not listening to you!" when it doesn't like what the petitions say?

That question briefly absorbed the nation's attention when in 1830 southern members of Congress combined with northern allies to pass a "gag rule" stating that no anti-slavery petitions could be received by Congress. Led by former president John Quincy Adams, anti-slavery members of the House finally obtained repeal of the rule. Today, any petition that is not "obscene or insulting" will be entered in the House journal if a member so requests.

Remarkably enough, during the Sedition Act crisis, the government prosecuted unoffending citizens for organizing and signing petitions calling for the legal repeal of the act. Today such a prosecution would be laughed out of court.

These then are the six rights (or more properly provisions, because the Establishment Clause, textually at least, is a *disability* directed at government, not a right vested in individual citizens) that form the First Amendment. These six have sparked a debate: are they simply individual stars shining against the dark background of a general governmental power to control speech, action, and society? Or do they make out a bright sky of presumed freedom, what the twentieth-century philosopher Karl Popper called "the open society"?

To oversimplify a vast scholarly literature, one side contends that the provisions of the speech-related clauses reveal an almost single-minded focus on speech to and about government, which is an indispensable condition for self-government. In this reading, the First Amendment protects almost solely what is called "core political speech" about constitutional government, and has little relevance to other kinds of expression, whether they are calls for revolution, depictions of sexuality, or seemingly nonpolitical artistic and literary work. Government remains free to regulate or suppress speech that is not near the "core" of the First Amendment's concern.

The other view is that the specific rights in the Speech Clauses are evidence of a commitment that, subject to a few small exceptions, citizens can write, print, and say what they want—whether they are discussing Karl Marx's *Communist Manifesto* or James Joyce's *Ulysses*.

A few points in the text bear on this question of scope. First is the categorical language of the First Amendment: "Congress shall make *no law*" abridging these expressive rights. There is no modifier or limiter—nothing like "the freedom of *political* speech" or "the freedom . . . of the press *to question and criticize government*," or "the right peaceably to assemble *for civic meetings*." The right to petition does mention government as either the audience or the subject of those petitions, making the omission of that kind of language from the other rights more striking.

Second, the amendment as a whole concerns more than speech, and far more than politics—it specifically discusses religious freedom as well as speech. Certainly no one would suggest that the right of "free exercise of religion" extends only to political aspects of religion—that the congregation may meet in the vestry to protest abortion but could be prevented from holding Mass in the sanctuary. Religious concern is as far-reaching a concept as are artistic freedom or the sexual impulse; why would a measure protecting such a broad concept in its first, religious half protect only a narrow one in its second?

The text would seem to put the burden of proof on those asserting that some kinds of expression are unprotected. "No law" abridging free expression may not in fact mean "no law at all," but it surely means something more than "no law except one that government really, really wants to pass."

Second Amendment

While some parts of the Constitution are as dry as the English law's ancient Statute of Frauds, others are as delicate and suggestive as a poem by Emily Dickinson, offering empty spaces we are invited to fill. Dickinson's poetry is deliberately terse and operates by image and suggestion far more than by narration or exposition. It forces us to read carefully, with an openness to the multiple meanings suggested by every word or phrase, and no certainty that how we read them is correct: generations of school children, have learned to read using poems like "I'm nobody. Who are you?" As Walt Whitman is the father of American poetry, Dickinson is the mother. Dickinsonian reading is as much a part of the American mind as is Fundamentalism.

What would reading the Constitution with a Dickinsonian eye entail? Certainly we must become involved as much in what is not said as in what is. The language of the Constitution is compressed—in 7,000 words it evokes an entire nation—and practical unpacking of that text necessarily involves some of the tricks we learn encountering poems as apparently simple, yet baffling, as these words, written by Dickinson in 1865, as the United States suffered through civil war and social revolution:

> Revolution is the Pod
> Systems rattle from
> When the Winds of Will are stirred
> Excellent is Bloom[16]

The poem proceeds by juxtaposing an idea—revolution—with an image—
the seed-pod of a plant. It does not contain a lesson about revolution; instead it
forces the reader to expand his or her idea of it, to see it in a new way.

Let's apply a Dickinsonian eye to an important provision of the Bill of Rights:

A well regulated Militia,
being necessary to the security of a free State,
the right of the people to keep and bear Arms,
shall not be infringed.

"Revolution is the pod" does not describe; the Second Amendment does not,
truly, prescribe. Instead, it evokes the image of a militia, then weds it to two
important concepts—on the one hand a "free State," on the other "the people"
and their rights. Generations of scholars and judges have puzzled over this verbal
collage. Who are "the people"? Are they an organized group of villagers assembled for "training day" on the village green, or solitary wilderness settlers toting
home-forged rifles for protection against bears and cougars?

Many readers find in the Second Amendment a larger unstated vision of
America as a polity in which an armed people "regulate" the state rather than the
reverse, in which the individual is empowered to resist with deadly force unwelcome interference by either the government or the neighbors. (Just to make
matters more confusing, a common usage in eighteenth-century America
defined a "regulator" as a member of an extra-legal band of violent vigilantes.)[17]
Others, equally plausibly, deny this image, finding instead the important meaning
of the amendment in the words "well regulated," and drawing from that the
image of a republic in which the states are collectively armed for defense against
rebels within and enemies without.

The duel of meanings is closely akin to the studied ambiguity of poetry. All
discussions of what constitutional scholar Sanford Levinson recently called "the
embarrassing Second Amendment"[18] are shaped by complex images, by notions
of what it is to be American, to be a citizen, or indeed to be a man. That it attracts
the mythic imagination isn't surprising; its text offers one of the most puzzling
conundrums in the entire Constitution.

"A well regulated militia being essential to the security of a free state," it begins.
This is the only provision of the Bill of Rights to have a preamble, and one of only
two provisions in the entire Constitution. (The other is the so-called Patent and
Trademark Clause, which introduces the congressional power to create limited
monopolies as designed "To promote the Progress of Science and useful Arts.")
It is also the only place in the Bill of Rights, indeed one of only three places in the
Constitution, in which the *present* tense is used—"a well-regulated militia *being*
essential." (In the Tenth Amendment, the powers not delegated to the federal

government "*are* reserved to the states respectively or to the people"; in the Citizenship Clause of the Fourteenth Amendment, "all persons born or naturalized in the United States, and subject to the jurisdiction thereof, *are* citizens of the United States and of the states wherein they reside.") This is in sharp contradistinction to what might be called the prophetic future tense of the rest of the document: "Congress *shall* have the power," or "the executive power *shall* be vested in a President." The first clause of the Second Amendment is matter-of-fact, almost offhand. *As we all know*, it seems to say, a militia is important to "a free state."

What is a "free state"? Does it mean a state of the Union, or any organized sovereign government? Is a well-regulated militia essential to the United States as a free nation independent of other nations, or to its constituent states, sovereign and to some degree independent of their federal father? If it were possible to determine what this means, it might answer the key question about the Second Amendment, which is: does the amendment protect (1) the power of the states to maintain militias as part of the "common," that is, national, defense; (2) the power of the states to arm themselves against possible federal oppression; (3) the right of individuals to "keep and bear arms" for militia service; or (4) the individual right to do so for personal protection?

If the amendment is a structural protection for *states*, then state governments would have had and would continue to have plenary authority to regulate weapons inside their borders. Nothing in the Constitution says that states *have* to maintain militias. If they chose not to, then possession of weapons by individuals would be of little use to the amendment's purpose, and they could ban them altogether. If they choose to maintain militias, they could limit any individual right to the kinds of arms it would be useful for citizens to possess in the event of emergency. They could perhaps even limit possession to people of military age, whose ownership of weapons would be useful. Or they might even have the power—as some communities in the American West have tried to do over the years—to *require* citizens to maintain a workable weapon in their homes so as to be ready for service at a moment's notice. The amendment would simply prevent the federal government from overriding these state choices.

On the other hand, if the right to "keep and bear arms" is a protection of the individual against tyranny from any source, then states, like the federal government, would be at least limited in (though not necessarily totally disabled from) the restrictions they wish to impose on individuals. The amendment's text speaks of a beneficiary of the right— "a free state," which implies an organized government; and a holder of the right, "the people," which implies possession and use in some collective form. What it never says is, "a person." The Fifth Amendment provides rights to individual "person[s]." The Second does not do so explicitly; this however cannot be conclusive, as the Fourth protects the right of "the people" against unreasonable search and seizure, and that right can only be meaningful if it is extended to individuals.

Here the Framers' overall rhetorical approach is spectacularly unhelpful. As we have noted before, both the 1787 Convention and the First Congress adopted a grudging, tight-lipped tone toward the states. In only one place in either the Bill of Rights or the original Constitution is a right explicitly given to the states at the expense of the federal government. Suggestively enough, that solitary "state right" (more properly a "reserved power") relates to the organization and leadership of the state militia. That suggests an unusual degree of solicitude toward state power in this area, an interpretation that makes even more sense when we consider the radical military structure set up by the original Constitution.

Under the Articles of Confederation, all military forces were to be raised, provisioned, and organized by the states. The Confederation had the sole prerogative of "determining on peace or war," unless a state found itself either (1) actually invaded by another country (preemptive war against sovereign nations by the states without congressional consent being apparently barred by omission); (2) forewarned of a plan by "some nation of Indians" to invade the state (preemption in this case being allowed without congressional consultation); or (3) "infested by pirates" (the language suggesting that raids by pirates from outside the state's territory would not permit state reprisal without congressional approval, but that an actual pirate base on state territory could be attacked without consultation).

But despite Congress's predominance in the area of *deciding* on war, the entire military force of the Confederation was to be maintained by the states. The Confederation was to defray "charges of war" by raising funds through a direct requisition against the states based strictly on the value of land within their borders. But the military units were to be raised by the states, and the state legislatures would also designate the "regimental officers" ("all officers of or under the rank of colonel") even in wartime, when the forces would presumably be under joint Confederation command.

In the event of war, the Congress would set a number of troops needed and send each state a requisition "in proportion to the number of white inhabitants of such State." The states were to raise the troops required and "cloath, arm and equip them in a solid-like manner, at the expense of the United States" and then march them to the "place appointed" to be taken into the national service.

A cumbersome system indeed, and it would be unworkable if individual states had no ready supply of trained men and materiel in case of emergency. Accordingly, the Articles required that "every State shall always keep up a well-regulated and disciplined militia, sufficiently armed and accoutered, and shall provide and constantly have ready for use, in public stores, a due number of field-pieces and tents, and a proper quantity of arms, ammunition and camp equipage."

Thus, under the Articles, the states not only could but must maintain fully combat-ready militias, while the Confederation would have no forces not directly supplied and staffed by the states. The prospect of the Confederation sending such troops against state governments, instead of foreign enemies, was virtually nil.

By contrast, consider the military setup under the 1787 Constitution. Congress could directly "raise and support armies," in time of peace or war. Congress could fund those armies by taxing the people of the states, without state consent. States could maintain militias and could appoint their officers. However, the organization and discipline of the militias was under congressional control at all times. In addition, the federal government could call the militias into the "actual service of the United States" at any time. When it did, the president would be their commander-in-chief. Once called into federal service, the militia could be used not only to "repel invasions" but to "execute the laws of the union [and] suppress insurrections"—in other words, to bend recalcitrant state governments to the federal will. Perhaps in no other area did the change from the Articles to the Constitution make a more drastic shift of authority from the states to the Union.

States were no longer *required* to maintain militias. The language seemed to take their existence for granted; but what would a state's "reserved power" to appoint officers avail if Congress, using its power to prescribe the discipline under which they would be maintained, were to overreach and order them disbanded? It's easy to imagine the horror of the veterans of '76 at the idea of a standing army kept by a Congress specifically empowered to take over, and perhaps disarm and disband, the state militias. The "shot heard 'round the world" had been fired when British regular troops, sent by a distant central government, marched to Lexington and Concord to seize the militia's weapons. Nothing in the Constitution would prevent that from happening again.

It would be quite logical, then, to read the Second Amendment as a direct response to this concern. The phrase "well-regulated militia" was directly lifted out of the Articles to refer to the state militaries ("every State shall always keep up a well-regulated and disciplined militia"). The Second Amendment could be read as reaffirming that state militias were essential, either to the state's freedom or to the well-being of the Union. Thus the federal power to discipline and call out the militia could not be expanded by construction to permit their dissolution. That reading is made even more logical when we consider that the Second Amendment, like all the provisions of the Bill of Rights, was initially read to apply only to the federal government. Nothing in it would apply to a state's power to regulate weapons ownership by its own people, if the state government so chose.

But this argument is far from conclusive. If the drafters of the Second Amendment were thinking purely of empowering the states and clarifying the status of the militia, then they have only themselves to blame for subsequent misunderstandings that have arisen. They could easily have said, "the power of the states to maintain a well-regulated militia, and to allow their people to keep and bear arms therefor, shall not be abridged." But they had trouble uttering the word "state" in the context of "power," as we have seen. Ensuring federal power, and limiting state authority, was a far more pressing concern of the Framers. And they chose the word "right," rather than "power"; if the word in this context refers to a state government, it would mark the only place in the entire Constitution—as written and amended from 1787 until now—where a state power is referred to as a "right." In every other context, the word "right" refers to an individual prerogative rather than a governmental power.

Constitutional historian Leonard W. Levy, a man of great learning and unambiguous opinion, deduced from the amendment's language that the Second Amendment must guarantee an entirely individual right:

> The very language of the Amendment is evidence that the right is a personal one, for it is not subordinated to the militia clause. Rather the right is an independent one, altogether separate from the maintenance of a militia. Militias were possible only because the people were armed and possessed the right to be armed. The right does not depend on whether militias exist.[19]

Levy is a historian, not a linguist, and a real grammarian (ever-popular as a party guest) might say that the Militia Clause actually *is* grammatically subordinate to the Keep and Bear Clause, with the participle "being" to imply a cause-and-effect relationship: "*Because* (or *since*) a well regulated militia is essential to the security of a free state, the right of the people to keep and bear arms shall not be infringed." That reading arguably makes more sense than reading them as coordinate phrases: "A well-regulated militia *is* essential to the security of a free state *and* (or *while we're on the subject*) the right of the people to keep and bear arms shall not be infringed." If there is no subordinate relationship between the two clauses, then why would not the drafters have used the same aspect for both? The Militia Clause is in the present tense; the Keep and Bear Clause is in the future.

Consider the difference between saying, "The financial situation is quite critical, and I will have macaroni and cheese for lunch," and "The financial situation being quite critical, I shall have macaroni and cheese for lunch." Levy would apparently accept subordination, either grammatically or conceptually, only if the drafters had said, "*Because and only because* the right to keep and bear arms . . ." The co-ordinate reading of the two phrases seems to arise from a disposition to find a personal right in the language, rather than from the language itself.

That disposition might legitimately arise from the history of the phrase. "The right to keep and bear arms" went back to ancient disputes between king and Parliament, and to attempts by Catholic kings to disarm Protestant subjects. After the Glorious Revolution of 1688, William III granted his subjects the Bill of Rights, which specified that "subjects which are Protestants may have arms for their defence suitable to their conditions and as allowed by law."[20] That language provides fodder for both sides of the argument. It says that the arms are to be kept, not for defense of the Realm but for "their (i.e., personal) defence," which supports the idea of a personal right. On the other hand, it grants a highly qualified right, one which is limited by (1) a subject's religion; (2) a subject's "standing," or rank in the English social structure; and, most important, (3) laws set by Parliament, which, since it can "allow" the bearing of arms, must very likely also be able to "disallow" it. The English right to bear arms thus is a qualified one, enforceable against the Crown alone, and perhaps designed to safeguard the authority of Parliament as much as the liberty of the subject.

The argument is complicated by the important constitutional fact that the Fourteenth Amendment, enacted much later, has the effect of providing that many if not all the guarantees of the Bill of Rights now apply against both the states and the federal government. If the Second Amendment protected only a state's right to maintain a militia, it would make little sense to regard it as applying against the state—"a well-regulated state militia is essential, and so the state shall not have the power to regulate weapons" is a classic non sequitur. On the other hand, if it created a personal right against the federal government that could be abridged by the state (as the English right was provided against the king but subject to Parliament), the very nature of the right is changed—from qualified and purposive to categorical and absolute—by saying that the state also cannot limit it.

In all, the textual and structural evidence is in equipoise, though, as the earlier Levy quote illustrates, very few commentators are willing to admit the depth of its ambiguity. The argument seems currently to be tipped one way or another by extratextual ideas of American history, the nature of freedom and even the essence of manliness. Many Americans profoundly believe that the American Revolution was won by a completely unorganized popular movement, in which self-sufficient yeomen in fur and homespun dusted off ancient flintlocks and deployed individually against the Redcoats from behind trees and walls. The actual struggles of Congress and the leadership of the Army to construct a professionally trained and supplied force display the Patriot movement less than gloriously. They have tended to be eclipsed by the myth of the self-sufficient country rifleman. If America won its independence with grandpappy's squirrel gun, then any threat to current personal armories is a dagger pointed at the national heart.

Other historical images are equally persuasive, perhaps at an unconscious level. If we regard the Militia Clause as having some relation to the "keep and bear arms" language, of course, it's not necessary to designate the state militia power as the sole purpose of the clause. A more refined question might be, what personal right to bear arms would further the end of providing a citizenry trained and equipped to serve the militia in time of emergency? And how would that right be balanced against the kinds of restrictions on personal possession of weapons that might actually be counterproductive by restricting the power of the militia to "execute the Laws of the Union, suppress Insurrections and repel Invasions" Personal possession of hand grenades, field artillery, armor-piercing bullets, or tactical nuclear weapons might reasonably be thought to undercut the militia function. Semi-automatic weapons and powerful handguns might or might not, in individual hands, further the purposes of the militia. These questions, like other important constitutional questions, are surely amenable to arguments more finely reasoned than most of those employed in popular discourse about the Second Amendment.

In 2008, the Supreme Court decided that the Second Amendment guarantees a personal, individual right to possess a handgun in the home for self-protection.[21] Two years later the Court decided that this right applies, by force of the Fourteenth Amendment, against the states as well as against the federal government.[22] The Court is now, for the first time in our history, committed to spelling out the extent of the personal right, and we can expect questions of this sort to come up. It is thus in the interests of everyone concerned with the role of firearms in society to contribute more than images and myths to a reasoned resolution of this question—and during such discussions, perhaps we should all keep our hands where others can see them.

Third Amendment

We move now from the Bill of Rights' most ambiguous and controversial provision to its clearest and most successful one. The Quartering Act of 1774, imposing troops as houseguests on Americans, was considered one of the "Intolerable Acts" that drove the colonies into revolt, and the Declaration of Independence recited as one of bad King George's sins "quartering large bodies of armed troops among us." Many states had adopted provisions in their own constitutions banning quartering, and now the new federal government would not be able to quarter troops either—at least not in time of peace. Householders could bargain for military lodgers and give their consent if the terms were right. In wartime, things would be different. Congress could enact general laws setting the terms for mandatory quartering; but those laws would as a practical matter almost certainly contain protections for the property owner and provisions for reimbursement.

That the Third Amendment addresses a problem we find somewhat recondite is a mark of its signal success. Its provisions are clear enough that any mind, military or civilian, can understand. Is this a private home? Yes. Is the nation at war? If not, then troops may not be quartered there without consent no matter what. If so, then we must consult the federal statutes to find whether Congress has authorized quartering. If quartering is authorized, the procedures set up in that statute must be followed.

Simply put, it's hard to violate the Third Amendment without understanding that's what you're doing. Substantial debate goes on about whether a government action "prohibit[s] the free exercise" of religion, violating the First Amendment, or is an "unreasonable seizure," violating the Fourth. But the idea of inadvertently quartering troops in a private home brings to mind a rule enunciated in Walt Kelly's *Pogo* when the Alligator, Albert, was accused of eating the Pup-Dog. Albert was innocent, but he at first tried to excuse himself by suggesting he might have eaten the puppy while sleep-walking. "People don't eat other people by MISTAKE!" was the response from his interrogator, Ol' Mouse.

Not that claims haven't been made under the Third Amendment. Lawyers have fertile minds, and the temptation to bring a Third Amendment claim where even remotely possible must be hard to resist. One set of litigants claimed that allowing military airplanes to fly over their land without permission amounted to "quartering." The District Court's response was succinct—"This argument borders on frivolous"—and arguably generous too.[23] An army reservist claimed that orders that he parade with his unit at a conservative veterans' organization convention somehow violated the Third Amendment; that court was curt: "inapposite."[24] Only once in the entire history of the Republic has a respectable Third Amendment article been made, in *Engblom v. Carey*,[25] which stands out in the case law the way a bump in the road towers over surrounding central Florida real estate.

Engblom arose when state correction officers at a prison in upstate New York went on strike. The state's governor ordered National Guard troops to the prison. Prison officials housed the Guard in small apartments that had been rented to the officers, ousting the strikers and their possessions.

The officers sued for a violation of their Due Process rights, but also added a claim that sending the Guard to live in their rented rooms was a "quartering," entitling them to money damages. Their claim succeeded in the way legal claims can succeed—that is, it produced a theoretical victory that led to no relief. The Second Circuit Court of Appeals considered the facts and concluded that the Third Amendment now applied to the states as well as the federal government, thanks to the Fourteenth Amendment; that National Guardsmen were "soldiers" within the meaning of the Third Amendment; and that the rental quarters were "private homes," thus making out a complete violation of the Third Amendment. However, under federal civil rights case law, the plaintiffs could recover money damages only if the right that was violated was "clearly established" at the time of the violation. It wasn't, and so they couldn't.

The *Engblom* court inadvertently illustrated the confusion that surrounds the Third Amendment when it lamented that "little illumination can be gleaned [about the amendment's meaning] from the debates of the Constitutional Convention." That relative lack of illumination is probably due to the fact that the amendment was neither drafted nor discussed at the Philadelphia Convention, but two years later during the First Congress—though one must admit that the judge's clerk would likely have found little of use even if he had been looking in the right place. The Third Amendment, being so relatively easy to apply, has been doomed to live a dusty and uneventful life on the constitutional shelf; but we can console ourselves with the knowledge that Alan N. Sussman, Esq., a distinguished civil liberties lawyer in Bearsville, New York, who served as counsel for the striking correction officers, lives among us as a god among mortals, the only lawyer in American history to win a case under the Third Amendment.

Fourth Amendment

"For most of us," an old legal saying runs, "the Constitution is the cop on the corner." So far in the Constitution, we have met armies, and soldiers, and judges. The cop makes his appearance in the Fourth, at least to contemporary eyes. The word "cop" for police officer is not recorded until 1859; its root, the word "copper" (meaning a policeman's truncheon) apparently didn't emerge until 1846. That's because in 1789, when the Fourth Amendment was framed, the concept of professional law enforcement was barely known. The word "policeman" had first been used, in Ireland, only in 1788. At the time of the First Congress, only Philadelphia had a paid force of law enforcers; New York, where the Congress was meeting, did not have such a force until half a century later. Law enforcement in the eighteenth century was carried out by sheriffs and marshals, mostly under the control of courts. These court officers would serve judicial arrest warrants and take the accused into custody. Most cities also had "night watchmen" and "thief takers," sometimes privately paid and sometimes on the public payroll.

Today, however, police officers are part of daily life. For that reason, the Fourth Amendment is a huge part of the Constitution as most citizens know it. Next to the First Amendment, the Fourth has probably spawned the largest case law and scholarly commentary.

Fourth Amendment rights belong to "the people," though the context suggests that his means "the people" as individuals. "The people" have the right to be "secure in their houses, papers, and effects." That security extends, though, only against "unreasonable searches and seizures," and though the language is stern—the right "shall not be violated"—the "reasonableness" standard is vague.

The amendment consists of two clauses—this time, in grammatical terms, fully independent. The first establishes the right to be free of "unreasonable" search and seizure; the second establishes a limitation on the power of government to issue warrants that authorize searches and seizures. The interplay of these two provisions is complex.

The Fourth Amendment clearly places limits on the means government can use to find and seize forbidden items ("contraband") and evidence of crime. But it also refers to another kind of "search and seizure"—the "seizure" of persons, what we call arrest and detention. (Government's power to detain individuals would not necessarily be unlimited even if "seizure" did not include "arrest." The Bill of Rights contains three other provisions that could apply to detention—the Fifth Amendment's protection of "liberty" without "due process"; the habeas corpus clause recognizing the right of an imprisoned person to demand legal justification; and the Eighth Amendment's ban on "excessive bail." None of these, however, might limit the power to arrest, or "seize," simply the power to hold a person once arrested.)

The Warrant Clause and the Search and Seizure Clause in this respect interrelate, but it's not entirely clear how. Neither has precedence over the other. The Warrant Clause does not say that there can be no "reasonable search" or "seizure" *without* a warrant. Nor does it say that every "search" or "seizure" *with* a warrant is automatically "reasonable." It simply limits the circumstances under which a government may grant its agents a warrant.

If all arrests and searches needed a warrant, many "reasonable" searches and seizures would be barred. A police officer may see one person attacking another. Even to restrain the assailant temporarily would be a seizure; would anyone expect the constable to rush to the magistrate and breathlessly seek a warrant to prevent a murder in progress? Officers may observe suspects on public or private property with weapons or contraband, or may see them clearly preparing to commit crimes; it would be most unreasonable to say that they could not intervene without an official paper.

The two clauses suggest instead that under certain circumstances a warrant may be needed to make a search or arrest reasonable. What if, for example, the police believe that one person has committed a specific crime, or that another is storing illegal drugs or weapons in his home? If they have seen the crime committed, or watched the drugs being carried into the house, it would be reasonable to grab the suspects and evidence on the spot. But what if they hear from someone else, not a policeman, that a person has committed a crime or stored contraband? What if the cop hasn't seen anything illegal, but concludes from what he does see that suspects are up to no good? A person may wear gang clothing; a given house may have been the scene of strange comings and goings. It may be—in fact, surely often is—unreasonable for a policeman to decide to arrest or search on those grounds alone. Displeasing policemen, without more, can't be an offense in a free country.

Under those circumstances, the Warrant Clause may offer a way to render an unreasonable search or seizure reasonable. The police officer takes his or her suspicion to another person, who decides whether there is "probable cause" to issue a warrant for the arrest or search. Warrants, furthermore, must "particularly describ[e] the place to be searched, and the persons or things to be seized."

The amendment doesn't say what kind of official is permitted to issue a warrant. It could be issued by another police officer, or even by the suspicious officer himself. Something about that plan doesn't sit exactly right. The Constitution rarely sets up procedures that give one official the power to initiate, adjudicate, and carry out any governmental procedure. At the highest level, another branch of government is usually involved. In the common-law system, since at least the sixteenth century, "warrant" had a specific meaning: "A writ or order issued by some executive authority, empowering a ministerial officer to make an arrest, a seizure, or a search, to execute a judicial sentence, or to do other acts incident to the administration of justice."[26] The word, then, clearly implied one party issuing the authorization and another party seeking it. Its major purpose was a defense, not for the citizen arrested or searched, but for the official conducting the bust, against tort claims for assault, trespass, or theft. So a warrant could almost certainly not "issue" without an "issuer" who was distinct from the person to whom it is issued.

This would mean that our police officer could not conduct a search or an arrest in many situations without asking permission from someone else in government. Or does it? What if at the beginning of morning patrol, the desk sergeant simply handed out blank warrants authorizing the officers to "search or arrest all and any persons who may in their reasonable belief be guilty of any crime, and to enter all premises upon which there may be concealed the roots, fruits, or instrumentalities of crime," leaving the officer to fill in the names and places?

That kind of warrant—called a "general warrant"—had been used extensively in British North America during the years before and during the Revolution. To prevent government from doing that in the new nation, the Fourth Amendment adds three restrictions on any valid warrants. First, they cannot issue except "upon probable cause." That term, from the common law, means yet again something like "reasonableness."[27] As our courts have developed it, it has come to mean in essence something that can be put into words and explained to another person, something based on facts rather than hunch, feeling, or "We don't like your kind around these parts."

The requirement of probable cause suggests that investigators must allege some facts to obtain a warrant. Did the facts have to be true? The question is not as strange as it may sound to a nonlawyer. The recitation of some legal facts, throughout the history of the common law, had become a mere formula designed to achieve a result. Thus, for example, the ancient writ of trespass always included a ritual allegation that the unlawful entry onto land had been accomplished by "force and arms, to wit, swords, staves, etc.," even when nothing of the sort had occurred. The allegation of force was necessary for the issuance of the writ, and all parties knew that the writ had to issue before a court could adjudicate the case, and so everyone winked at the suggestion that Farmer Ethelbert had led an armed invasion of Farmer Edilfred's pastureland.

Of course, ritual false allegations would not be as benign in a criminal-law context. So the allegation of facts amounting to probable cause had to be "supported by oath or affirmation." To this day, investigators seeking arrest or search warrants must submit affidavits, sworn statements, setting out in specific detail the facts that they believe support probable cause. These are not pro forma—in complicated cases, they may run to hundreds of pages. False swearing in a warrant application can (at least in theory) subject an officer to prosecution.

Having laid out probable cause, a warrant must also specify exactly what the officers hope to obtain with it—what types of items of evidence and who, or at any rate what kind of people, will be seized when it is served.

One final requirement has been read into the Fourth Amendment, though the text does not clearly include it. We know that a warrant must be supported by specific facts amounting to probable cause, must be sworn to by the person seeking the warrant, and must specifically describe what and who are being sought. But who decides if these conditions have been met? The desk sergeant? Or (as is the case in many European countries today) the prosecutor? It's easy to see that either of those officials might be readily disposed to find probable cause in relatively sketchy facts alleged by an investigator they know well and rely upon. All the formal requirements could be complied with without any skeptical evaluation of the warrant request. Federal courts have read the Warrant Clause as requiring that the request be made to an official who is "neutral and detached," not part of the investigation or of the law enforcement apparatus. The general term for an official empowered to assess a warrant application is "magistrate," which can mean a federal judge but can also mean a magistrate, or some other official who is sufficiently distant from the investigators that in theory he or she will make an independent evaluation.

A perennial question about the Fourth Amendment is what happens or should happen when the government violates it. This happens every day, either because investigators make a conscious choice to ignore the rules or because they make a mistake or misjudgment. Some arrests and searches, as we said earlier, must be made on the spot—but they must then be assessed for reasonableness, not on the naked word of the officer but by some neutral official.

Sometimes the situation is fairly easy to assess—law enforcement officers stop and arrest an innocent person out of malice or sloppiness, or they break into and search an innocent family's home because of a stupid mistake as to name or address. Legally, the remedy for these errors is straightforward (though as any litigator specializing in such cases will tell us, *practically* they can be quite difficult): the innocent party is due money damages for the suffering and loss.

But what about cases in which officers search or arrest without reasonable grounds—and nonetheless discover evidence of crime? The controversy over this situation is one of the longest-lasting in criminal procedure. One side of the discussion suggests that the remedy for this kind of misconduct is the same as for the search and seizure of the innocent—tort damages for the person injured and, in egregious cases, criminal prosecution of the offending officer.

However elegant theoretically, however, this solution is often practically worthless. Civil juries are understandably reluctant to assess money damages against police who arrest guilty people. Prosecutors, who work daily with police officers, rarely want to send them to prison for excessive zeal in catching criminals. This leaves a gap in the constitutional order, for the rights guaranteed in the Fourth Amendment are not reserved to "the innocent people" or "those who deserve security"; if they were, they would be of very little use to ordinary citizens. As Hamlet points out, "use every man after his desert, and who should 'scape whipping?"[28] The Fourth Amendment does not present itself as a means by which sheep may be separated from goats, but as a limit on how the blue-clad shepherds may sort the sheep.

The courts over the years have evolved—and then limited—what is called the "exclusionary rule," which provides (in grossly oversimplified form) that evidence acquired by illegal search and arrest may not be used at trial. This is a strong remedy, and one with many detractors. It seems to smack of a game between criminals and cops, in which, as Judge (later Justice) Benjamin Cardozo once wrote with some asperity, "the criminal is to go free because the constable has blundered."[29] It is this rule, more than any other, that has given rise to the popular belief that hardened criminals often escape punishment out of what is called "a technicality."

Its supporters, on the other hand, defend the rule as the only practical means by which the police can be discouraged from heavy-handed tactics. If they can find something on most people they stop or search, they have little incentive to stay clear of the constitutional limits.

The full scope of this decades-long argument is beyond the scope of this essay. But it illustrates the general question of how constitutional rules are ordinarily to be enforced. We have noted that the Constitution throughout generally uses the prophetic future—in this case, "The right of the people to be secure in their persons, houses, papers, and effects . . . *shall* not be violated." In this context, only the most naïve reader would mistake prophecy for prediction, and we may assume that constitutional drafters are not naïve. Constitutional rules are violated every day; how shall they be vindicated? None of the provisions of the Bill of Rights carries in its text an enforcement mechanism. What is to happen when government violates the rules against abridging free speech, or quartering troops in homes in time of peace? Under the practice that has developed, if the violation takes place by means of a statute, the remedy is fairly clear: a federal court should (even if it doesn't always) hold the law invalid and prevent its enforcement. But most constitutional violations aren't written in the statute books—they arise out of hasty or ignorant bureaucratic decisions that affect only a few individuals at a time. When those individuals are innocent or admirable, the remedy of a civil lawsuit is available, and Congress and the courts have fashioned statutes and causes of action that will award damages and deter future violations.

But constitutional rights extend to the guilty, the despicable, and the unpopular as well. Is it humanly possible for a legal system to vindicate their rights? Or are there to be two classes of people in society—those who "deserve" rights, and have them, and those who do not? The language of deserving enters the discourse of rights uncomfortably often, whether it concerns the treatment of alleged terrorists in custody or of semi-literate citizens who simply desire to cast meaningful votes. Mechanisms of enforcement will always contain an irreducible quantum of subjectivity and bias, and both legislatures and judges must daily decide how much disadvantage and inconvenience they are willing to undergo in order to continue living under a regime of rights rather than of government-granted privilege. And once we move past the rhetorical invocation of rights to the business of implementation, the answers are seldom obvious.

Most of us believe strongly that police should not routinely knock at (or knock down) our doors by mistake, or on mere suspicion; that our "persons, houses, papers, and effects" should be left alone unless government has a reason. We tend to be a bit less solicitous of our neighbors' person and property when, rightly or wrongly, we suspect that they are up to no good. The balance between security and suspicion is a moving target, and history often seems to move inexorably toward the suspicion side of the scale. Constables often blunder, and when their blunders carry no consequences, they tend to persist in them.

Fifth Amendment

The Fifth Amendment is almost a miniature Bill of Rights; at more than 100 words, it is the longest provision of the Bill of Rights and covers at least five different guarantees, three related to criminal proceedings, one related to property rights, and one applicable to all government dealings with individuals. Even though 100 words is not very long, the text of the Fifth Amendment draws on formulas from the common law, like an epic poet using well-worn tropes, to generate some of the most intriguing textual riddles in the entire Constitution.

The Fifth Amendment rights are (1) indictment by grand jury in major criminal cases; (2) protection against double jeopardy in criminal prosecution; (3) protection against being required to testify against oneself in criminal prosecutions; (4) protection against any adverse governmental action without due process; and (5) a requirement of compensation when government condemns private property by eminent domain. In each case, however, the wording creates interesting puzzles, especially in relation to wording elsewhere in the Constitution.

To begin with, a grand jury must provide the charges before any person can be prosecuted for "a capital, or otherwise infamous crime." The grand jury is one of the most fearsome investigative mechanisms available to a contemporary prosecutor. Nearly a century ago, the Supreme Court described it as "a grand inquest, a body with powers of investigation and inquisition, the scope of whose inquiries is not to be limited narrowly by questions of propriety."[30] Less than twenty years ago, the Court said,

> the grand jury can investigate merely on suspicion that the law is being violated, or even just because it wants assurance that it is not. The function of the grand jury is to inquire into all information that might possibly bear on its investigation until it has identified an offense or has satisfied itself that none has occurred. As a necessary consequence of its investigatory function, the grand jury paints with a broad brush. A grand jury investigation is not fully carried out until every available clue has been run down and all witnesses examined in every proper way to find if a crime has been committed.[31]

A grand jury functions under the guidance of a federal prosecutor. It may summon any citizen to appear, bringing with her any requested papers and records, if it believes she has information relevant to its investigation; the witness need not be a "target," a person facing potential indictment. In fact, a "target" may refuse to appear; an innocent citizen may not. Every witness before a grand jury, even a target if she chooses to appear, must appear before the grand jury in private, and must undergo questioning by the prosecutor without her own counsel in the room. Targets occasionally choose to appear and even more occasionally manage to convince a grand jury that they are guiltless; but in general, lawyers say, a good prosecutor can persuade a grand jury to indict a ham sandwich.

But grand jurors are not government employees, and there is at least the possibility that they will ask inconvenient questions if a prosecutor overreaches; if they become convinced that the prosecution does not have "probable cause" to proceed, they can refuse to return an indictment, which is known as "no bill." There is thus the remnant of the constitutional principle that more than one pair of eyes must look at any major governmental decision.

The alternative is a system in which criminal charges are begun by sole decision of the prosecutor, at a time of his choosing, for any charges he believes the facts will support. That is the system followed in most world legal systems—and by a number of American states, in which criminal proceedings begin with what is called an "information." Other provisions of the Fifth Amendment—freedom from double jeopardy, for example, or seizure of private property for public use without just compensation—have now been interpreted to apply to the states through the "due process" clause of the Fourteenth Amendment. The Supreme Court, however, in 1884 held that the general right of "due process" did not bar the use of an information in a state felony indictment.[32] Since then, many cases have held that "due process" does incorporate specific guarantees of the Bill of Rights; the grand jury clause, however, has not been revisited and applied against the states.

The Constitution provides that a grand jury may hold an individual to answer by means of "indictment or presentment." The indictment is a charge initiated by the grand jury at a prosecutor's request; the presentment was a charge initiated by a grand jury itself in a report directly to a federal court. The presentment as a legal proceeding is now obsolete.

The Fifth Amendment grand jury guarantee applies only in the case of a "capital, or otherwise infamous crime." Capital crimes are clear—any charge that could carry the death penalty, which in today's world means only murder. But what is an "infamous" crime? Do crimes really fall into the categories of admirable and infamous?

Here the text is in every respect perfectly ambiguous, for the word "infamous" at the time it was written had two contrasting legal meanings. The first definition of an "infamous crime" focused on the moral quality of the criminal. Obviously, as a matter of common sense, there is a gradation among crimes. Murder, for example, tells us worse things about its perpetrator than does shoplifting, or even securities fraud. But murder was not an infamous crime at common law, and fraud was. That's less paradoxical than it sounds—in the eighteenth century, intentional murder was a *capital* crime, whose conviction carried with it an automatic sentence of death. In addition, fraud does tell us for certain something that murder does not; a swindler is perfectly willing to lie. And the infamy that certain crimes brought on one convicted was a public, official stamp of untruthfulness. A person convicted of an infamous crime would be thereafter ineligible to take the oath as a witness, a juror, or a public official. One historian of the criminal law notes that by the early seventeenth century, "three categories of "infamous" crimes . . . rendered a witness incompetent to testify—treason, felony, and *crimen falsi* (crimes of falsehood)."[33]

The other meaning of "infamous," however, focused not on the soul of the criminal during the crime but on what happened to the body after conviction. In this definition, some non-capital crimes carried with them "infamous punishments," which meant, in the sixteenth century and now, "punishment by imprisonment, usu[ally] in a penitentiary."[34] The two sets of crimes are not necessarily the same.

The ambiguity in the text persisted until 1885, when the Court heard a habeas corpus petition from a prisoner in the federal "house of correction" in Detroit. James Wilson had been convicted of passing a counterfeit United States bond. The federal prosecutor had proceeded against him without a grand jury indictment, and he had been sentenced to 15 years imprisonment.[35]

The government argued that passing forged bonds was not an "infamous crime" at common law, because a defendant convicted of that crime could still testify in other trials. The Court ordered Wilson released. Justice Horace Gray quoted an eighteenth century English treatise: "There are two kinds of infamy: the one founded in the opinions of the people respecting the mode of punishment; the other in the construction of law respecting the future credibility of the defendant."[36]

Gray then analyzed the text and history of the Fifth Amendment to conclude that Madison and the other framers intended the latter meaning. As for an "infamous crime" in 1885, he made this observation, which would be unacceptable to modern "originalists":

> What punishments shall be considered as infamous may be affected by the changes of public opinion from one age to another. In former times, being put in the stocks was not considered as necessarily infamous. . . . But at the present day either stocks or whipping might be thought infamous punishment.[37]

The meaning of infamy again was tested in 1906, when Charles Walter Moreland was convicted of willfully failing to provide for his own children. After an information was brought, the juvenile court of the District of Columbia sentenced Moreland to six months in the D.C. "workhouse," a farm in Occoquan, Va. The government argued that the workhouse was not a penitentiary, and thus the punishment was not "infamous." The Court disagreed and ordered Moreland released.[38] Justice Louis Brandeis, joined by two other judicial giants, Oliver Wendell Holmes Jr. and William Howard Taft, dissented: Moreland's s time in the workhouse, Brandeis argued, had been spent "[o]n the farm, in healthful and attractive surroundings," doing work "such is ordinarily performed under favorable conditions in farms, in factories, and in the mechanical trades." The prisoners worked an eight-hour day. "There is a school, a library, and a hospital," and "there is no wall, cell, lock or bar." The work required was "compulsory education," not "hard labor," and served the purpose of allowing delinquent parents to earn the money they owed to their children." Thus, he reasoned, "even if imprisonment at hard labor elsewhere than in a penitentiary had, in the past, been deemed an infamous punishment, it would not follow that confinement, or rather service, at a workhouse like Occoquan, under the conditions now prevailing should be deemed so."[39]

The requirement of grand jury indictment, under the Fifth Amendment, does not apply to serving military personnel, or to those in "the militia, when" called to actual service "in time of War or public danger." Those in the military are liable to military justice (a system that the French journalist and statesman Georges Clemenceau once wrote "is to justice as military music is to music").[40]

We now come to the Double Jeopardy Clause. It provides that no person may be "twice put in jeopardy of life or limb" for the same alleged crime. The translation of "jeopardy" into "on trial" is not hard; what is fascinating is the predicate level of danger: "of life or limb." Most defendants, even for the most serious crimes, today are not in jeopardy of losing their lives. Many state legal systems have no capital offenses at all.

What about offenses requiring long prison terms? Double jeopardy certainly, as a practical matter, does attach. But look at the actual text—the clause protects only against double jeopardy "of life or limb"—that is, of offenses potentially requiring execution or mutilation by chopping off of hands, and so on. This raises two questions, both significant for the way we read the Constitution generally: first, does this mean the Constitution *authorizes* governments to enact mutilation as criminal penalty? And, second, can it possibly be that double jeopardy does not protect against multiple trials for the same offense if that offense carries "only" a potential penalty of prison?

The questions relate to the problems of inclusion and of omission, respectively. To begin with the inclusion of "life," both in the Double Jeopardy Clause and in the subsequent Due Process Clause, no less a textualist that Justice Scalia has argued that the mention of the word "life" as a penalty guarded by Fifth Amendment protection "clearly *permits*" the death penalty. The late Justice Harry Blackmun routinely dissented from the Supreme Court's decisions not to review death sentences with an argument that capital punishment, at least as currently administered in the United States, violates the Eighth Amendment's prohibition of "cruel and unusual punishment." In a 1994 case in which the Court denied review, Justice Scalia wrote a separate opinion blasting Blackmun's practice: "The Fifth Amendment provides that '[n]o person shall be held to answer for a capital . . . crime, unless on a presentment or indictment of a Grand Jury, . . . nor be deprived of life, . . . without due process of law.' This clearly permits the death penalty to be imposed, and establishes beyond doubt that the death penalty is not one of the 'cruel and unusual punishments' prohibited by the Eighth Amendment."[41]

One could respond that the argument, in a much-used lawyers' phrase, "proves too much," especially in this context, because the text of the same amendment, as we have just seen, references a criminal penalty that involves loss of "limb." Could this possibly mean that the Eighth Amendment "clearly permits" chopping off the hands of a thief, or as was commonly practiced in the South the foot of an escaped slave? Does a prohibition always or even usually operate as an authorization?

And anyway, might it not help to regard the phrase "life or limb" as yet another old formula inserted in our national epic here to signify something like "very serious penalty"? If it is read that way, it authorizes no particular punishment, but operates to limit the government's ability to punish. A phrase of limitation surely makes more sense read thus than as a Da Vinci-code style authorization. Nothing else in the Fifth Amendment is an authorization for punishment; "life or limb" probably isn't either.

Next in the text comes the provision which is the source of the popular phrase "taking the Fifth": it provides that no person "shall be compelled in any criminal case to be a witness against himself." (In passing, let's note that the masculine pronouns "he," "him," and "himself" appear fifty-one times in the Constitution, while the feminine pronouns do not appear at all, even in the Nineteenth Amendment extending the right to vote to women.) As practiced, what lawyers call the Fifth Amendment *privilege* against self-incrimination extends more broadly than a strict reading of the text would require. It could be read simply that a criminal defendant cannot be called to the stand in open court to testify as part of the prosecution's case against him. (Obviously the text has no implication for a defendant's choice to testify as a witness *for* himself.)

This would have three implications: first, other witnesses could be compelled to appear and to answer questions even if the answers to the questions would create legal jeopardy for the witnesses as well as for the defendant—because the witnesses would not be testifying against *themselves* in that specific case. The testimony could be used in accordance with the law of evidence in later proceedings against the witnesses as long as they were not called to the stand in that case.

Second, a criminal defendant could be questioned vigorously outside of court, and his statements or silence could be used, because he would not be a "witness," giving sworn testimony, in the courtroom proceeding himself. Third, a defendant's refusal to testify in a case against himself would be fair game for the prosecution, allowing the prosecutors to argue to the jury or judge that an innocent defendant would surely be willing to be a witness.

In practice, the Fifth Amendment bars all of these things. No person can be punished for refusing to testify in any kind of sworn proceeding, even if it is against another person or (as in the case of congressional hearings, for example) "against" no specific person at all. First, if a witness believes that answering a question could expose him or her to the danger of prosecution, he or she may simply refuse to answer by citing the Fifth Amendment. (Only the Fifth will do, by the way: some witnesses have refused to testify on the sole ground that politically loaded questioning violated their First Amendment rights; those witnesses are liable to penalties for contempt.) Second, a defendant may not be forced to answer police questions outside of court, no matter who is being investigated, and a defendant's refusal to answer questions is not admissible as evidence of guilt. (As the well-known saying explains, of course, if a defendant does choose to answer questions, those answers may be used at trial, even if incriminating.) And, finally, prosecutors may not comment on a defendant's failure to testify at trial—to do so is grounds for a mistrial—and criminal juries are routinely instructed that they must not draw any negative conclusions from a defendant's failure to testify.

That last conclusion sometimes irks nonlawyers (and some lawyers); why wouldn't an innocent person offer an account of what happened? But it accords with text: the amendment doesn't say, "no *innocent* person shall be compelled" to testify, but "no person," a category that obviously includes the guilty and the innocent. And an innocent person might have many reasons for choosing not to testify (as a lawyer for such a person might have many reasons for advising the client not to testify): he or she may have a strange or repellent personality, liable to alienate the jury. He or she may have a record of unrelated crimes, which the prosecution couldn't introduce as evidence of the charged crime but *could* use to "impeach" his or her testimony, suggesting to the jury that a defendant is guilty of the current offense as well. Last, in the American system of justice (and indeed in most civilized systems), a defendant is presumed to be innocent until found guilty. No defendant must prove his or her innocence; the state must prove his guilt. A defendant, in consultation with a lawyer, may simply believe that the prosecution has not proved its case. In that case, testifying is just asking for trouble, as a slip of the tongue or factual error may open the defendant up to the appearance of guilt.

Double jeopardy and the privilege against self-incrimination are specifically criminal provisions. The next clause applies to all court proceedings, and indeed to every dealing citizens have with government: "No person shall . . . be deprived of life, liberty, or property, without due process of law." The phrase "due process of law" comes from an English statute of 1354 codifying the guarantees of the Magna Carta (1215): "That no Man of what Estate or Condition that he be, shall be put out of Land or Tenement, nor taken, nor imprisoned, nor disinherited, nor put to Death, without being brought in Answer by due Process of the Law."[42]

This clause is fundamental to the American system, and a central axiom of limited government; it is so central that it reappears, word for word, in the Fourteenth Amendment as a limitation of the states. When the state wants to do something to you, it must jump through some hoops to do it. The number and width of the hoops differ depending on how much "deprivation" the state is inflicting. Parking fines (which deprive a person of money) can be assessed without a trial, as long as the car owner has a chance to show later that the meter was broken; tools and objects used to commit crimes can be confiscated on the spot, as long as the owner is given a chance to get them back if not convicted; defendants can't be put in jail (and certainly not executed) without a wide range of procedural protections.

Finally, the Fifth Amendment provides an enigmatic protection that applies entirely in civil matters. It is a substantive protection, not procedural, and it has given rise to controversy from the dawn of the Republic up until the present day: "[N]or shall private property be taken for public use, without just compensation." At its core, this protection is easy to understand—if the government needs to build a road through your house, it has to pay you for it; and not simply a payment of its choice, but a "just compensation." That's not textually the same as "the market price"; the notion of a "just price" has long roots in Western thought, stretching back beyond Thomas Aquinas. The logic of capitalism is that the price the market sets, if the market has worked freely, is the *best* price for everyone concerned, because it is the most efficient. But economics as a science did not emerge until the Enlightenment at the earliest. And before it did, pricing was seen as having an ethical component. Extracting high prices for property just because the buyer really needed it was seen as a kind of usury, which Christians were forbidden to practice. Though the demand might be great for something— food in time of famine, fuel in a cold winter, or land in the path of a needed road or bridge—it would not be "just" to charge a premium for it. For centuries, government had set the price of certain necessities of life (bread, for example) to prevent private parties from gouging the poor. That raises an intriguing paradox, because one of the meanings of "just price" was "the price set by government."

What is "just compensation" for private land? Most of the time, the negotiation between owner and government is a relatively well understood dance around a number that estimates what the private market would pay if the property were on the market. Obviously sometimes government's muscle can distort the negotiations, and courts are often called on to set a fair price for property taken by eminent domain. Usually the courts interpret "just compensation" to mean "fair market value."

The text of the so-called Takings Clause contains two intriguing puzzles, both of which bedevil courts today. First, what does it mean to say that private property is "taken"? In the case of our roadway through a private home the "taking" is easy to see and define—the government has extinguished the property owner's title and evicted the owner from possession, and now uses and occupies the land entirely and exclusively. But what if the government leaves the owner in occupation and possession, but simply makes it harder and more expensive to use the land? What if government restricts the uses to which the property can be put— barring the building of a strip mall, for example, while permitting the owner to build a house and live in it? What if government does not buy the property, but simply regulates it so heavily that the owner cannot use it at all? Which if any of these is a "taking" requiring compensation?

Government makes decisions every day that affect the value of property. When a new highway goes one way, land near the route becomes more expensive, while land near the rejected alternate route may decline in value. When government designates some property as environmentally sensitive, it can't be sold anymore as potential factory sites, and so its price will decline. When the City closes the old downtown office building, the leasehold value of the vacant restaurant space nearby plummets—no more guaranteed customer base at lunch hour.

Textually, the simplest way to interpret the clause would be to say that "taking" means exclusively the entire seizure of property and removal of title from the original owner. That definition stirs some uneasiness, however, because everyone knows that the value of property can be destroyed without a forced sale. Our next-door neighbor may run a meth lab in his home, pushing down property values and finally forcing us to leave entirely to avoid toxic pollution. The business across the street may decide to add twenty stories to its structure, cutting off light and air to the quaint country retreat we thought we owned. What is the role of the Takings Clause when government is (from our point of view at least) the bad neighbor?

We might say that the clause says "taken" and not "spoiled" or "hurt." If government takes the property away, the clause applies; if not, not. That rule might not be as harsh as it seems at first: nothing in the Fifth Amendment, or anywhere else in the Constitution, says that the representative branches of government, particularly the legislatures, could not create and enforce rules for the other cases. If property owners believe that they are being mistreated by government, they have the resources to make their voices heard.

The counterargument would be that protection of property rights was and is a central concern of liberal self-government. Kings and tyrants made a practice of seizing property, keeping it for themselves or doling it out to favorites for their use. One defining characteristic of government is a kind of amoeba-like greed, a desire to expand its domain and control over people, places, and things. Legislatures and regulators have a built-in incentive to suck the value out of private property without actually paying if they can; that leaves them more money to spend on other projects. A textual restriction on the power of seizing property, in this analysis, is to be taken quite seriously and should be enforced by the courts broadly rather than grudgingly.

The kind of partial taking we are discussing is called a "regulatory taking." The leading case on the meaning of the Takings Clause in this context was written by Justice Oliver Wendell Holmes Jr., who was justly renowned for coining memorable phrases even though some of them are not entirely clear. In this case, he came up with the pithy rule that "while property may be regulated to a certain extent, if regulation goes too far it will be recognized as a taking."[43] Got that? Perhaps not surprisingly, the combination of this Delphic language and the rise of environmental regulation have triggered a wave of lawsuits claiming that certain kinds of restrictions go "too far." When the courts recognize such a claim, they are often accused of being hostile to government regulation in general; reading the rhetoric of some opinions, it's hard not to agree with some of the accusers. On the other hand, the case law is clear on at least one thing: there can be cases where government goes "too far," and it is the job of the courts to decide what they are.

A second phrase in the clause also stirs popular passion. Read the clause again—"nor shall private property be taken *for public use*, without just compensation." This could be read two ways. The first would be that "public use" is limiting language—as if the clause read "nor shall private property be taken except for public use and never without just compensation." In that case, there would clearly be a rule for courts to test whether the "taking" was for "public use" or for some impermissible, presumably "private," purpose. But "for public use" could also be simply a phrase synonymous with "by the government, by the public bodies." This wouldn't mean an unlimited power by government to seize land on a whim—deprivations of property must still be by "due process of law," which would mean that an exercise of the power would have to be justified by some statute or rule, and that a court could examine whether that rule is being properly applied and whether the procedure has been appropriate. The courts, however, would not inquire into the purpose for which the property was being taken; that determination would be left to the political process.

That rule is like a lot of rules that suggest that decisions with constitutional dimensions be made by the political process: many people, and even many lawyers, instinctively react that this is no rule at all, that it simply means that government can do anything it wants. That's not precisely correct. If the political process sets rules for seizure of property, those rules have to be vetted and approved by representatives of the people. There's an argument that elected officials are very sensitive indeed to public displeasure and wouldn't approve a rule that resulted in arbitrary or widespread seizure of property. On the other hand, thinkers in the eighteenth century and before were concerned about government taking private property—defined often not simply as land or personal property but as a wide variety of personal rights—from one citizen and giving it to another.

The current doctrine by the Supreme Court is that "public use" doesn't mean "public ownership." As it recently stated the rule,

> Two polar propositions are perfectly clear. On the one hand, it has long been accepted that the sovereign may not take the property of A for the sole purpose of transferring it to another private party B, even though A is paid just compensation. On the other hand, it is equally clear that a State may transfer property from one private party to another if future "use by the public" is the purpose of the taking.[44]

These words came in a decision that set off a furor. In *Kelo v. City of New London*, the municipal government condemned a small house owned and occupied by a nurse, Suzette Kelo, to be sold to the Pfizer Corporation as part of a large industrial park and mixed-use development. The purpose of the scheme was to reinvigorate the tax base of an exhausted northeastern city by providing opportunities for new jobs, new businesses, new stores, and new apartments. That purpose was not simply a benefit to Pfizer, the Court reasoned, and thus fulfilled the requirement of "public use."

Ordinary citizens, property-rights activists, and talk-radio and TV hosts protested that the Court had "given" government the power to seize property from ordinary citizens and give it to powerful private parties. But what the Court actually said was a bit more carefully shaded. First the Takings Clause does not say "government shall have the power to take private property." "Eminent domain" was a power that government had always had in England and in British North America. The states had limited it in different ways in their state constitutions. The Court was not "approving" eminent domain, but construing limitations on it—in other words, deciding on what in another category might be called "state's rights" to set up their own legal system. Second, the Court was not saying that the kind of land deal at issue was a good idea. (In fact, it wasn't; Pfizer ran into financial trouble and never moved into the gleaming campus that was to be built over Suzette Kelo's neighborhood.) It was, in essence, saying that every use of the term "public use" should probably not become a literal federal case, in which life-tenured federal judges make a decision on whether they think a given government program will really benefit the public. Is a railroad a "public use," while a new mixed-use development is not? Is this the kind of decision judges, of all people, are equipped to make? It could be viewed as an open invitation for judges to vet democratic decisions by applying their own personal political philosophy; libertarian judges would strike down most takings, believers in robust government few.

There's a case to be made that supplying the meaning of such an ambiguous term can and should be done by elected legislators as much as by federal judges. In fact, that is exactly what has happened in the wake of *Kelo*. As the property scholar Joseph William Singer recently wrote, "In response to the Kelo decision, almost all states have passed legislation or constitutional amendments that limit the power of municipalities to take property for economic development purposes."[45] Perhaps this is a better way to work out the definition of "public use."

On the other hand, of course, that happy ending is unlikely to provide much consolation to Suzette Kelo, who lost a house that she loved, and called out to the Constitution for help, and found none there.

Sixth Amendment

The Fifth Amendment is a Cracker Jack box of immunities, civil and criminal. The Sixth Amendment, by contrast, makes clear from the beginning that it concerns only "criminal prosecutions." This amendment is the closest thing the Constitution has to a list of "positive rights," things government has to do for a person. It's a fairly limited list, though one that has proven to be of crucial importance to defendants over the past 225 years. The amendment as a whole, however, protects both accused and community. It requires a public, reasonably accurate system of assessing guilt and imposes requirements not only on the government but on the community, which must supply evidence when it is sought and must also serve as jurors.

The right to criminal trial by jury was already guaranteed by Article III. The Sixth Amendment provides two refinements to that guarantee. First, the jury must be "impartial." Article III made no mention of this requirement. The 1787 Constitution also guaranteed "trial . . . in the State where the said Crimes shall have been committed." The Sixth Amendment's guarantee is slightly different—it governs not the physical location of the trial but the composition of the jury, which must be "*of* the State and district wherein the crime shall have been committed." It is a requirement that may or may not protect the accused, but it definitely mandates community involvement in the criminal process.

All told, the Sixth Amendment shapes a system of criminal procedure that is highly protective of the accused but that clearly if imperfectly also takes the rights of the community into account. The jury as regulated in the amendment is not simply a device that protects the accused; it is also a representative body, specifically rooted in the community affected by the crime, whose members exercise political authority of a kind that belongs to every free American. Jury service is thus a duty as well as a right, and in both senses it is of constitutional dimension.

It might be more useful to think of the "rights" guaranteed by the Sixth Amendment as "procedures," designed to produce a just outcome. Depending on how you count, the Sixth Amendment provides six or seven of these. The first is "a speedy and public trial." Defendants are not to languish for years awaiting charges and a chance to be heard. Of course, "speedy" is not defined in the Constitution and thus must be defined by courts in the contexts of specific trials. Speed does not always favor the defendant, in fact: the prosecution has often had time to gather evidence before an arrest is made. Courts must continually decide whether too much delay on one side unfairly favors the other. Congress has given shape to the clause by enacting a federal Speedy Trial Act that sets maximum and minimum times for certain stages of the proceedings.

The trial must also be public. As we noted in the discussion of Article I, the Framers were a lot more comfortable with the idea of secrecy in government than democratic theorists are today. But it was widely agreed that government must not be allowed to adjudge criminal guilt in the dark. Though we speak of the "right to a public trial," this "right" (unlike, say, the right to a "speedy" trial) is one that a defendant cannot waive. A "right" that can't be waived is in some sense not a right but a general rule designed to benefit the system and the country as a whole. In fact, the public nature of the trial is an entitlement of the public, which has an interest in knowing how justice is done.

Unlike the right to a public trial, a defendant may waive the right to trial by jury. A defendant may plead guilty and waive trial altogether; but a defendant may also ask to be tried without a jury, with the judge acting as "trier of fact" and finding guilt or innocence.

The jury is often called a "jury of one's peers," but that word does not appear in the Constitution. The notion of a peer, meaning a person of equal legal rank in society, was not translated into American law. English law recognized all kinds of stratified juries, including the "jury of matrons," an all-female assemblage charged with discovering whether a female prisoner facing the gallows was pregnant, in which case her execution would be delayed until after childbirth.

The Sixth Amendment requires only that a jury must be "impartial." In contemporary trial jurisprudence, the pursuit of "impartiality" has become an elaborate ritual. It begins with voir dire—from the law French, meaning "to speak truth." In voir dire, either judge or jury asks the potential jurors (called "the venire" or "the jury pool") about their ability to judge the case "impartially." In some jurisdictions this takes the form of multi-day examinations of each member of the jury pool, beginning with their knowledge of the specific case before the court and progressing to their social, racial, and economic attitudes. Each side may have made use of public records to determine their socioeconomic status, criminal record, and everything from where their children attend school to what magazines they read. The two sides may make use of psychologically trained "jury consultants" who combine the public information with assessments of their body language and vocal intonations to divine what they are thinking. At the end of voir dire, either side may challenge a juror "for cause," arguing that there is some objective reason that that person cannot be impartial. The two sides then exercise what are called "peremptory challenges," which permit either side to demand the dismissal of a certain number of potential jurors without giving a reason at all. The result of this tortuous process can hardly be considered a cross-section of the community. Both sides try to stack the jury with those they think will favor their side.

In recent years, in a series of cases beginning with *Batson v. Kentucky*,[46] the Supreme Court has held that basing peremptory challenges on the race or sex of a juror is barred by the Fourteenth Amendment's Equal Protection Clause. The reason is not so much that the new rule will make the juries more impartial but that the exclusion of the potential jury members because of their race or sex violates *their* rights. Jury service is a kind of public office, and allowing lawyers— even lawyers for a private person like a criminal defendant—to exclude anyone from that office on the basis of race or sex is unconstitutional.

If carefully observed, these new rules vastly complicate the process of using peremptory challenges. Under the Court's new procedure, if one side suspects that the other is using one of the forbidden criteria to strike jurors, it may raise the issue in a motion. If the Court shares the suspicion, it may order the other side to explain its decisions. If no satisfactory innocent explanation appears, then either the challenged juror must be seated or the jury-selection process must begin all over again with a new venire. *Batson* creates a right that applies not only to the defendant; the state itself, as the prosecuting party, has a right to a jury selected without bias, and thus may use *Batson* to challenge defense challenges. There is a difference, though. If a judge improperly denies a defense "*Batson* motion," then an appellate court will return the case to the trial court, for a hearing on whether the error was "harmless," and if it was not, to conduct a new trial.[47]

On the other hand, if a defendant uses improper criteria and wins an acquittal, double jeopardy prevents an appeals court from ordering a new trial.

This summary of the unsettled state of current law is relevant only because of the light it sheds on the concept of "impartiality." As some justices have pointed out, the elaborate dance occasioned by *Batson* would not be necessary if neither side had peremptory challenges. The inevitable subjectivity of jurors is assessed by a correspondingly subjective process of selection by counsel. In those circumstances, the attempt to restrict one or two bases of subjective selection while permitting so many others seems almost impossible. In the long run, the answer may be the abolition of the peremptory challenge.

There's no reason that a jury picked without peremptory challenges could not be "impartial"—in English law, where the concept of the jury arose, the term has a much more limited meaning. It meant simply a jury in which the members had no previous relationship with or conflict of interest about the case or the parties. Voir dire is either nonexistent or much more limited in England and the Commonwealth countries. In a jury picked from a proper jury panel, a system that allowed challenges only for cause might result in a fairer cross-section of the community, which is the modern equivalent of the "jury of peers" from medieval Britain.

The interest in a "fair cross-section" of the community has a textual basis, flowing from the amendment's next requirement, that the "impartial jury" must be "of the State and district wherein the crime shall have been committed." This is to some extent a protection of the accused—a criminal defendant facing charges of selling obscene material in Manhattan cannot be carried off to face "justice" from a jury selected from the God-fearing folk of Gadsden, Alabama. But it would seem to operate as much as if not more than a protection of the community. Local residents cannot be whisked away to the seat of government to answer for local offenses; the local community must participate as jurors, and on some occasions their presence will frustrate the desire of government to criminalize and punish its enemies.

The court may be all the closer because the jury must come from the "district" where the crime occurred, referring to the geographical boundaries drawn up for federal trial courts' jurisdiction. But the "district" requirement may not prevent an accused from being tried far from home. Districts are based on population rather than geography. Consider that Alaska, with more than 660,000 square miles, is all one district. Even the largest states, New York and California, each have only four. The government's drawing of districts has to be done on a general basis; the Sixth Amendment provides that it can't suddenly vary the size or location of a district either to prejudice the accused to exclude the affected community from participation.

The accused must "be informed of the nature and cause of the accusation." Kafka's Josef K. never quite learns what he is supposed to have done wrong, which of course makes it impossible for him to defend against the charges. A person charged with a crime should know not only what crime is being charged but also the evidence that supports the charges. The government cannot ordinarily drag a person into court and then call surprise witnesses or introduce secret evidence, giving the defendant no time to prepare to rebut them.

This right of the accused also serves a public accountability function, however. The public can also know what conduct the government considers criminal, what evidence is considered sufficient to charge or convict of that crime, and how that evidence was gathered.

The accused must have "compulsory process for obtaining witnesses in his favor." Before and during a criminal trial, defendants and their counsel are delegated the power of the government to issue subpoenas to potential witnesses. People may have knowledge that will be helpful to an accused, tending to show, for example, that the accused was somewhere else when the crime was committed or that someone else admitted to the crime. But they may be reluctant to come forward, either out of fear of the government's displeasure or of retaliation by those their testimony would incriminate. If the defense cannot persuade them to testify voluntarily, it can require them to come forward. In practice, this right is a two-edged sword; compelled witnesses may turn forgetful on the stand, either out of pique or out of fear. But the threat of a subpoena is a useful tool in pretrial investigation. The right to call witnesses had often been abridged in British law. It is now a firm part of the American criminal justice system.

Finally comes the right "to have the Assistance of Counsel for his defence." It is not the right to "obtain" or "retain" counsel, but the right to "*have*" a lawyer to assist during a criminal trial. If ever there was a textual basis for a "positive right," this would certainly seem like one: such a right would not seem to contain the qualification "when he can afford one or find one willing to work for nothing." Nonetheless, for much of the nation's history this clause was treated as purely negative: that is, if a defendant could hire or find counsel, the government could not prevent it; but society had no obligation to provide a lawyer at its own expense. The narrowness of this interpretation was changed—at least for serious crimes—in 1965, in a case called *Gideon v. Wainright*,[48] which is the subject of Anthony Lewis's famous book, *Gideon's Trumpet*.[49] Clarence Earl Gideon was convicted of breaking and entering in a small Florida town and sentenced to five years in prison. At his trial, Gideon had asked the trial judge to appoint a lawyer for him, but the judge refused, because Florida law at that time permitted appointed counsel only in capital trials. Gideon insisted to the court that "The United States Supreme Court says I am entitled to be represented by Counsel."[50]

Gideon's language, and the Court's subsequent treatment of his claim, bear on our quest for the meaning of the Constitution's text. He did not say, "The United States Constitution says I am entitled to be represented by Counsel," although its plain words certainly seem to. There is no basis in the Sixth Amendment's text for restricting the right to capital cases (or indeed to charges which can result in a sentence of six months' imprisonment or more, which is basically where the Court draws the line now). This is not to say that the restriction is incorrect, even as a matter of constitutional law; it is simply to say that it is not textual.

The issue as the Court saw it in *Gideon* was whether the Sixth Amendment right to appointed counsel was a "fundamental right," one that was required by the Fourteenth Amendment to be observed by the states. In 1938, the right to appointed counsel had been guaranteed to federal prisoners. That decision, in *Johnson v. Zerbst*, had been written by Justice Hugo Black.[51] Exactly twenty-five years later, Justice Black wrote an opinion in *Gideon* stating that "reason and re-flection require us to recognize that in our adversary system of criminal justice, any person haled into court, who is too poor to hire a lawyer, cannot be assured a fair trial unless counsel is provided for him."

Since *Gideon*, the right to appointed counsel has been firmly rooted, and police are required by another case, *Miranda v. Arizona*, to notify defendants of this right the moment they are arrested.[52] It is an irony that this right took so long to be recognized, just as it is an irony that it appears at the end of the Sixth Amendment; for it can be argued that without counsel, the other rights are at best hollow. Most of us cannot plan and conduct a criminal defense, no matter how entitled we may be to do so. Justice for the accused begins with counsel; but in the Sixth Amendment, counsel comes last.

Before leaving the Sixth Amendment, we should note a feature of defendants' rights that is not mentioned at all. While criminal juries must be "impartial," nowhere does the Constitution explicitly state that the state must prove criminal charges "beyond a reasonable doubt." Two rights are implicated here. First, it is axiomatic that criminal defendants are presumed to be innocent until the state has proved them guilty.

The United States Supreme Court did not weigh in on the issue until the 1895 case of *Coffin v. United States*.[53] A defendant who had embezzled funds from the bank he worked for objected to the trial court's jury instructions. In those instructions, the court had waxed eloquent about the need for proof beyond "reasonable doubt," but had refused to instruct that "[t]he law presumed that persons changed with crime are innocent until they are proven, by compe-tent evidence, to be guilty." The Supreme Court concluded that "[t]he principle that there is a presumption of innocence in favor of the accused is the undoubted law, axiomatic and elementary, and its enforcement lies at the foundation of the administration of our common law."

But a presumption of innocence need necessarily not embody the principle of "reasonable doubt." The "reasonable doubt" standard is the second right implicated. That's a heavy burden for the state to carry. "'Reasonable doubt,'" Chief Justice Lemuel Shaw of Massachusetts wrote in 1850, "is a term often used, probably pretty well understood, but not easily defined. It is not a mere possible doubt; because every thing relating to human affairs, and depending on moral evidence, is open to some possible or imaginary doubt. It is that state of the case, which, after the entire comparison and consideration of all the evidence, leaves the minds of jurors in that condition that they cannot say they feel an abiding conviction, to a moral certainty, of the truth of the charge."[54] Simply as a matter of constitutional text, then, criminal courts might allow convictions on a lesser showing—"preponderance of the evidence," say, which is used in civil trials, or "clear and convincing evidence," a standard used in some First Amendment cases which is greater than a preponderance but less than "beyond reasonable doubt."

Again, however, the "reasonable doubt" standard is so venerable that no one today questions that it is of constitutional dimension. In a leading case on the subject, the United States Supreme Court in 1970 in essence threw up its hands and just said the idea was really, really old: "The requirement that guilt of a criminal charge be established by proof beyond a reasonable doubt dates at least from our early years as a Nation."[55] One intriguing theory comes from Professor James Q. Whitman, of Yale Law School, who wrote in 2005 that

> "In the Christian past . . . there was more at stake, in a criminal trial, than the fate of the accused. The fate of those who sat in judgment was at stake. The famous injunction of Saint Matthew—*Judge not lest ye be judged!*—had a concrete meaning: convicting an innocent defendant was regarded, in the older Christian tradition, as a potential mortal sin. The reasonable doubt rule was one of many rules and procedures that developed in response to this disquieting possibility. It was originally a theological doctrine, intended to reassure jurors that they could convict the defendant without risking their own salvation, so long as their doubts were not "reasonable." "Beyond a reasonable doubt" was originally a rule for anxious Christians, living in an age haunted, as our world no longer is, by the fear of damnation."[56]

Our world may or may not be haunted by fear of damnation, but the fear of punishing the innocent still haunts the dreams of conscientious people and nations. Whatever its origins, the "reasonable doubt" rule is another principle so fundamental that it need not be spelled out in the Bill of Rights. Those who sometimes insist that a right must be written in the Constitution to be binding against government might ponder this example.

Seventh Amendment

As we've seen, the Sixth Amendment guarantee of trial by jury was only a refinement on a guarantee already in the original Constitution. But that guarantee applied only to *criminal trials*. One of the burning controversies during the ratification debate of 1787–88 centered around the lack of a similar guarantee for *civil* juries, panels that decide disputes between private parties, or private parties and the government.

Critics of the Constitution made much of the document's silence about the civil jury. In response to this criticism, the Framers of the Bill of Rights composed an amendment that is entirely backward looking. "Due process of law," or "freedom of religion" are concepts that evolve—in general parlance, at least, whether or not we believe that intellectual evolution should affect constitutional interpretation. But the civil jury is to be "preserved," kept as it was in 1789.

Suits "at common law" were (and are) those in which a court could give money damages. (Suits for injunctions were, and are, actions "in equity.") The Seventh Amendment says only one thing—that this right shall be "preserved." There is no language in the amendment extending the right or finding new dimensions of it. If juries had been responsible for making these decisions previously, and the amount at issue was twenty dollars or more, juries had to decide them in the new republic. Depending how we calculate, that would probably correspond to a present value of somewhere between $500 and $5,000—not a high threshold.[57]

The function of a jury was, and is, to decide factual questions. That's why we say that a jury "finds" a defendant guilty in a criminal trial, or "finds" a defendant liable in tort. The guilt or liability is a fact—she did the crime, he failed to take adequate precautions. Judges, by contrast, decide matters of law; for this reason, we usually say that a judge "rules" (on a motion) or "holds" in deciding the proper meaning of a legal concept. The distinction between the law (what is the rule in cases like this?) and the facts (what happened in this case?) is easy to state, and from a distance it can appear clean cut. The closer we get to individual cases, however, the fuzzier the border looks.

To begin with, at common law, a judge must decide whether a case can even go to a jury. This is a particular kind of lawyer's reasoning, which requires thinking that things are true even when they may not be and then concluding that they wouldn't matter even if they were. Basically, it means that a judge must assume that everything the plaintiff says is true—the defendant did everything the plaintiff claims she did, the plaintiff suffered every bit of harm she says she did—and then decide whether that would make out a legal claim. Even if the plaintiff can't raise her arm since the accident, what she says the plaintiff did wasn't negligent. Even if what the defendant said about the plaintiff wasn't true, it would still constitute protected First Amendment speech rather than action-able defamation. It's easy to claim that this kind of determination simply deter-mines "matters of law"; that's the way lawyers put it. But that's just a simple label on a complex phenomenon.

"If you can think about something which is attached to something else with-out thinking about what it is attached to," the puckish twentieth-century scholar Thomas Reed Powell once wrote, "then you have what is called a legal mind."[58] Just so, if you think you can decide whether facts would matter without deciding whether they are true, you are fooling yourself. Judges resolve matters of fact all the time. Under some circumstances, in fact, they can even set aside facts found by juries. If a jury finds for the plaintiff (thus explicitly, or by implication, finding that the defendant was at fault in some way) a judge not infrequently will just set that verdict aside and order a new trial, on the grounds that no "reasonable" jury could have reached that verdict from the evidence presented to it.

The amendment assumes that will happen. It doesn't forbid courts to reexam-ine matters of fact; instead, it says that reexamination shall be done only "accord-ing to the rules of the common law." This is an intriguing command. The common law at the time the amendment was written was more than six centuries old and had already spawned libraries full of Year Books, case reports, and treatises. But at the same time, the common law was and is a changing, evolving thing.

It is understood by all to be "judge-made" law—though the polite fiction is that a common-law judge "finds" the law, pulling it from the mind of God or what Justice Oliver Wendell Holmes Jr. once derided as the "brooding omnipresence in the sky."[59] Thus the wording of the Seventh Amendment could be read as in-corporating an expectation that judges will continue to "find" and refine the common law, including changing the rules about reexamination of facts, as time wears on and conditions change. Of course, it could also mean that the division of labor between judge and jury is to be frozen as it was in 1789, when the amend-ment was written, or 1791, when it was ratified.

I find this at best unlikely and at worst absurd: to take a reference to a forward-looking set of doctrines and claim that it is a single backward-looking command; to take a reference to something that is by definition mutable and claim that it must be unchanging. It is as if we were to define a property right by the line of high tide (as in fact a number of states do when dealing with privately owned beachfront property) and then insist on interpreting it by trying to deter-mine exactly where high tide fell on the day that the property deed was executed. That is to say, it's both essentially impossible and, in some sense, silly.

What the Seventh Amendment says, in essence, is that we live under a common-law system; the civil jury (which has all but disappeared even in Britain) cannot be abolished; and courts must work out how much power a jury has in each case. The amendment at once preserves a right and gives it permission to change.

Eighth Amendment

The Eighth Amendment has made what is perhaps the Constitution's most widespread contribution to the American language, a phrase that has become a new epic formula, "cruel and unusual punishment." Even children can invoke the concept as a protest against losing cell phone privileges. "That sucks! All the other kids have phones!" is a recognizable variation on the formula.

Giving the term a useful meaning, however, is not as easy as invoking it. To violate the amendment's prohibition, a punishment must fulfill two conditions. First, it must be "cruel"—which, to most ordinary speakers, means something more than "unpleasant" or even "very painful." Doctors may inflict pain in the course of treatment, for example, yet we would seldom think of calling them "cruel." "Cruel," to most people, carries a connotation of gratuitousness, of a desire to inflict purposeless suffering for its own sake.

How do we locate "cruelty" in our practice of criminal justice? The business of punishing and deterring crime is by definition harsh and painful. Punishment, without more, must involve some suffering. Though we sometimes like to claim that we punish criminals for the same reasons we punish our children, in truth there is a difference. At least as practiced by normal parents, the punishment of children is designed to equip them to remain safe (we punish children caught playing with matches), and morally whole (we punish those caught telling lies).

At one time in our nation's history we liked to pretend that these same aims motivated criminal punishment. Most states and the federal government call their prison agencies departments or bureaus of "corrections," implying that their task is to set offenders on the path of righteousness. A state prison today is usually styled a "penitentiary," a word drawn from medieval church law that originally designated a priest or cardinal specially designated to hear and absolve extraordinary sins.

In fact, the notion of a "penitentiary" and the United States were born at almost precisely the same moment. The English reformer Jeremy Bentham, writing in the late eighteenth and early nineteenth centuries, exposed the wretched conditions in local jails and prisons in England and on the Continent. He and other reformers suggested a substitute facility where offenders would be housed in clean individual cells and encouraged to reflect upon and repent their offenses. The penitents would be trained to support themselves honestly. Then they would be returned to society to sin no more.

One of the first official penitentiaries on this model anywhere in the world was the brainchild of Thomas Jefferson. At Jefferson's urging, the state of Virginia in 1797 commissioned an English architect newly arrived in the United States to design what became a truly futuristic prison complex by the James River in Richmond, the state capitol. The architect, Benjamin Latrobe, succeeded so well at this commission that he was then hired to design the United States Capitol.

Penitence, however, is far from the primary goal of criminal punishment. Criminal-law theorists explain that the system aims at "incapacitation" and "deterrence." We wish to make sure that a dangerous criminal will not have the opportunity to harm anyone else. (Years ago, I testified before a legislative panel that in my judgment the death penalty was not an effective deterrent to crime; one alert senator pointed out a flaw in my logic: "Have you ever known anyone who was executed to commit another crime?") We also hope that the severity of his or her fate will serve as an example that will terrify other potential criminals—in the phrase made popular by TV shows, to "scare them straight."

So criminal punishment always by definition includes inflicting some pain that is not intended for the offender's own good. Cruelty, it seems likely, would relate to pain inflicted for no good reason at all—not by mistake, not erroneously proportioned, not informed by an unwise policy, but just because it gives pleasure to those who inflict it. When does harshness become wanton cruelty? That inquiry is a subtle one. But it is only half of the Eighth Amendment's standard. To fall within the prohibition, a punishment must not only be "cruel" but also "unusual." Two questions arise. First, how rare does a punishment have to be to be "unusual"? Second, does the amendment mean that a punishment must be unusual by today's standards, or by the standards of 1791?

Perhaps we can answer the second question by reading the Eighth Amendment as a whole. In fact, it contains three prohibitions, not just one: "Excessive bail shall not be required, nor excessive fines imposed, nor cruel and unusual punishments inflicted." These are relative terms, directing the reader to make a comparison among bail amounts, fines, and punishments, to determine which of them are outliers, "excessive" or "cruel and unusual." What set of possible bonds, fines, and punishments are to furnish the grounds of comparison?

Some have argued (particularly with relation to the "cruel and unusual punishments" language) that the Framers were directing us to canvass the practices of *their* day and to interpret the amendment to forbid only those bonds, fines, or punishments that were agreed to be outliers at that time. If we accept that definition, it gives the clause some meaning—namely, that government exactions in the criminal justice context are not to grow more savage over time than they were in 1791. If the Eighth Amendment really meant nothing more than that, it would still be a welcome rule; we do not want to hurtle back to the early eighteenth century or earlier in our practices.

But can that really be all that the amendment means? If the "cruel and unusual" language is read in isolation from the rest of the amendment, the 1791-practices argument has a certain surface plausibility. After all, it at first glance seems possible to find out what punishments were not imposed in 1791 and to agree that we won't impose them now (though, as we shall see, that inquiry is by no means as easily conducted as we at first may imagine). But the

amendment begins with two prohibitions on *excessive* monetary exactions—
bail and fines. Would we research the practices of 1791 to give meaning to the
term "excessive"? Would we go back and research the table of statutory fines
imposed for crimes, and analyze the practice of colonial courts as to bail, and
conclude that nothing worse than those can be imposed? Assuming we have assembled that information, how would we interpret it?

Let's pick a number out of the Constitution itself: remember that the Seventh
Amendment defines the right to jury trial as applying to all disputes over $20 or
more. In 1791, evidently, $20 was a significant amount of money. So then should
we consider a rule than no fine or bail could amount to more than $20? That
would be absurd; today, $20 will barely buy dinner at McDonald's. Surely a
defendant accused of a serious crime can be required to post more than $20 to
guarantee his or her appearance at trial; surely a defendant convicted of a serious
crime—perhaps of stealing thousands or even millions of dollars—can be fined
more than $20.

Okay, then, let's take an amount that is ten times the threshold of the jury trial
right in 1791—a whopping $200. That result is as absurd as using $20; it renders
both bail and fines essentially meaningless as tools of the criminal justice system.
How then would we create a present equivalent of 1791's $200? Perhaps we
could determine what $200 means today by using the Consumer Price Index to
establish how much money would be needed today to buy $200 worth of goods
in 1791. Extending the Consumer Price Index (established in the twentieth century) backward to 1791 involves a fairly complex mathematical-historical economic calculation, one that creates a number of widely divergent answers. Entire
books have been written to document those answers.[60]

But beyond the complexity of the mathematics, there is the question of
whether it even makes any sense to regard "purchasing power" as a meaningful
concept for comparing a market where most goods were made at home and
most food was locally grown with one in which electronic symbols indicating
cash are the main method of exchange, and this "cash" is used to buy computers
made in China, clothing stitched in Malaysia, digital film downloads animated in
Mexico, and computer software code written in India.

The comparison could be drawn another way—say, by taking the average
daily wage in 1791 and comparing it to the median wage paid in 2009. Again,
given that we are comparing a largely noncash economy with one that runs entirely on cash and credit, there is a similar question of whether the comparison
has any meaning at all.

If our goal was to find an objective rule for "excessiveness" in the Constitution, we are failing. And in the process of failing, we have ceded the query to
specialized technicians—statisticians and economic historians—whose techniques are incomprehensible not only to ordinary citizens but even to lawyers

and judges. We might do better to interpret the word "excessive" simply in light of what we today would consider to be too much, or disproportionate to the risk of flight (for bail) or the gravity of the offense (for fines). That inquiry is no less subjective, but it is also no more so—and it has the advantage of being a process of interpretation that anyone (particularly judges) can use intelligibly.

If the quest for "excessiveness" leads us to present practice, then why shouldn't the interpretation of "cruel and unusual punishment" do the same? It is a more complicated question, to be sure, because to violate that clause a punishment must be both "cruel" *and* "unusual." How do we give meaning to those terms? We could, of course, go to historical records to try to figure out whether slitting of noses was a common criminal penalty in 1791. There's no question that it's cruel, and very little question that it was cruel then: but was it "unusual"? How could we assemble a reliable picture of what punishments were doled out in colonial and post-revolutionary courts? And even if we assembled reliable data about the frequency of judicial nose-slitting, how many slit noses would make a cruel punishment "usual," and thus permitted?

The alternative is the sort of inquiry conservative legal thinkers like to deride—a searching look at current society, to assess what has happened to notions of cruelty in the two centuries since the drafting of the Bill of Rights. There's the danger of subjectivity here, to be sure—but it's subjectivity in the interpretive of subjective terms. And it's much easier to assess criminal-justice practices today than to assess what they were two centuries ago; there is more integrity in assessing the attitudes of the society we actually live in than in trying to understand those of a society that may be the distant ancestor of this one, but that we can never even visit.

"The past is a foreign country," the British novelist L. P. Harley once wrote. "They do things differently there."[61] A number of constitutional interpreters angrily deny that the US Constitution should be interpreted using the contemporary law of other countries. Some of the same people nonetheless also insist that it should be interpreted by the law of that most foreign of all countries, the past.

Ninth Amendment

"Why, may that not be the skull of a lawyer?" Hamlet asks in the graveyard before he learns the skull is Yorick's. "Where be his quiddities now, his quillities, his cases, his tenures, and his tricks?"[62]

The Ninth Amendment is the grinning skull beneath the smooth skin of the Constitution.

Its language is deceptively simple: "The enumeration in the Constitution, of certain rights, shall not be construed to deny or disparage others retained by the people." The Ninth Amendment is one of a small number of places in the Constitution where the document discusses itself, its meaning, and its validity. In Article V, it tells us how to amend it; in Article VI, Section Two, it tells us that it is among the valid sources of law; in the Ninth Amendment it tells us how not to interpret it. The latter command is so oracular that many interpreters are tempted to skip over it altogether.

Lawyers believe in rules, in the idea that human foresight and goodwill can create "domestic tranquility" for all to enjoy. But the rich disorder of life can never be fully reduced to writing; no more can any bill of rights, no matter how promethean its authors, contain the full spectrum of yearning free souls can generate.

The Ninth Amendment stands as a signboard pointing to the unknown country of the future, with the label "Terra Incognita." Wishful constitutional prospectors, seeking a source for some nontextual liberty they prefer, often decide that its mother lode lies in that unknown territory. *Here is my land,* they say: *here is my right to park my car when and wherever I want, here is my right to smoke in public or to forbid others from smoking in public, here is my right to take the bar exam even though I have not graduated from an accredited law school, here is my right to remain in my home even though I do not pay my mortgage, here is my right to censor the curriculum of my child's public school, here is my right to grow and use marijuana.*

They seem to imagine, as the eminent scholar Walter Dellinger once remarked, that Madison, lodged in some cramped rental flat in New York on the night before the opening of the First Congress, sat down to draft a complete list of individual rights but found the task tiresome. Reaching eight amendments, he despaired of finishing by daylight, so he quickly dashed off a final one, consisting in essence of the words "everything else."

But that is not what the amendment says. The language in the first eight amendments requires that rights "shall not be abridged" or "shall be preserved." Those rights are to have immediate effect in the world. By contrast, the Ninth governs *discussion* of rights, not rights themselves. It is a rule of construction, warning future interpreters not to "deny or disparage" rights not listed in the Constitution. It is directed to society in general, not specifically to courts or even to legislatures.

The Framers all more or less subscribed to the idea Jefferson phrased memorably in the Declaration of Independence: "that all men . . . are endowed by their creator with certain unalienable rights." Jefferson did not attempt to enumerate them; he noted only that "among these are life, liberty and the pursuit of happiness." There were others, most people agreed, but no one could quite agree what they were.

But in a self-governing republic, such rights were not boons granted by sovereign to subject; they were individual property, immune from seizure by the state. The Constitution might list some of these rights, but it did not create them by listing them, and it did not extinguish them by omitting them. (The Ninth Amendment, unlike the Tenth, does not mention states at all; its interpretive principle governs only claims of rights "retained by the people.")

In 2007, then-Attorney General Alberto Gonzales testified that there was no real constitutional right to habeas corpus. "[T]here is no express grant of habeas in the Constitution. There is a prohibition against taking it away," he told the Senate Judiciary Committee. "But . . . the Constitution does not say every individual in the United States or every citizen is hereby granted or assured the right to habeas."[63]

Here, baldly stated, is the authoritarian logic the Ninth Amendment is designed to guard against. The Constitution, and through it the government, is the grantor of individual rights. Unless the Constitution says *all citizens are hereby granted and guaranteed this right*, there is no such right. Government may observe it out of choice, or grace; but government is in no way disallowed from limiting or extinguishing the "right" when circumstances warrant.

The Gonzales principle is the one method of interpretation the Ninth Amendment forbids. Textual ambiguity, or silence, about an individual right does not empower government, the amendment asserts. That idea is profoundly threatening to some legal imaginations, which, as we have seen, tend to prize rules over anything else. If we permit unenumerated rights to enter the discourse, this mind-set frets, soon we will have court decisions proclaiming polygamy a basic right, or infant sacrifice.

Yet surely there is some position intermediate between *only those rights the Constitution grants in so many words* on the one hand and *anything goes* on the other. Earlier, for example, we discussed the presumption of innocence. How would we meaningfully discuss whether the Ninth Amendment suggests the existence of that right? We could argue about it many ways. Historically, we could note, Anglo-American courts have developed this protection not only to defend the rights of the accused but also to make the results of criminal trials more accurate. Logically, we could note that our system of procedure, which accords the preponderance of power to the government, makes little sense if the system places the real burden on the citizen. As contemporary legal thinkers, we could look to the evolving consensus of other systems; most advanced democracies observe this presumption. Most advanced legal systems guarantee it. International human-rights instruments, like the Universal Declaration of Human Rights and the International Covenant of Civil and Political Rights, explicitly embody the right.

As textualists, we could ask ourselves whether the presumption is akin to the rights explicitly guaranteed in the Constitution: could, for example, a jury be an "impartial jury" if it were permitted to presume guilt? As citizens, we could consult our common sense, informed by more than two centuries of failure and success at self-government, to determine whether an asserted right is important to life in a free state.

If the Ninth Amendment does not contain an invisible list of rights, it does embody a useful *burden of proof*, a principle that government cannot restrict us unless it first shows that our conduct is *not* covered by a constitutional right. That burden can be borne, and in some cases fairly easily, but the exercise is a useful lesson to those who govern and who too often see individuals as obstacles to the greater good.

The Ninth Amendment may best be understood as akin to the mathematician Kurt Gödel's famous Incompleteness Theorems. These two theorems demonstrated that no formal logical system summarizing arithmetic can be consistent; and that each such system must contain at least one theorem that cannot be proved inside the system.

In fact, Gödel did *not* claim that arithmetic was not consistent—his last proof, published a quarter-century after the Incompleteness proof, showed that in fact the system of arithmetic *is* consistent. But the meaning of incompleteness was that the proof could not be completed drawing only on axioms and rules *within the system*; some assumption from outside (called "metamathematical") was essential to constructing a valid proof of completeness.

Gödel is uniformly considered to be the greatest mathematician of the twentieth century, and many serious mathematical thinkers call him the greatest of all time; Albert Einstein once wrote to a friend that he had come to Princeton, where Gödel was in residence, "in order to have the privilege of walking home with Gödel."[64] Gödel's proof arose precisely because completeness, formality, and a consistent system were qualities he prized and strove for all his life.

Many lawyers, scholars, and judges are as obsessive about consistency and completeness as Gödel. The temptation is strong to treat the Constitution the way logicians treated the system of arithmetic—as a set of axioms from which answers can be derived in logical fashion, using only concepts within the Constitution. This is the impulse behind constitutional scholars' wistful talk of "neutral principles" that will resolve constitutional issues in a way that does not involve underlying political or moral values. That effort seems as noble but as doomed as the effort to demonstrate the consistency of arithmetic from within the system itself.

The Constitution does *not* tell us how to interpret itself. The only hint it gives is in fact the Ninth Amendment, which seems to me to be an incompleteness provision, a warning that we will not find within the text the answer to many of the most important questions the Constitution was written to address, at least as it pertains to human rights.

Like arithmetic, the Bill of Rights can be complete, it can be consistent—but it cannot be so without meta-constitutional postulates from outside it. We must go outside of the formal relationships among constitutional provisions and draw our overarching assumptions from the society the Constitution describes. In a political document, those must be political values. The "model" must be one of a free, self-governing society; and not just *some* model, some imagined Platonic republic, but a republic that Americans might conceivably build and might imaginably want to live in.

Some judges and scholars have a libertarian model of America, drawn from the history of American resistance to centralization and regulation—their model resembles what political thinkers have dubbed "the night watchman state."[65] Further government interventions in market and social relations, libertarians believe, threaten tyranny. Others, making different assumptions about human nature and social behavior, believe that government behaves tyrannically when it tolerates gross imbalances of wealth—even if reducing that imbalance requires taxing some to spend for the benefit of others. Yet others believe that racial and sexual subordination are America's original sin, and that a system that shrinks from confronting this kind of oppression is not truly free.

The text of the Bill of Rights may seem complete and consistent to each of these interpreters; but their interpretations will be different.

Is this a flaw in the system? I don't think so. The Constitution is about a country, about people, about specific political arrangements, and most of all about the idea of a self-governing democratic republic. The job of constitutional interpretation is to bring that vision to life, to make it as real as flawed humanity can make it. That cannot be done by a system of rules; it takes more.

Tenth Amendment

In the 1942 film *King's Row*, Ronald Reagan memorably plays Drake McHugh, who wakes from anesthesia to find that a surgeon has cut off both his legs. "Where's the rest of me?" he screams. A quarter-century later, Reagan used that line as the title for his autobiography, as if, having once intensely imagined that loss, he had still not gotten over it.

The Tenth Amendment for many Americans functions as the site of a phantom limb, the aching point of absence of a country they imagine they once had and have now lost.

"The powers not delegated to the United States by the Constitution, nor prohibited by it to the States, are reserved to the States respectively, or to the people," says the text. What the amendment says is perhaps best approached by noting what it does *not* say.

Most obviously missing is one word: "sovereignty." In this regard, the amendment really is an amputation site. "Sovereignty" is a pretty big word to lawyers, and was even more important in the eighteenth century than it is now. Consider the very first words of the Articles of Confederation: "Each state retains its sovereignty, freedom, and independence, and every power, jurisdiction, and right, which is not by this Confederation expressly delegated to the United States, in Congress assembled." Two other words from the Articles are missing too: "expressly" and "right."

Under the Articles, the Confederation was not a national government—indeed, not wholly a government at all. It was a plural being—"the United *States*, in Congress assembled." Like the United Nations today, it was a league of sovereigns; and like any other international body, it had no power that was not spelled out in so many words in the treaty that created it. The omission of these words, "sovereignty," "expressly," and "right," suggests a very different type of union than under the Articles.

In the Articles, the powers are delegated *by the Confederation*—that is, by the group of states themselves "in Congress assembled." In the Tenth Amendment, the delegation is made by *the Constitution*, a document written by "we the people." The states, in the wording of the amendment, are not the *sources* of power delegated to the new government.

Where does that power—and perhaps that vexed "sovereignty"—reside? To phrase it differently, when powers are "reserved" by the Tenth Amendment, to whom or what do they belong? The Tenth Amendment does not explicitly reserve *any* power solely to the states. Powers are "reserved to the States respectively, *or to the people*." There are powers that the federal government may not have, it seems to say; and those powers reside somewhere else. That's it. Nothing specifically "reserved" to the states alone, and no hint that the states are the creators of the Constitution, nor that the Union was created as the agent of the state governments. When advocates of "state's rights" claim the Tenth Amendment as their authority, they are experiencing phantom limb, mistaking the Constitution, as amended by the Bill of Rights, for the Articles—a flawed charter of government that lasted less than eleven years and nearly brought about the collapse of the entire American experiment.

Something more radical is latent in the text. The amendment discusses three classes of powers (without specifying what any of them are). The first are powers "delegated to the United States by the Constitution." These are powers that are surrendered to the federal government by virtue of ratification—surrendered, that is, not just by the states but also by the people. Without a constitutional amendment, the federal government cannot lose or give up those powers, even if a majority of the people at some moment would prefer that it didn't have them.

The second class (again unspecified) are those "reserved to the states respectively." Those powers (whatever they are) cannot be taken by the federal government, nor withheld by the people. The third class are "reserved . . . to the people."

Neither the state nor the federal government has any claim to ownership of these. They are the people's, to be used as they see fit.

What powers would fall into the latter class? It's easiest to imagine that these "powers" reserved to the people must be the rights we have learned to revere, rights which no government can abridge (at least without a very good reason)— free speech and assembly, religion, and so on. But the term used is "powers," not "rights," and though the two concepts are related, they are not the same.

In common usage, I have a right to do something if government cannot stop me from doing it, whether that thing is to vote, to attend church, or to publish a powerful daily newspaper. But I may or may not have the *power* to do any of those. I may need a ride to the polls, or to church, and if I cannot find one, no one has denied me my "right" to vote or worship; I may need millions of dollars to become a press lord, and if I do not have them, no one has denied me my right to freedom of the press. A right—the absence of any legal block—does not create or imply a power.

In the realm of law and politics, the distinction is equally sharp. Power relates to "[d]ominance, control, or influence over another."[66] Citizens may have a *right* to vote; but they do not have the *power* to conduct an election. To be an official election, it must be organized and controlled by the governmental body with the *power* to conduct it.

As a matter of shorthand (recognizing that all definitions are oversimplifications), individuals have *rights;* groups or governments have *powers.* A right is mine; no one can take it away. I may exercise it or not, as I choose. But I can't lend, sell, or delegate it—giving someone else, for example, two votes.

A body that holds power, however, may exercise it or delegate it. State governments have the power to build roads or run prisons, for example; they may (and often do) hire private companies to do it for them, subject to their control. If the companies do a bad job, the state government may revoke the delegation of power and do it themselves, or give it to someone else.

If that is valid, what does it mean that "powers" are "reserved . . . to the people"? In this reading, it means that the final ability to delegate or withhold a given power is with the people; that they may, if they choose, decide that no one shall use it at all; or that the state government shall use it; or that the federal government shall use it. It is theirs to withhold, but it is also theirs to bestow.

This sheds a harsh light on the popular idea that the Tenth Amendment *bars* the federal government from acting under any power other than those "specifically" delegated to it. In this reading, the powers textually given by the Constitution to the federal government cannot be denied to it; but other powers, reserved to the people, might also be, in addition, given to the federal government on loan, to be reclaimed whenever the people so decide. The loan, or the revocation, would be carried out by the people's representatives; that is to say, by Congress.

So if powers are reserved to the people, the people may delegate them through their representatives. If their representatives approve a delegation to a given level of government, that level of government may exercise those. The residuum of the reservation would be the people's sovereign prerogative to take their powers back, simply by having their representatives repeal or alter the delegation.

Of course, there would be some powers the people could not delegate to the federal government—those, and only those, "reserved to the states respectively." What are those? The Tenth Amendment doesn't add any new ones, and (as we have seen) the original Constitution explicitly reserves only one power to the states—the power to designate officers of their militias. No amendment subsequent to the original ratification has either enlarged the powers of the states or contracted the power of Congress over them.

In text and structure, the Constitution (as we have seen) seems to be mostly concerned with *empowering* the federal government and *limiting* the states, and if the Tenth Amendment is an exception to that overall scheme, it is a half-hearted and ambiguous one. Justice Harlan Fiske Stone once wrote for the Supreme Court that "[t]he amendment states but a truism that all is retained which has not been surrendered."[67]

But if it is a truism, many find it a difficult truism. Surely the limb is still there!

Quick Fixes

Eleventh and Twelfth Amendments

Amending the Constitution isn't easy. A change in our fundamental law is something Americans approach with fear and trembling.

That habit of mind had set in as early as 1848, when Abraham Lincoln, then a member of the House of Representatives, publicly opposed an amendment to empower Congress to build "internal improvements" (a public works program Lincoln strongly favored):

> As a general rule, I think, we would [do] much better [to] let it alone No slight occasion should tempt us to touch it. Better not take the first step, which may lead to a habit of altering it. Better, rather, habituate ourselves to think of it, as unalterable. It can scarcely be made better than it is. New provisions, would introduce new difficulties, and thus create, and increase appetite for still further change. No sir, let it stand as it is. New hands have never touched it. The men who made it, have done their work, and have passed away. Who shall improve, on what *they* did?[1]

Indeed, Lincoln was born, grew up, and served his political career in a culture that dared not alter the work of "the men who made it." Only during a cataclysmic war, when the nature of the Republic had changed forever, did he champion an amendment, the Thirteenth, that outlawed slavery.

Between 1787 and 1804, however, the Constitution was amended no fewer than twelve times. The first ten we have seen: they were basically designed to operate from the start. The last two address flaws or ambiguities in the 1787 document that only became apparent after it had been in action a few years. Like the Bill of Rights, they were the work of a founding generation that apparently saw their work as open-ended and far from untouchable. Their text, to most readers, is opaque and tedious. Both, however, are important. The Eleventh is mostly the preserve of lawyers. The Twelfth still governs the way we pick presidents today.

Eleventh Amendment

In May 2003, Representative Marilyn Musgrave introduced in the House a proposed amendment to the Constitution that read "Marriage in the United States shall consist only of the union of a man and a woman. Neither this Constitution or the constitution of any State, nor state or federal law, shall be construed to require that marital status or the legal incidents thereof be conferred upon unmarried couples or groups." The amendment was known as the Marriage Protection Amendment. The proposed amendment was written by three prominent conservative legal scholars; one of them was rejected Supreme Court nominee Robert Bork, one of the first and most respected advocates of "originalism."

Almost as soon as the amendment was introduced, a squabble broke out over what it meant. The second sentence said that neither state nor federal constitutions, "*nor state or federal law*, shall be construed to require that marital status or the legal incidents thereof be conferred upon unmarried couples or groups." Did this mean that states could not legislatively pass bills allowing "civil unions" between same-sex couples?

The questioners pointed out that a state civil-union law would have to be "construed" in order to take effect, and that a civil-union law would "confer" at least some of the "lawful incidents" of marriage. Any law must be read by government officials, who "take its words in such an order as to show the meaning." That is the dictionary meaning of "construe."[2] And since the law couldn't be "construed" to allow "incidents of marriage," it could not take effect.

Strikingly, this question came from some of the amendment's *supporters*, who disagreed on what it would mean if enacted. And in fact, the question split *the very three scholars who had written it*. Bork insisted that the amendment would simply stop "liberal activist courts" from imposing gay marriage on an unwilling people, while allowing state legislatures to enact gay marriages if they chose. The other two disagreed, saying that *any* kind of civil union, legislatively or judicially created, state or federal, would be barred. "If the Constitution forbade states from creating 'navies,' they clearly could not establish 'flotillas' or 'armadas,' either," one of Bork's co-drafters explained.[3]

The disagreement had political consequences, because opinion polls showed that many of those who opposed gay marriage actually approved of creating civil unions for same-sex couples. The movement to ban gay marriage found itself split between those who wanted to ban anything like civil unions and those who did not. When the amendment failed to pass either the House or the Senate, proponents came back with another version, designed to allay the civil union fears. This time it read: "Marriage in the United States shall consist only of the union of a man and a woman. Neither this Constitution, nor the constitution of any State, shall be construed to require that marriage or the legal incidents thereof be conferred upon any union other than the union of a man and a woman." This, the sponsors said, would fix the problem.

But once again, others in the movement to ban gay marriage disagreed. They told their supporters the new amendment would still block civil unions in the states. Why? Because the first sentence *already* banned gay marriage. Thus the second sentence must ban more than gay marriage; in effect, it must ban any-thing *like* gay marriage, whether created by courts or by state legislatures. Again, the bickering weakened the movement and the amendment failed.

The rise and fall of the Marriage Amendment is a cautionary tale for Consti-tution readers. First of all, it suggests that reading texts, even the kind of fine parsing we are doing in this book, really matters. Some opponents of the Mar-riage Amendment tried to suggest that its flaws arose from poor draftsmanship (one called it "linguistic goo"),[4] but its language is actually no vaguer than many provisions that *are* in the Constitution. And that brings us to the second point. The first proposed amendment was written by a small group of like-minded scholars; and yet within months, the three of them flatly disagreed about the "original intent" or the "original meaning" of their own words. In this small exer-cise in constitutional interpretation, the "framers" were still alive and even they didn't know for sure what they "intended" or "understood."

The point is that when we try to understand the Constitution, the words are all we have, and the words themselves are very seldom clear. The Eleventh Amendment is a case in point—and the tortured history of the Marriage Amend-ment is particularly relevant here, because the elusive meaning of the Eleventh Amendment also centers around that mysterious word "construed."

The Eleventh Amendment was approved by the states in 1794 and formally added to the Constitution in 1795. To this day, it holds the record for shortest interval between proposal by Congress and ratification by state legislatures. The amendment's language says something, but anyone reading it is bound to wonder exactly why it is where it is and what its framers were about.

Article III begins by discussing "the judicial power of the United States," and then listing a number of kinds of "cases or controversies" the power "shall extend" to. One of these is "controversies . . . between a State and Citizens of another State." Seems straightforward, yes? If a citizen of one state wants to sue the state government of another state, Article III says the case can be heard in federal court. In 1793, the Supreme Court upheld the judgment in the first such suit, and the state governments reacted angrily.

Chisholm v. Georgia[5] involved a merchant, Robert Farquahr, who had patrioti-
cally but unwisely sold military uniforms to the state of Georgia during the Revolution. After Independence, the state refused to pay him, and the dispute wound
on for seventeen years. Farquahr died, and his executor, Alexander Chisholm,
tried to collect the money the state owed. South Carolina's courts had no jurisdiction over a case against another state; and Georgia's courts would not hear the
case because of a doctrine called "sovereign immunity." This doctrine came from
the British law maxim that the king, the sovereign, could do no wrong and could
thus never be haled into court without his consent to account for his acts. After
the Revolution, many states held themselves out as the new sovereigns, immune
to suit or accountability to individuals. Chisholm's case was stalemated until the
new Supreme Court held that under the new Constitution, he could pursue his
remedy in the new federal courts. In the new union, the states were not the
sovereigns any more.

State governments and their supporters were outraged, and the Eleventh
Amendment is the result. Less than a decade after the ratification of the Constitution, state governments and the people used the Article V process to overrule
the Supreme Court (*Chisholm* was its first major constitutional decision) and to
give instructions on how to read the Constitution. The way they did that leaves
us a textual puzzle—actually, two.

The first and most directly related to the words is the language that "the judicial power . . . shall not be *construed*" to reach cases in which a citizen from another state (like Chisholm) sued a state. The framers could have said "the judicial
power . . . shall not *extend*" to such cases. That would have made it clear that ag-
grieved parties like Chisholm could never look to the federal courts for relief,
and that Congress could do nothing to change that by statute. However, the
language says only that the power shall not be "construed." This could be read
two ways; the first is that the judicial power never extended to suits by out-of-
state citizens against states in the first place, and that allowing such suits was an
illegitimate "construction" of the power. The second is that the power still *extends*
(remember Article III explicitly says it does) to at least some suits of this kind,
but that Article III should not be "construed" to reach all of them.

"Construe" comes from a Latin root related to building, meaning the assembly of materials into a whole. *The Oxford English Dictionary* lists nine meanings, all closely related to the idea of carefully parsing the grammatical meaning
of a phrase or sentence. These include "to explain or interpret for legal purposes," and "to expound, interpret, or take in a specified way (often apart from
the real sense)." The detailed entry includes one example from the seventeenth
century in which the word means its own opposite—to analyze wrongly, to
misconstrue. Black's Law Dictionary gives its meaning as "to analyze and explain
the meaning of."[6]

So here's our first textual puzzle. If Article III says the power "extends" to cases brought by a citizen of another state against a state, and the Eleventh Amendment says that the power "shall not be construed to extend" to the same set of cases, how do we read the two together? As I said earlier, if the framers of the Eleventh Amendment thought that the original grant of jurisdiction was a mistake, they could easily have revoked it. Does what they did write mean "Article III doesn't mean what it says," or does it mean "when there is a doubtful case, don't adopt a meaning not in the text of whatever provision or statute you are interpreting to allow such a suit"?

The two readings would have very different effects. If Article III doesn't mean what it says, then Congress couldn't allow such suits no matter what. There never was power in the courts to hear them. *Chisholm* was wrong, and the amendment is a mere correction. If on the other hand, the amendment means that Article III is just not to be *interpreted* that way, then Congress might still be able to authorize these suits simply by *saying clearly* (in a way that required no "construction") that the judicial power should extend to certain suits. That would mean that if Congress wanted citizens to use the federal courts to enforce its statutes against state governments, it would have to say so. If the earlier meaning is correct, however, that means that nothing Congress says can make a difference.

Historians, scholars and judges have read the amendment both ways. Some of the divergence results from a disagreement over history, and some is the result of a choice between ways of reading. One group says that Article III means what its words mean, and the Eleventh Amendment means what its words mean. There is power to hear some suits by individuals against states, as long as the jurisdiction doesn't come out of some doubtful "construction" of the law. That's not purely a "words mean what they say" reading; it also takes note of the overall text of the Constitution. The Constitution explicitly blocks the states from doing many things, such as debasing the currency or altering the meaning of contracts. Why shouldn't we read it elsewhere as restricting their prerogative to buy uniforms from a hapless low-country mercer and then telling him to whistle when the bill comes due?

Then there's the philosophy of a lot of the Framers: their concern that state governments were acting irresponsibly and dishonoring treaty obligations and economic agreements. But in the end, this reading relies most heavily on a kind of "Horton Hatches the Egg" philosophy of reading—the text meant what it said and it said what it meant.

The other philosophy is equally popular. It holds that what the words on the page seem to say is only meaningful if we read them in terms of what we "know" the Framers were thinking. In its recent cases, the Supreme Court has said that what should be read are not the bare words but the "the background principle of state sovereign immunity" that was on the minds of those who wrote them.[7] (The dissent argued instead that the Court was erroneously "holding that a nontextual common law rule limits a clear grant of congressional power under Article I.")[8]

For that reason, over the years, the Court has read the amendment to bar federal suits by citizens of a state against their *own* state government (where there is no issue of "Citizens of another State"). It has held that citizens cannot sue states even in *state* court when the case arises under a federal statute (where there is no issue of "the judicial power of the United States"). It has held that a citizen cannot proceed against a state in a federal *administrative agency* (where there is no issue of *judicial* power, state or federal, at all).

The Court has allowed one sharply limited exception. The Thirteenth, Fourteenth, and Fifteenth Amendments, as we will see, contain language conferring new power on Congress to enforce them. The Court has allowed Congress then to authorize some suits under these amendments. That's because, the Court said, these three amendments were passed after the Eleventh, and so can be read to have modified its limit on the judicial power.

But the Court has not simply affirmed Congress's power under the later amendments; instead, if Congress passes a statute authorizing such lawsuits, the Court insists that judges must decide whether the inequality or restriction the statute is aimed at is really, in their view, an important one. If it isn't, then the later amendment doesn't authorize the lawsuit. Vindicating the equal-protection rights of the disabled, for example, is an interest the Court finds insufficiently important.[9] True, disabled people are discriminated against; but the Court itself doesn't see that kind of discrimination as particularly serious under the Fourteenth Amendment. Congress can outlaw discrimination against the disabled; but it may not permit direct lawsuits against states by disabled employees who have suffered discrimination. On the other hand, discrimination by race, or sex, is a serious violation of the amendment, and thus those lawsuits can proceed.

The point of this discussion is not to parse the Supreme Court's case law on this seemingly arcane (though in practical terms quite significant) point. It is instead to show that when the Court must directly interpret the words of the Constitution (instead of its own decades of case law), it has to use the same expedients we do. Do we follow what the words say, or what we think those who said them meant?

One might wish that the drafters of the Eleventh Amendment had been clearer about what they were up to; the truth, however, is that no set of words can ever be self-explaining. Draw the net as tightly as we will, the old devil "construction" appears in the spaces between.

Twelfth Amendment

Of all the parts of the new government set up by the Constitution, none has needed more repair than presidential selection and succession. The electoral-vote system in the original Constitution had a kind of musty flavor even when adopted, a tinge of the decadent Holy Roman Empire. The original system worked just fine—as long as there wasn't any real contest between candidates. But almost any voting system can adapt to unanimity; the test is how it handles opposition, and the original Article II system failed its first major test.

The Twelfth Amendment was adopted almost a decade after the Eleventh, and it flowed directly out of an episode in which the electoral system failed, bringing the country—not to put it too dramatically—to the edge of civil war. It's not surprising that the people felt the necessity of changing it back then. What is surprising is how much the revised system resembles the balky electrical system on an otherwise fine car. As we learned in 2000, some manufacturing defects never quite get fixed.

Here's a bare-bones historical background for the Twelfth Amendment. In the original Article II, the electors meet on a set day in their individual states and vote "for two persons." The only restriction was that one of them had to be "an inhabitant" of a different state from the elector's. There was no ranking or nota-tion. The votes were counted and a list of the totals was to be sent to the "the president of the senate," who was in fact the vice president unless that office was vacant. That figure would count them. If one had a majority, then he became president, and "[i]n every Case, after the Choice of the President, the Person having the greatest Number of Votes of the Electors shall be the Vice President." Pretty straightforward, like a prep school popularity contest. If two candidates both had a majority, but one had more votes than the other, "the person having the greatest number of votes shall be president." If nobody had a majority, then the House would choose from among the top five.

But if the top two candidates (1) both had a majority and (2) had the same number of votes, then the House would choose between those two only. In any case, the vice president would be the candidate who received more electoral votes than anybody except the president—so that even if the House ended up choosing between two tied candidates, the other candidate would become vice president.

If one candidate had majority support, then of course he should win. If no candidate had majority support, then the choice should come from Congress. And if two candidates had equal support, then the people's representatives, voting by states, would break the tie.

The Framers may have thought they had covered all the bases. But wise as they may have been, they didn't understand how politics is truly conducted when ultimate power is the stake. Political parties appeared almost as soon as Congress assembled in 1789, and by the time Washington retired in 1796, the parties wanted to run candidates for president, rather than leaving the choice to the high-minded whims of electors. And the winners and losers did not roost quietly together atop the executive branch.

John Adams, Washington's vice president, succeeded Washington. His opponent in the race, Thomas Jefferson, was the electoral runner-up. Vice President Jefferson spent the next four years plotting the downfall of Adams, and in 1800, Jefferson's new Democratic Republican Party swept the electoral vote in what became known as "the Revolution of 1800." For perhaps the first time in Western history, a new leader was elected to replace a living head of state without revolution or coup d'état.

But there was one problem: which new leader had been elected?

Jefferson had a running mate, Colonel Aaron Burr, a Revolutionary War hero and charming knave. Burr secured votes in the North for an informal ticket in which he was to be Jefferson's vice president. But because the electors did not rank their selections, Jefferson and Burr got the same number of votes. Offered the chance to withdraw in favor of Jefferson, Burr refused. The choice of the new president was thrown into the old House of Representatives, dominated by the political enemies of both men. It was as if the Republican House in 2000 had been given the choice between Al Gore and Joe Lieberman.

For thirty-five ballots, Jefferson's enemies dithered about whether they feared him or Burr more. The country drifted toward civil war; Jeffersonian militias were mustering for a march on Washington and a coup d'état. In the end, Alexander Hamilton persuaded his allies that they hated Burr more, and Jefferson became president. Only a little more than a decade after the Constitution took effect, the flimsiness of Article II had nearly destroyed the entire edifice.

The Twelfth Amendment was the result. Under its provisions, when the electors meet, they are to vote by "distinct ballots" for president and vice president. This will result in two "distinct lists," one of presidential and the other of vice-presidential candidates. Both are forwarded to the "President of the Senate" (the vice president) and opened in front of a joint session of Congress as before.

In Article II, there was a provision for dealing with a total in which two candidates both had a majority of "the electors appointed." In that case, the House was to choose among only those two candidates. There was also a plan for a scenario in which no candidate got a majority at all; if that happened, the House would choose among the top *five* vote getters. But under the Twelfth Amendment, each elector now has only one vote for president, so by definition, only one candidate can have a majority.

The second possibility, in which no candidate has a majority, remains. In that case, the Twelfth Amendment now restricts the House to choosing among the top *three* candidates. Once again, the vote is to be conducted by states. Now remember that under Article II, if the election was thrown into the House, the electoral-vote runner-up automatically became vice president. The chaos of 1800, however, revealed the flaw in this plan: depending on whether Burr or Jefferson won the vote in the House, the other, as the runner-up, would be vice president. But that meant that while the House toiled through its inconclusive thirty-five ballots, nobody knew who would be either president or vice president. And if March 4, the end of John Adams's term, arrived before the House could make up its mind, there would be no president and no vice president to step into the void.

Under the new Twelfth Amendment, there were two possibilities. First, because there were "distinct ballots," one candidate for vice president might get a majority even though no candidate for president got one. (That actually occurred, in 1824, the only other presidential election ever thrown into the House. Andrew Jackson and John Quincy Adams were the two presidential candidates. Both had selected John C. Calhoun as their running mate, and Calhoun coasted to an electoral-vote victory.) But if no vice-presidential candidate got a majority of the electors, the "Senate shall choose the Vice-President."

Here was an elegant adaptation. Selection of the vice president by the Senate preserved the principle of state equality after electoral-vote stalemate. But it also made it much less likely that there would be neither a president nor a vice president by the March 4 deadline. Why? Well, remember that voting in the House is "by states," meaning that if a state's House delegation is evenly divided, the state does not cast a vote. And since "a majority of all the states shall be necessary to a choice," each state that doesn't vote makes it less likely that any candidate will get a majority.

But in the Senate, a divided delegation still casts two votes. So the body is much more likely to make a timely choice—even though a winner needs a majority of the "whole number" of senators, not simply of those voting. The result of this feature was to make it much more likely that a vice president would be selected by March 4. Thus, the amendment says, "if the House of Representatives shall not choose a President" by March 4, "then the Vice-President shall act as President, as in the case of the death or other constitutional disability of the President." Here, in an attempt to clarify procedures, the framers of the amendment introduced two potential new ambiguities: as before, it's unclear whether the vice president in such a case should become the new president or just an "acting President." Linked to that is a second possibility—what if the House finally selected a new president on March 5, after the vice president had begun his service as head of state? Does the newly selected president replace the vice president, or has he missed his chance?

Luckily, this question has never arisen. The ambiguity, though, still lingers, even though the provisions for presidential succession have been amended twice more.

In fact, despite repeated quick fixes, this portion of the Constitution still works so badly that the election of 2000 produced a standoff nearly as corrosive as that of 1800, as if two centuries of constitutional government had not intervened. The only change this time was that the Supreme Court, which is never mentioned anywhere in any of the provisions about presidential selection, took it upon itself to resolve the issue rather than leave it to Congress, which is clearly charged by the Constitution's text. Readers must judge for themselves whether the judiciary handled the job better than Congress would have.

Democratic Vistas

Thirteenth, Fourteenth, and Fifteenth Amendments

When Americans think of the Constitution, they think of 1789, of a small elegant room in Philadelphia and serious-minded revolutionaries in broadcloth and wigs. But, as George Orwell wrote, "To see what is in front of one's nose needs a constant struggle."[1] In front of our noses—written right into the document—is the plain fact that, in many ways, we do not live under the Constitution those men wrote, and that they didn't write much of the Constitution we live under. By my own count, as many as 400 of the original 4,400 words of the 1789 Constitution—nearly 10 percent—no longer apply because they have been directly repealed by amendments passed after the adoption of the Bill of Rights. Many other parts of the 1787 Constitution have taken on quite a different meaning because the institution that inspired them, slavery, has been abolished. The differences are great enough that it no longer makes sense—though many still do—to speak of the Framers' "design" or "vision."

Amendments to the Constitution have come in waves. For two generations after the Twelfth, there was nothing. Then, in the aftermath of the Civil War, there were three. The Progressive era, a generation or so later, spawned five, three that are important today and two—one to prohibit liquor and one to undo that—which cancel each other out. Two technical amendments—one altering the president's term and another limiting his service—came during the New Deal era. Then the civil rights and youth revolution of the sixties gave us a series. At the end, strangely enough, the Constitution's most recent amendment is one of Madison's original thirteen.

The Thirteenth, Fourteenth, and Fifteenth Amendments are the most important changes ever made in the Constitution. The Thirteenth profoundly subverts and reinvents the values of the 1787 document; the Fourteenth radically alters the structure of the government created in 1787; the Fifteenth begins a transformation in the relation between voting and citizenship. These three

"Civil War," or "Reconstruction Amendments" are, as some scholars have said, a second Constitution. Rhetorically, they are quite diverse—at times speaking in the voice of biblical prophecy, and at others faintly echoing the epic diction of Article I.

Thirteenth Amendment

In 1864, the Union Army of the West, commanded by William Tecumseh Sherman, flooded through Georgia and later, the Carolinas, doing their best, as they passed, to destroy the infrastructure of daily life in the Confederacy. The next year, a songwriter named Henry Clay Work immortalized Sherman's March in a Song, "Marching Through Georgia," which included the refrain,

Hurrah! Hurrah! We bring the Jubilee!
Hurrah! Hurrah! The flag that makes you free!

The flag in the song was in two ways not the old flag of the Union. The new flag had thirty-five, not thirty-three, stars; when the southern states had "left" the Union in 1861, neither Kansas nor West Virginia was a state. But Old Glory also now stood for a radically different social and economic system from the one symbolized by the antebellum flag. The Union armies that marched through Georgia brought with them new constitutional values. That new Constitution and those new values formally entered our nation's fundamental law in December 1865, after the fighting had ended. They were embodied in the Thirteenth Amendment, which had been drafted by Congress in 1864—under the sponsorship of the man who not so long before had viewed the Constitution as "unalterable," Abraham Lincoln.

Of the three Civil War amendments, the Thirteenth is the most radical. Its forty-seven words lay out a new vision of the nation, the Constitution, and the law. The radicalism lies not simply in the fact that the amendment outlaws slavery—though, as we have seen, that in itself was a major change in the import of the Constitution. It lies too in the very language: "Neither slavery nor involuntary servitude . . . shall *exist*" anywhere the flag flies, it says.

Nothing previously in the Constitution has presumed to define the existence of anything except the institutions of government. The original Constitution creates a government, then tells it how to organize itself, and how to act toward citizens. Beyond its reach, by implication, is a private realm.

The Thirteenth Amendment, for the first time, extends "thou shalt not" to the private citizen. It says, "thou shalt not hold slaves." But that aim could be achieved simply by saying "slavery by law is hereby abolished and forbidden." The actual text goes further, to say, "You *do not* hold slaves. The human beings you seek to hold are free at this moment. Slavery does not exist. *Freedom is not just the law; it is the fact, now and forever.*"

For the first (and so far only) time, the Constitution radically redefines daily life. The prescriptive diction ("The executive power shall be vested . . .") and the prohibitory voice ("Congress shall make no law . . .") are now supplemented by the prophetic voice, foretelling not just government's powers and duties but the nature of the world. The authors of the amendment were familiar with the voice of prophecy. At this turning point in American history, their words echo those of the Old Testament Prophet Micah:

> . . . they shall beat their swords into plowshares,
> and their spears into pruning hooks;
> nation shall not lift up sword against nation,
> neither shall they learn war any more;
> but they shall sit every man under his vine and under his fig tree, and
> none shall make them afraid.[2]

So the scope of the Thirteenth Amendment is large, running from the government to the relations between people on American soil—and not just on American soil, but in essence, wherever "the flag that makes you free" should fly Slavery is abolished "within the United States, or any place subject to their jurisdiction." This means not only within areas admitted to statehood but within areas acquired as territory (such as, after the Civil War, Alaska and later Hawaii), or even as the fruit of conquest and war, like the Philippines, Puerto Rico, or the islands of the South Pacific. The United States must no longer tolerate slavery; wherever the nation's power flows, the flag must bring the Jubilee.

What is slavery? The amendment offers no definition as such—Americans in 1865 surely understood that term, having lived with it through most of a century of social nightmare. But a slave by any other name must also not be held: not only slavery is outlawed, but "involuntary servitude, except as a punishment for crime whereof the party shall have been duly convicted." Prisoners may be set to hard labor; but that labor cannot be exacted without a conviction of a crime. Some southern states after the Civil War passed debt peonage laws; workers (usually but not always black) signed contracts to work for a period of time. If they were unable or unwilling to complete that service, the state would seize them and force them to fulfill the contract. The Supreme Court struck down those laws, saying they prescribed "involuntary servitude" for debt, and debt is not a crime.[3]

Even criminals may not be set to labor until they have been "duly convicted." The word "duly" is the first stirring of an idea that will become explicit in the Fourteenth Amendment. We've seen that the Fifth Amendment binds the federal government to observe "due process of law"; the amendment, however, did not bind the states. Here in the Thirteenth is a hint that "due process" will now apply everywhere. Since slavery does not exist anywhere except on one condition, that condition must bind the states: the conviction must have been "duly" reached. The states had formerly been dry land; "due process" now laps at their shores.

The second section of the amendment also offers something new, a textual puzzle that judges and scholars continue to worry at today: "Congress shall have power to enforce this article by appropriate legislation." The original Bill of Rights is a set of prohibitions, and nowhere in the list of prohibitions is there mention of what power shall enforce them. Observing them might have been left to the good faith of legislators (early state bills of rights often contained language saying, for example, that "the liberty of the press *ought to be* inviolably preserved,"⁴ which reads today like an appeal to conscience, not a categorical command). Or it might be (as it has become today) the special province of the courts, adjudicating disputes between individuals and their rulers.

The Thirteenth Amendment, however, does not say that individuals have a *right* not to be held as slaves. It surely meant that much; but as we've seen, its sweeping language implies much more. It imposes an obligation on government to cleanse society of the disease of slavery. And with that obligation comes power. Congress is to have that power, and thus, it seems, to take the lead in extirpating slavery.

This is the first new power Congress has been given since 1787. What is its scope? The scope of Congress's powers under Article I is broad—to "make all Laws which shall be necessary and proper for carrying into Execution the foregoing Powers, and all other Powers vested by this Constitution in the Government of the United States, or in any Department or Officer thereof." Can the power offered under the Thirteenth Amendment be narrower?

It's an important question and will come up again with later amendments, particularly the Fourteenth. Consider these two views. First, the Constitution describes congressional power in sweeping terms—"necessary and proper" amplifies not only the enumerated powers of Congress but "all other powers" given by the Constitution to any branch of the federal government anywhere in the Constitution. This would clearly apply to the new power granted in Section Two of the Thirteenth Amendment. The word "appropriate," then, would have no meaning unless it served to indicate that the Section Two power was in some way more limited than others. A law enforcing the Thirteenth Amendment (or, later, the Fourteenth, the Fifteenth, the Seventeenth, the Eighteenth, the Nineteenth, the Twenty-Third, the Twenty-Fourth, and the Twenty-Sixth) is thus to be held to a stricter standard of constitutionality than is one passed under the enumerated powers of the original Constitution. Courts have, at times, subjected

laws passed under the Fourteenth Amendment to exactly such a stricter standard. A law enforcing the amendment, they have written, is only valid if the
Court finds it "appropriate," which means more than merely "necessary."

But there's a different way to look at it, one that involves reading the entire
document. The "appropriate" language is used in every case in which an amendment gives a new power to Congress. Does it make sense to imagine that the
framers of each new amendment drew it to give Congress only a very limited
power? Does it make sense for courts—who are not even mentioned in the
amendments, much less given any new textual power—to set themselves up as
stricter arbiters of the new powers than of the old?

In this second reading, the word "appropriate" is a cross-reference. This is
what linguists call *deixis*, meaning pointing or indication. "Discourse deixis"
refers the reader to another term or concept in the document. In this case, it
refers us back to "necessary and proper." If it stands in for "necessary and
proper," then it indicates that this power is linked to the powers granted in the
original Constitution. Could a power be "necessary and proper" but also "in-
appropriate"? The repeated use of the word "appropriate" by different amendment drafters thus avoids acquiring a new meaning by its frequent or infrequent
use. We also thus avoid giving to the amendments that grant power some
lesser status than we give to original grants of power; by doing so, we avoid
contradicting the provision of Article V that states that amendments are "valid
to all Intents and as part of this Constitution"—not to be read differently or
disparaged as inferior.

"Amendment" means change—and while we cannot understand a change
without understanding what is changed, we have no real logical reason to begin
analyzing a change by presupposing that it is first and foremost not a change. As
we said before, this amendment and the next two are sweeping and fundamental. If an amendment's overall nature makes major changes in the Constitution,
then it seems wrong to assume that the changes made by its parts are narrow.

Fourteenth Amendment

In 1987, the 200th anniversary of the Philadelphia Framing, the San Francisco
Patent and Trademark Society invited Justice Thurgood Marshall to address its
annual professional meeting in Maui, Hawaii. The address they got surprised
some of them and upset a few.

Marshall, who died in 1993, was the greatest civil rights lawyer in American
history, the man who had argued and won *Brown v. Board of Education* in 1954.
A decade later, President Lyndon Johnson, had named Marshall first solicitor
general and then associate justice—the first African American to serve in either

post. In 1987, after more than two decades on the Court, Marshall told the assembled lawyers that the nation was "celebrating the wrong document."

The original Constitution, he said, had collapsed in 1861, with the advent of the Civil War. "While the Union survived the Civil War, the Constitution did not," he said. "In its place arose a new, more promising basis for justice and equality, the fourteenth amendment, ensuring protection of the life, liberty, and property of *all* persons against deprivations without due process, and guaranteeing equal protection of the laws."[5] To Marshall, one of the greatest constitutional lawyers in American history, the Fourteenth Amendment did not simply alter, or even transform the Constitution—it *became* the Constitution, eclipsing the original document.

Tony Mauro of *Legal Times* reported that

> back in Washington, where his speech text was handed out, Marshall's remarks were viewed as anything but humdrum. For the first time in this bicentennial year, a jurist of prominence had said a disparaging word about the celebration. . . . The speech made page one of *The Washington Post*, *The New York Times*, and *USA Today*. It electrified the bicentennial celebration—as much as it can be electrified. Daniel Popeo of the conservative Washington Legal Foundation actually called for Marshall's resignation, proclaiming the speech was a "terrible revelation of what goes on in Marshall's mind. There's a deep bitterness and bias there."[6]

It is hard for most Americans to grasp a view that argues that the Constitution is not only not perfect, but not even really the Constitution. But the Fourteenth Amendment marks such a change in the meaning, structure, and workings of the original document that few lawyers would be surprised by an argument like Marshall's. They may agree or disagree that the Fourteenth Amendment is "the second Constitution," but the thought is not outlandish.

Almost no one reads the entire Fourteenth Amendment at one sitting any more. Law textbooks immediately direct students exclusively to Section One, and they break even that section down into discrete parts—the Citizenship Clause, the Privileges or Immunities Clause, the Due Process Clause, and the Equal Protection Clause, each of which gets its own section in the course. Lay readers find sections Two through Four all but incomprehensible. But it is worth reading the entire amendment at once, with some idea of the historical circumstances that spawned it. A wholistic reading detects some echoes of the epic mode of Article I; indeed, one can read the amendment as a political epic—with all five sections describing a new political system for the reborn Union—that contains a social epic, Section One, which describes a new, democratic society that will rise in the states. "A Union of truly democratic states" is the description of its aim given by Carl Schurz, who was active in its passage and ratification.[7] Considering that equality and democracy were both absent from the Constitution before, the amendment represents an enormous change.

SECTION ONE. Article I described a government that ruled two houses, the house of trade and the house of war. Section One now gives us images of American life that Article I ignored: Who is an American? What does it mean to be an American? How are the states to treat their own people? How are they to treat strangers from other states, and even from other countries? The parts together paint a picture of inclusion and equality that was entirely absent from the Constitution heretofore.

Who is an American? A great deal of soaring rhetoric is lavished on the 1787 Constitution—its greatness, its endurance, its supposed promises to all Americans of equality, or liberty, or safety, or unity, or whatever social good a political leader wishes to extol. But for all that, the document itself is a bit short on soaring phrases and broad principles. In fact, after the Preamble, it spends thousands of words distributing powers and works its way only crabwise, and by implication, into the values those powers are intended to further.

That began to change with the Thirteenth Amendment, with its declaration of what shall and shall not exist within the Republic's reach. The Fourteenth also begins with a broad universal proclamation. Not only are there henceforth to be no slaves under the Flag, but "*all* persons born or naturalized in the United States and subject to the jurisdiction thereof, *are* citizens of the United States and of the State wherein they reside." This is a breathtaking change in rhetoric: even the Thirteenth Amendment was prophetic, decreeing that slavery "*shall* not" exist; the Fourteenth begins with the present tense: "*are* citizens of the United States."

Not since the Tenth Amendment has the document spoken in such explicitly denotative terms. It does not change the present, it describes it—and perhaps describes what has always been the case, even if some people before the Civil War did not recognize that fact. It speaks in universal terms, of "all *persons*," of whatever description, without qualification of race, religion, sex, or social status. Remember Article I, Section Two, Clause Three, which begins with a base number of "free persons," condescends to count "persons held to labor for a term of years," proclaims the irrelevance of "Indians not taxed," and then grudgingly enumerates a fraction of "other persons"? The new language begins with "all persons." By definition they are "free persons"—the Thirteenth Amendment says *they cannot be anything else*. The original Constitution worked by addition—defining a core of real persons and then adding some of the rest and excluding others. The Fourteenth begins by throwing a national aegis of protection over all.

Then there is an enigmatic limitation. To be "citizens of the United States," people must not only be "born or naturalized" in the United States, but also "subject to the jurisdiction thereof." Much current debate focuses on the meaning of these words. In our time (as it was in the time the Fourteenth Amendment was written), immigration is a bitter cultural and political issue. It is galling to many that anyone born in the United States now has American citizenship, even if born to parents who entered the United States without permission or who have remained here without authorization. These children are called "anchor babies," from the popular impression that parents of citizen children are somehow immune from deportation. (The entire point of this book is that words matter; note that those who coined the term "anchor baby" have transformed a newborn American child into a lead object whose only significance is in relation to other people.) Many citizens (a majority, in some polls) would like to change the law to withhold citizenship for the children of "illegal" immigrants. Some legal scholars who agree with them argue that the words "subject to the jurisdiction" must mean "legally present."

The problem with this argument is that the framers of the amendment used the word "jurisdiction." That word, in 1868 as today, refers most commonly to the power of government to set rules and to try those who break them. There's no implication of consent or allegiance by the person "subject to the jurisdiction": and indeed, a common-law court in England, and a court in the United States, had—and still has—the power to detain, try, and sentence an offender if that person is found in its territory; the power to summon such people and hear civil complaints against them. This would suggest that anyone born in the territory of the United States is "subject to the jurisdiction" and thus "is" a citizen.

But if that covers everybody, is the phrase "subject to the jurisdiction" meaningless? No, because in 1868 it did not cover two groups, and even today does not cover at least one. In 1868, the government still had extensive dealings with what Article I, Section Two, Clause 3 called "Indians not taxed"; these were the Indians living on reservations (and the so-called "wild Indians," tribal bands who had not yet been confined to reservations) who lived in United States territory but were recognized to be under their tribal governments. Citizens with complaints against these Indians were required to present them to the United States, which could either deny them or pay them and then pursue a government-to-government claim against the tribal government. These Indians were not "subject to the jurisdiction."

The second category of persons present in US territory are those covered by diplomatic immunity. Diplomats, including many of the staff of embassies, are and have for hundreds of years been known to be, not "subject to the jurisdiction" of the courts of the countries where they live and work on official business. A joy-riding ambassador may total your car; you cannot sue him or the embassy. Instead (like a mid-nineteenth-century settler on the Great Plains with a claim against an Indian band), you must go to your own government and ask it to pursue a claim against the foreign government. Diplomats' children, even when born in the country to which their parents are assigned, are not considered citizens of that country. By a legal fiction, they formally "reside" outside the United States, even when they are within it.

As for other categories of persons not "subject to the jurisdiction," either in 1868 or now, I can't think of one. It is true that in 1868, there was no concept of an "illegal alien." The term came into use, as near as can be told, only in the years after World War II. But it is also true that "illegal aliens" in the United States are "subject to the jurisdiction" of both state and federal legal systems. They can be, and are every day, arrested, prosecuted, and sentenced (even to death) in American courts for crimes committed here; they can be sued for their debts or for damage they cause with their cars or on their jobs. By the ordinary and natural use of the term, that means that they are "subject to the jurisdiction"—and that their children are citizens.

Some who argue for a narrower reading claim that, in the words of John Eastman, a prominent legal scholar, the Citizenship Clause "was drafted after the Civil War to guarantee that the recently freed slaves rightfully received full citizenship rights"[8] and thus has little to say about the status of nonslaves who are the children of aliens. Anyone who has a history textbook knows that that must be at least part of the reason the clause was drafted: the pro-slavery majority on the United States Supreme Court, in the Dred Scott Case, had held that persons of African descent were not American citizens and *could never be* American citizens, no matter what Congress said.[9]

But though the language obviously overrules *Dred Scott*, the drafters did not frame the provision to focus on "recently freed slaves" or African Americans. It would have been easy enough to do, using language they used in other legislation: "all persons of African descent born or naturalized in the United States are citizens etc." The striking thing about the clause, and about Section One of the Fourteenth Amendment in general, is that it carefully does not limit any of its concepts to any racial group. As we will see shortly, Section Two actually does contain some references that limit the scope of that provision—which has to do with voting rights—by race and sex. That makes their omission in this clause even more striking.

I incline more toward a broad reading. It seems to have more direct relationship to the text. The original Constitution had no real definition of citizenship, only a grudging enumeration of who "counted" for representation purposes. The tone of the Citizenship Clause seems much different—inclusive, universal, and comprehensive.

This is yet another way that the Citizenship Clause evokes the tone of the Preamble. Once more, the Constitution has become an invitation, a document addressed to all people in the United States and many outside it, who can dream that someday their children will live as equals in America's yet "more perfect union."

What is America? In its first sentence, the Fourteenth Amendment revolutionizes the membership of the American Republic. But that is just the first sentence of the first section. The second sentence of Section One, in fifty-two words, now radically alters its nature. This sentence has three parts, each of which has developed its own rich literature and case law. They are called (1) the "privileges or immunities" clause; (2) the "due process" clause; and (3) the "equal protection" clause. It is possible to quarrel and dispute over the meaning of this or that phrase, to question whether a given clause applies to a given case (and lawyers and scholars get paid to do so). But textually they appear together, in a breathless rush; and each one is written broadly. It is difficult to deny the sweeping import of the clauses taken together.

Privileges or Immunities. The first sentence having told us who is a citizen, the first clause of the second tells us that states must respect that citizenship. The language of Article I, Section Ten, announced a list of very specific prohibitions on the states—things "no state shall" do. Most of them concerned offenses they could not commit against the federal government—forming alliances, signing treaties, debasing the currency, maintaining state armies. A few, however, concern constitutional rights of individuals—no bills of attainder, no ex post facto laws, no laws altering legal contracts.

In Section One of the Fourteenth Amendment, "no state shall" appears again, and its force is now directed entirely in behalf of individuals and their rights. Their first clause concerns citizens; the next two deal with "persons." The effect is subtle, but the choice is hardly random. The first clause seems to reference, in deictic fashion, a set of rights that belong especially to citizens: more precisely, a set of "privileges or immunities." This language explores more deeply the meaning of what we call "rights." Some are "privileges"—things government must allow us to *do*, whether it wants us to or not. What could these be? Later in the Fourteenth Amendment, we read for the first time in the Constitution the phrase "the right to vote." That "right" would also be a "privilege." In the Bill of Rights, we can see some: freedom of speech, free exercise of religion, freedom to assemble, freedom to petition would be a "privilege."

But some of the rights are "immunities." The prohibition on "establishment of religion," for example, takes its meaning from the immunity it grants each citizen from certain incidents of a religious establishment: immunity from church taxation, for example, or the involuntary jurisdiction of religious courts. The Second Amendment's "right to bear arms" is a privilege; the Third's guarantee against peacetime quartering of troops would be an immunity.

Every privilege, the right to do something, carries with it a shadow immunity—freedom from restraint upon that thing. Every immunity, the freedom from government action, carries in its train a privilege—the ability to act in some way, unmolested by the state. Where one stops and another begins is a vexed question: by putting both into the clause, the framers suggested that it covers the full universe of what we lump together as "rights."

But what *are* those rights? The phrase, as noted above, *must* be deictic: in its own words it references rights but gives not one specific. It seems very unlikely that the phrase "privileges or immunities" could refer simply to the principle of "comity," or equal treatment. That's true for two reasons. First, there is an earlier clause, the "Privileges *and* Immunities" Clause of Article IV, that has been read to guarantee that each state must treat out-of-staters as well as it treats its own people. There would be no reason to repeat that command as a "Privileges *or* Immunities" Clause. That conclusion is strengthened by the different wording that follows. In Article IV, "citizens of each state" are "entitled" to the privileges and immunities of "citizens in the several states." That can be read as directing states to do something—to give out-of-staters the incidents of state citizenship and rights guaranteed by state law. The new clause sternly orders states to keep hands off "the privileges or immunities of citizens of the United States." This deictic language certainly points toward a federal source of rights.

What are the rights it points to? Where are they to be found? Two theories have emerged. The first is that there is a set of "privileges or immunities" that relate solely to the federal government and to the national character of American citizenship. This reading finds in the language a direction to states not to inter-fere with any citizen's relations to the national government. That is to say, no state can pass laws taking away a citizen's right to petition the federal govern-ment, or barring a citizen's right to travel from state to state, or voiding the right to counsel in federal trials. On the other hand, the clause, in this reading, would say nothing about whether states themselves had to permit citizens to petition the state government, or move freely about within the state, or permit counsel in state trials.

That reading comes from putting major emphasis on the phrase, "citizens of the United States," allowing it to carve out something exclusively called federal citizenship, over and apart from state citizenship, which is regulated in the Constitution, if at all, by a looser standard.

The second reading, however, would regard the Citizenship Clause as cre-ating a logical structure for the Privileges or Immunities Clause, in this way: first, it defines who is an American citizen; second, it absorbs state citizenship into national citizenship, making them one and the same; and finally, it indicates that states must respect the same limits as the federal government when they deal with any American citizen, their own citizens or not.

In that reading, then, the rights in the Constitution—all of them—would operate upon the states. This would mean that the Bill of Rights would bind the states. If that was the meaning, why didn't the drafters simply say, "no state shall make or enforce any law that violates the first eight amendments to this Constitution"? Well, in this reading, there would be three possible reasons: first, the Bill of Rights is not the sole provision of the federal Constitution guaranteeing individual rights—as we have seen in the clauses relating to bills of attainder and habeas corpus, for example—and so the language would include all of those; second, the Ninth Amendment commands that no drafter should be audacious enough to announce completion of a closed set of them; and, third, statutes themselves can produce rights. Thus, if Congress chose to use its old or new powers to guarantee a privilege or create an immunity for all citizens, those statutory rights would also apply against a state.

The two readings clash in the case law of the Supreme Court. Soon after the amendment's ratification, the Court adopted the first, restrictive reading. That decision was not based on what the Constitution said so much as it was on the idea that the Framers could not have really meant what they said. Imposing federal rights on the states, the Court said, would "fetter and degrade" the states.[10]

The problems with the first reading, though, are at least two, one theoretical and one practical. In constitutional theory, to say that the clause bars states from taking away their citizens' federal rights is, in legal terms, like saying that I will graciously not take away your right to fall toward the center of the earth. Under Article VI, Section Two, anything in federal law or the Constitution already trumps any state law. So the "federal rights only" reading in essence reads the clause out of existence.

The practical problem is allied to that. The Fourteenth Amendment clearly changes something. Courts have been stuck with the "federal rights only" reading—once the Supreme Court announces a doctrine, it takes five votes to overturn it. But in practical terms, the new nation that emerged from the Civil War could not exist as a self-governing, democratic republic without strong federal monitoring of individual rights. As a result, courts began to "find" individual rights "incorporated" in the Fourteenth Amendment—but in the "due process" clause, not the Fourteenth Amendment.

Due Process. The Privileges or Immunities Clause deals with the rights of "citizens of the United States." The Due Process and Equal Protection Clauses cover *persons*, not citizens. The word "person" reinforces the "all persons" language in the Citizenship Clause, deepening the universal, sweeping tone of Section One. While much of the Constitution is written in terms of niggling analysis and subdivision, this section sets up a rhetorical world in which broad concepts— "equal protection," "due process"—apply to everyone.

At first glance, though, the "due process" clause seems more straightforward than the "privileges or immunities" language. This phrase should have a pretty clear meaning. Like some earlier terms, "due process of law" refers us outside the document; but unlike some of them—such as, for example, "cruel" in the Eighth Amendment or "unreasonable" in the Fourth Amendment—it does not reference general intuition, or moral theory, or political science. It is "due process of *law*," surely a term that lawyers can easily parse.

This seems doubly true because the Bill of Rights already uses the phrase in the Fifth Amendment. "Process" is a legal term. Lawyers had been coping with the concept for half a millennium before it ever entered the Constitution.

But remarkably enough, the term still has no technical meaning that can be looked up or consulted. When most Americans think of "due process," they think of the rights afforded to a criminal suspect—trial by jury, and so on. Of course government can't take our lives without a trial, or our liberty either if that is defined only as the right to move about from place to place. But government can "deprive" us of many things without a criminal trial. Parking officers can issue tickets; building inspectors can fine us, department of motor vehicles officials can revoke our drivers' licenses, and so on. None of these things can happen without "due process," but much of constitutional law turns on the issue of what process is "due." And despite a near-millennium of precedent, that question must be argued afresh in case after case.

But does "due process" refer only to procedures? Let's imagine a state (call it Lilliput) that is split between the two parties depicted in *Gulliver's Travels*—the Big Endians, who believe that one should break open boiled eggs at the large end, and the Little Endians, who believe the reverse. A Big Endian majority in the Lilliputian state legislature enacts a ban on opening the small end of a boiled egg. A Little Endian (let's call him Lemuel Gulliver) is apprehended by the Egg Patrol (pursuant to a valid warrant to search his house) in the act of eating a little-end opened egg. He is indicted by a state grand jury, tried by a petit jury of twelve, represented by counsel, offered the opportunity to testify on his own behalf—and convicted and sentenced to three to five years in prison.

The State of Lilliput has complied with every procedure provided by the Constitution, even furnishing Mr. Gulliver with appointed counsel of the first rank. He has been given a fair shake. And yet—and yet. Isn't there some problem with a law that sends an otherwise model citizen to prison because the majority doesn't like the way he eats his eggs? What business is it of government which end he opens? If Mr. Little in fact ends up in prison for the "crime" of heretical egg-opening, has he in fact received "due process of law"?

This mental process leads us through the actual invention of constitutional law's most famous oxymoron, "substantive due process." The famous scholar John Hart Ely once compared this phrase to "green pastel redness"[11]—not just self-contradictory but actually nonsensical. And yet, to paraphrase Justice Potter Stewart's famous dictum on obscenity, many Americans believe they know it when they see it.[12] Some laws are just stupid, repressive, mean, and goofy. We may not agree fully on which laws fall under that description, but nobody doubts they exist. These laws violate "substantive due process." My ninth-grade civics teacher, who was in his way a genius, once summarized "due process of law" as "fair laws fairly applied." Substantive due process is a concept by which courts strike down "unfair" laws.

The idea is easier to explain than to illustrate. That's because, as noted earlier, no two people would compile exactly the same list of "unfair" laws. At one time, many federal judges believed that any law protecting labor or labor unions was so outrageous that it required invalidation. More recently, the Court has held that laws outlawing abortion before viability violate substantive due process, and so do criminal penalties for engaging in private, consensual sex with another adult, regardless of sex. On the other hand, the Court briskly rejected the claim that states violate substantive due process when they forbid willing physicians to assist terminally ill patients in ending their lives. The reasons one claim succeeds and another fails can seem, to say the least, opaque.

For this reason, many legal thinkers argue that the courts should get out of the substantive due process business. If a law is silly and oppressive, they suggest, the political process will get rid of it sooner or later. Eventually the Big-Endian majority in Lilliput will be overcome with chagrin at the cost and foolishness of persecuting their Little-Endian neighbors and will elect legislators who will repeal the Egg Laws.

That's certainly true for many—though certainly not all—silly, vicious, and oppressive laws. But even if it were true for all laws, there is the problem of Mr. Gulliver, who must do his entire prison sentence for an offense that no reasonable government would punish. The plight of America's Gullivers ensures that substantive due process claims will continue to be brought, and that some will succeed. That courts are not wholly predictable, nor always "right," in their decisions in this area will not stop citizens from asking for their help, or judges from giving it.

Equal Protection. The next clause forbids any state to "deny to any person within its jurisdiction the equal protection of the laws." This is the first time in the Constitution that the word "equal" is used to apply to human beings. In Article I, Section Three, the first senators are to be divided "as equally as may be" into three classes for purposes of assigning reelection dates. Later in the same section, the vice president is given a vote when the Senate is "equally divided." In Article 2, Section One, each state's number of electors is "equal to the whole Number of Senators and Representatives" assigned to that state; later in the same section, procedures are given if presidential candidates have "an equal number of votes" from the electors. Article V provides that "no State, without its Consent, shall be deprived of its equal Suffrage in the Senate."

Conspicuous by its absence was Jefferson's principle that "all men are created equal." The Philadelphia Framers (Jefferson being safely off in Paris) were not convinced of that.

And yet, Jefferson's words haunted the American imagination, until, by 1863, Abraham Lincoln retold the story of the Founding: "our fathers brought forth on this continent a new nation, conceived in liberty, and dedicated to the proposition that all men are created equal." The Fourteenth Amendment was born out of Lincoln's violent death, and the violent death of slavery, when the victors of the Civil War took that version of history and wrote at least some of it into the Constitution.

But doesn't their phrasing seem curious? Modern constitutions often proclaim equality as their central value and their goal, and that idea is not hard to convey. Jefferson managed in 1776 with "all men are created equal." In 1793, the Marquis de Lafayette wrote language that was enacted by the French Constituent Assembly: "Men are born and remain free and equal in rights."[13] The Congress that wrote the Fourteenth Amendment certainly had the knowledge and ability to write language like that, and, as a matter of history, several such provisions were offered by its members. What eventually found its way into the document is a considerably more ambiguous phrase. What is to be equal is not the human beings, or even necessarily the laws themselves, but the "protection of the laws." What does that mean?

To begin with, we must assign some meaning to the term "equal." In mathematics, that's not a difficult proposition; in human terms, it seems insoluble. Every day, parents ask themselves: how do I treat my children "equally"? If one is four and one is seven, do I give them equal amounts of food? Do I make them both take naps? If both want to play with a complicated toy, am I oppressing the toddler by permitting his sister to use it while forbidding him to do so?

On the one hand, one can say that *equal rules* are all that can be called for; on the other, one can say that equality demands a concern with human circumstances. "One law for the lion and ox is oppression," wrote William Blake.[14]

The question is made a bit thornier by the timidity of the phrase "equal protection." Do the words enshrine a principle of equality in the Constitution? In this reading, "equal protection of the laws" might be read to mean something like "equal laws, equally enforced."

But that's not the only possible reading. What does "protection" mean? It is largely a negative. Laws as a class do more than "protect." Some empower: citizens are able to enter into contracts, sue and be sued, acquire property, and do many other things because they are licensed to do so by law. Could "equal protection" omit this class of laws? Could it mean no more than "equal enforcement" of laws, regardless of how oppressive those laws may be?

It's common to say that the Equal Protection Clause outlaws "discrimination"— but without more, this is nonsense. Drivers' licenses are available to drivers at sixteen years of age; fifteen-year-olds feel the sting. Criminal laws stigmatize those who steal and kill, branding them unequal to the law abiding. Owners of valuable land pay more property tax than owners of scrubland. Without discrimination there is no law.

What then is "the equal protection of the laws"? If "equality" or "equal protection" is the commandment, then it must rationally mean equality *in certain ways*. What axes of inequality does the clause forbid? Constitutional scholars and judges have struggled for a century and a half to find some limited set of inequalities that can be cabined off and made the exclusive province of the clause. Many claimed that the clause applies only or primarily to *racial* inequality. The Civil War, they think, was *about* race, or racialized slavery. Others suggest that "sex" should be included—and other forms of discrimination are argued by advocates for gays and lesbians, or for the disabled.

If the clause was intended only to cover race, the Framers did not say so. As we'll see, they made at least oblique reference to race later in the amendment, and the next Congress used "race" explicitly in the Fifteenth Amendment. And if they intended to cover sex, it's striking that in the next section of the amendment, they explicitly recognized (without quite authorizing) discrimination by sex in the right to vote. But can that be taken as evidence that the phrase doesn't "include" sex? Can we read the language as in some ways a code phrase for some form or forms of discrimination hidden somewhere in law or history—or is it, like "due process," a general command to find and give effect to an ideal of human equality amid the wide variety of discriminations worked by law?

In this reading, the task of interpreters is to separate the ordinary and unavoidable work of law from the excessive or unjust creation of classes among people. If that reading is correct, the task of interpretation is to give present meaning to a value of equality—of asking which distinctions are forbidden because they make it impossible to run a democratic society. And one indication of how we should ask that question might be the general tone of Section One—the unusual (for this Constitution) expansiveness of its language and structure, which begins by extending citizenship and ends by embracing not only citizens but persons.

SECTION 2: WHO VOTES AND WHO COUNTS? Section Two today is not much read. But it repays close attention. First, it tells us something about the general tone of the Fourteenth Amendment and the changes it made in the federal system; second, it introduces some new words into the language of the Constitution. Those new words give us a new look into the democracy the Civil War produced—on the one hand, into its breadth and vision, and on the other into the limits of its reframers' vision.

The first new but now familiar phrase appears right away: this section concerns "the right to vote." Voting until now has not been a constitutional right at all. The idea of popular voting had been mentioned only once in the 1787 Constitution, and that obliquely—the House of Representatives is, according to Article I, Section Two, to be "chosen by the people" of the states. The decision of who votes is entirely in the hands of those state governments; the "qualifications" of the "electors," or voters, in elections for the House must be "the Qualifications requisite for Electors of the most numerous Branch of the State Legislature." States chose their voters, with the proviso that whatever choice they made at the state level must apply at the federal level at once. Voting, for individuals, was not a right, but a governmental function, like holding office, for which a potential voter must possess "qualifications."

The language in Section Two of the Fourteenth Amendment is quite different. It assumes that voting is the default position and prescribes a penalty for violations of it. The language does not suggest who votes, but it does suggest who is expected to vote.

Who is that? Well, here is where the second new word in the lexicon appears, because Section Two focuses our minds on states' action in "deni[al]" or "abridg[ment]" of the "right to vote" to "any of the *male* inhabitants" of a state "being twenty-one years old, and citizens of the United States." A presumption is created here: if a citizen is male and twenty-one, he is presumptively a voter. The only exception is for those who have "participat[ed] in rebellion, or other crime." Anything other than that is an anomaly. (Note that the language does not say, as the Thirteenth Amendment did, "crime whereof the party shall have been duly convicted." Why not? Perhaps because there was no prospect of mass trials of former Confederate officials and soldiers. But under this language, they could be excluded by states from voting as a class without the need for individual convictions.)

The word "male" is the first real appearance of sex in the Constitution. The original document used the word "he" to describe the president; but that seemed like an almost absent-minded assumption (even today, the president has always been a "he"). This choice of gender terms is clearly conscious and advised. The model set out in this section is of a country in which male citizens over twenty-one can vote. It does not say that all who meet this description can vote, nor does it say that those who don't—women, aliens, those under twenty-one—cannot. (States, by the terms of this section, could still apparently allow women or eighteen-year-olds or—as many of them did until the early twentieth century—aliens to vote.) Instead, it says that adult male citizen suffrage is the norm, the minimum below which voting should probably not go.

But in the act of opening up the vote, it at least permits that door to close too. Women are not included. A constitution that has been silent on gender speaks for the first time to give tacit approval to exclusion of women. The language is a blot on the Fourteenth Amendment, and a melancholy token of a historical truth: revolutions that liberate often at the same time also restrict.

The implicit democracy contained in the "right to vote" in Section Two is restricted in another sense. The section does not, as we said earlier, actually guarantee "the right to vote." It describes it (at least its lower limits) and then prescribes a penalty for states that don't conform to the description. Individuals may have a right to vote, but that individual right does not receive direct federal protection.

That's because the real subject of Section Two is not who votes but who counts. Or, to put it another way, it does not concern the allocation of political power to individuals but its division among political actors in the federal government. Its aim is not to ensure voting, but to take power away from states that restrict the ballot.

Many things in the states needed fixing after the revolution that we now call the Civil War. Some people thought that the "right to vote" should be extended to all; but more urgent was the effect of the "three-fifths clause" of Article I, Section Two. Remember the hierarchy of personhood in Article I. Slaves were not "free persons," and they were not "Indians not taxed." They were "other persons," and states with slave populations got House seats for three-fifths of them, even though they didn't vote.

But the Thirteenth Amendment had done away with slavery. There were no more "other persons." Thus the former slave states would get House seats not for three-fifths of their former slaves but for all of them. Meanwhile, in the wake of the Civil War, none of the former Confederate states had any plans to allow these new "free persons" to vote. (As a historical note, in fact, the new president, former slave owner Andrew Johnson, had issued an executive order to those states specifically limiting the vote to persons who would have been qualified to vote at the time of secession—in other words, to white men.)[15]

The result would be a windfall of House seats for the former Confederate states. Having almost wrecked the Union and lost a bloody Civil War, they would now be more, not less, influential than before. One obvious solution would have been to require all states to allow black people to vote. But the votes in Congress for black suffrage weren't there when the Fourteenth Amendment was drafted. So the result was a provision that aimed at House apportionment. In effect, it said that barring a population within a state from voting would mean that that state would lose the House seats it would otherwise be entitled to. It was a perhaps too-gentle nudge toward inclusive voting.

Did that choice of words mean that under the new constitution, states were *granted the authority* to exclude groups from voting? We have seen this puzzle before. It's a penalty for doing something, which is not quite the same as permission to do it. The penalty, if enforced, was actually quite severe—states that lose House seats (and electoral votes) lose significant amounts of power. (Even today, bloody legal battles are fought out in the Supreme Court over the allocation of even one House seat between different states.) On the other hand, Section Two did not empower anyone to vote or offer voters turned away at the polls a remedy for their injury. It limited the penalty to the loss of voting power.

Would that have worked? Would it have impelled the southern states to open the voting rolls? We'll never know. The earliest any new apportionment could have been made was 1870, after the next census. But the political situation changed much more quickly than that. In the 1866 congressional elections, Andrew Johnson's all-white Reconstruction plan was rebuffed by the voters, and the next Congress proposed the Fifteenth Amendment, which was promptly ratified. That amendment, as we'll see, specifically took from states the power to impose racial qualifications on voters.

It's customary, then, to say that the Fifteenth Amendment "superseded" Section Two. But as a matter of text, that's not exactly true. As we will see, the Fifteenth makes it unconstitutional to deny the vote on the basis of race; but Section Two does not mention race. It suggests that adding *any* qualification for voting other than age, sex, citizenship, and criminal status would trigger the provisions for reducing state representation. Thus, for example, Section Two could easily have been interpreted to require penalties to states that (as many did during the segregated era of the twentieth century) imposed poll-tax requirements or literacy tests on prospective voters. Illiteracy is not "rebellion, or other crime," and neither is failure to pay a tax.

But that didn't happen. And one reason is that the text leaves open how the penalty is to be enforced. By the text of Article II, we infer that it is Congress who is to apportion the "Representatives and direct taxes." Thus, if the penalty in Section Two is ever to be invoked, it would have to be done by vote of Congress. Since many of the members would have been from states that didn't want to allow voting by illiterate voters or the poor at whom the poll tax was aimed, it seems hardly surprising that no attempt was ever made to extend Section Two beyond race.

The most important thing about Section Two for us today is its introduction, however backhanded and apologetic, of a "right to vote." As we will see, the term "the right of citizens of the United States to vote" appears a full four times more in the amended Constitution. Yet its first recognition in our Constitution came amid exclusive and oblique language. The Constitution always seems to back grudgingly, like a crab, away from the eighteenth century and into democracy.

SECTION THREE. Growing up in the segregated South half a century ago, I would sometimes notice on the walls of friends' houses a document, as proudly framed as if it were a diploma, granting to an ancestor "full pardon and amnesty for all offenses by him committed." Pardons for crime are not usually objects of family pride. But these individual pardons were a sign that one of the family's forebears had been a leader of the Confederacy, either in its military branch or in the civilian government set up after secession in 1861.

Simply as a matter of constitutional text, these Confederate officials were traitors. Treason is "levying War against" the United States, which the Confederacy did far more effectively than any foreign government ever has. Between 1861 and 1865, more than 260,000 uniformed Army and Navy personnel died in suppressing what was then known in the North as "the Rebellion." Anger against the Confederacy and its leaders ran deep in many northern homes.

When the war ended, however, an embittered Virginian killed Abraham Lincoln, and Andrew Johnson became president. In 1865 he began issuing pardons to Confederate officials and inviting them to reassume control of their state governments and to run for federal office.

Northern members of Congress were far less forgiving. The spectacle of former gray-clad generals and Confederate governors sitting in Congress was one they resented and feared. (Some Northerners actually feared that General Robert E. Lee would be the Democratic presidential nominee in 1868.) Section Three addresses this concern. It is the only amendment to the Constitution that explicitly restricts any power of the president.

Under Article II, Section Two, Clause One, the president has the power to "Grant Reprieves and Pardons for Offenses against the United States, except in Cases of Impeachment." Section Three does not take away that power. My friends' forebears were immune from criminal prosecution for any part they may have played in the war. (My own ancestors, being smaller fish, were covered by a blanket pardon issued by Johnson in 1867 that covered all those who owned less than a certain amount of property and held no high office.)[16]

A pardon ordinarily restores all civil rights, including the right to vote, to serve on juries, and to hold public office. But Section Three was designed to ensure that *Congress*, not the president, would decide who wielded political power after the Civil War. And political power, beyond the mere act of voting, would be withheld from that group of people who had sworn an individual oath before secession to support the Constitution and had then violated that oath by joining the Confederacy.

There were three classes of such people: (1) former members of the United States Congress; (2) appointed federal officials and US military officers (both were "officer[s] of the United States"); and (3) state officials, whether judges, legislators, or executive officials, who had taken the oath prescribed for all state officials in Article VI, Section Two, to regard the Constitution as "the supreme law of the land." If anyone meeting this description had joined the Confederate cause by "engag[ing] in insurrection or rebellion against the same, or giv[ing] aid or comfort to the enemies thereof," he was barred from certain political offices. These forbidden offices are, in order, (1) member of Congress; (2) presidential elector; (3) officer of the United States, meaning an appointed official either in the military or in the civil government; and (4) *state* officer of any kind.

This text makes two major constitutional changes. The first is that, for the first time, the federal Constitution now assumed the role of dictating who could hold *state* office, reaching into the state's own laws and constitutions to add an additional qualification for office. Nowhere before in the Constitution has there been a *federal* qualification for state office. True, under Article VI, Section Two, state officials must swear to uphold the federal Constitution. But there's no bar against persons of any age, sex, religion, or immigration status, as long as they were willing to swear or affirm. Those qualifications were the concern of the states. But now the Constitution takes from states at least one part of that decision, and tells them who may serve in their legislatures, in their courts, and in their governments.

The second change is that a small part of the president's pardon power is shaved off and given to Congress. The only way that a former Confederate official can become eligible for federal office is by a two-thirds vote of both Houses of Congress. (In 1882, the postwar political crisis over, Congress enacted a measure providing blanket pardon for any former Confederates who still wanted to serve in office.)[17]

In practical terms, Section Three has no impact today. But it sheds light on the Fourteenth Amendment generally. First, like Section Two, it is concerned with political power, a huge theme of the entire amendment. Second, it cuts back the president's power—power that had grown during the Civil War, as it does during all wars—and shows a desire to expand Congress's power. Third, it restricts the authority of the states to run their own affairs—just as does Section One.

One useful exercise in reading the Fourteenth Amendment is to note the number of changes it makes to the original document. Each one may be small, but together we might read them as making not just change but actual transformation.

SECTION FOUR. "Follow the money," Deep Throat hissed in the film *All the President's Men.* Good advice in all matters political. Politics, even at the constitutional level, is at its heart about money: who prints it, who pays it, who gets it. Money is a theme in the original Constitution, written by men who understood it and who feared that the new nation would never have enough. The government may tax; it may borrow, repay, and spend. It may control the flow of money to and from abroad, with Indian nations, and among the states; it may determine who gets the protection of bankruptcy, and how that protection will apply. It may issue coin and currency, and punish those who counterfeit it. ("To counterfeit is death," read a legend on much early American money; in medieval English law, counterfeiting was treason, and in contemporary international law, it is, when done by a government, a crime of war.) It may grant limited monopolies to artists and inventors. Like all legislatures, Congress governs through money and controls the states with it. (Most federal programs work by granting money to states, which they may accept and spend only if they agree to Congress's conditions.) Government has been defined as a monopoly of violence; in peaceful times, it may more usefully be described as a monopoly on money.

Section Two of the amendment shows an anxiety about who will be allowed to vote and what states will exercise power in the new government; Section Three expresses worry over who will represent and govern those states; Section Four's fearful language expresses concern over what will happen to the public treasury when the slave states return to full status in the Union. Section Four lays down unbreakable conditions about expenditure of money, and those conditions bind the states as well as the federal government.

Historically, the United States had almost no debt between about 1830 and 1861. But the Civil War was financed almost entirely by borrowing, and the debt had expanded by more than thirty times during the war years. With peace, the bill would come due.

Note the debt that is most explicitly protected: "debts incurred for payment of pensions and bounties for services in suppressing insurrection or rebellion." The fear seems to be that the wrong people will win office; that they will be over-represented in Congress; and that they will repudiate the war debt.

But the language is sweeping. It doesn't say that the debt "must be paid," or "shall not be repudiated." It doesn't even say that it shall be "paid on time" or "in full." It says the debt "shall not be questioned." This almost seems like another command directed at private citizens as well as the government, as if it ruled out of public discussion any questioning of the national debt. Michael Abramowicz, one of the foremost scholars of this section of the Constitution, quotes in his work a *New York Times* report from the mid-1980s of a lone protester who stood near the White House holding a sign reading "Arrest Me. I Question the Validity of the Public Debt. Repeal Section 4, Fourteenth Amendment to the U.S. Constitution."[18]

The Supreme Court, in the only case to interpret this section, read it as an unqualified command to the government:

> While this provision was undoubtedly inspired by the desire to put beyond question the obligations of the government issued during the Civil War, its language indicates a broader connotation. We regard it as confirmatory of a fundamental principle which applies as well to the government bonds in question, and to others duly authorized by the Congress, as to those issued before the amendment was adopted. Nor can we perceive any reason for not considering the expression "the validity of the public debt" as embracing whatever concerns the integrity of the public obligations.[19]

Drawing on this sweeping language, some constitutional scholars (I was one)[20] suggested during the debt-ceiling crisis of 2011 that, if the Congress refused to approve borrowing necessary to repay the interest and principal due on US securities, the president might have not only the power but the duty (under the provision requiring him to "take care that the laws be faithfully executed") to continue borrowing despite the debt-ceiling statute's prohibition. Absurd as it may seem, return to the claims made for presidential authority under Article II. While Congress clearly has sole authority to *appropriate* funds, the text is not so clear about *borrowing* money to repay debts incurred for previous appropriations. Beginning with Alexander Hamilton, executive hawks have claimed for the president any power "executive in nature" that was not forbidden in so many words. For a few weeks the question of the meaning of this obscure provision of the Fourteenth Amendment was the center of public attention. When President Obama publicly said that "my lawyers" did not believe that was a "winning argument," the interest subsided.[21]

Beyond the fear that government would not repay its debts, Section Four also shows a fear that government will pay too much.

The first clause of Section Four lays out what debts must be paid; the second sets out debts that can never be paid: no "debt or obligation incurred in aid of insurrection or rebellion against the United States, or any claim for the loss or emancipation of any slave." Just like the Union, the Confederate States of America (CSA) had run its war on debt and paper money. Confederate state governments, too, had issued bonds and notes, and bought uniforms and food and weapons with them. The Confederate promise could not be kept, but those who had accepted it still quietly hoped to be paid by the Union. Some were wealthy Southerners who had staked their all on a victory for the slave confederacy; others were cold-eyed European speculators who held large amounts of Confederate cotton bonds.

Section Four tells them, in the words of the Man in Black in the film *The Princess Bride*, to get used to disappointment. The CSA's debts would never be repaid, even if former Confederates eventually took over Congress and the White House. The money borrowed by the "seceding" states would never be repaid either. In addition, no former master would ever receive government indemnity for loss of slaves to the Emancipation Proclamation and the Thirteenth Amendment—a provision that to some Southerners abrogated the Fifth Amendment's promise of "just compensation" for the loss of "private property."

All together, the first four sections tell the South that it could not reassemble the oppressive state governments of the antebellum era; it could not gain federal political power for "representing" citizens it treated as lacking rights; it could not empower the old pro-slavery leadership; and it could never hope to turn government's financial monopoly to its advantage. Legal scholar David Strauss once characterized the Civil War Amendments "as something in the nature of a treaty, reflecting the outcome of the war," and the Fourteenth Amendment can certainly be read as the conqueror dictating terms to the conquered, much in the manner of the Constitution of Japan.[22] From now on, it says, politics will be played by victors' rules. The norms will be democracy, inclusion, freedom, and equality. The United States Congress will interpret and enforce them. And those who seek in state governments a base and a weapon to subvert the new rules will pay a price.

SECTION FIVE. But when the treaty's terms are violated, who presents the bill? Over the past century and a half, the courts have monitored compliance. In the twenty-first century, the Supreme Court has fashioned a doctrine giving itself control of interpretation of Section One, with Congress playing a subordinate role. Civil rights statutes can be enforced against the states, Justice Anthony Kennedy wrote, only if they satisfy the courts that they possess "congruence and proportionality" to the violation of rights they address.[23]

This idea is one of the curiosities of American constitutional law. It is not simply that those words appear nowhere in the amendment, or indeed in the Constitution. It is that the amendment makes *no reference at all* to courts as central to its workings, while over and over it references Congress as the focus of its concern: congressional representation in Section Two; congressional membership in Section Three; congressional appropriations in Section Four. Section One, however, is the part that is chiefly at issue in disputes today. When does a state law violate "due process" or "equal protection"? How, and by whom, is this to be decided?

Section Five provides the only guidance, and it points to Congress as the enforcer of all four sections. Just as in Section Two of the Thirteenth Amendment, Congress now has the power, "by appropriate legislation," to enforce the amendment. That could be taken to mean that Congress, representing the people, would now determine by open debate and majority vote the civil rights the states must grant and the political rules the states would follow. This reading is logical in textual terms and corresponds to the history. The authors of the amendment were members of Congress struggling to assert authority amid postwar chaos. They were also profoundly distrustful of federal courts, which had—as in *Dred Scott*—been bulwarks of slavery during the years before Fort Sumter. The words Congress wrote seem to have placed itself in the center of the new American republic.

The courts, however, have placed themselves there instead. The result has been to delay the expansion of civil rights and equality, sometimes by many decades. In 1883, the Supreme Court voided Congress's Civil Rights Act, designed to prevent the growth of a segregated system in the South. The Court, not Congress, would decide the extent of federal authority and the reasonableness of racial restrictions, it declared.[24] The result was nearly a century of segregation, violence, and exclusion in the Old South—of a kind of uncanny victory of the defeated. And in 1964, when the nation finally mustered the political will to reestablish Union victory in the South, Congress was forced to use the Commerce Power rather than Section Five as the basis of its power.

The court in the past twenty years has cut back on the enforcement power of the Fourteenth Amendment again, seizing on one word, "appropriate," in a 400-word amendment, and using it to establish themselves as its sole arbiters. "When I make a word do a lot of work like that," says Humpty-Dumpty to Alice in Lewis Carroll's *Through the Looking Glass*, "I always pay it extra."[25]

Fifteenth Amendment

Consider this instruction to a house-sitter: "Don't let the dog out at night. Don't feed the dog dry food." The homeowner returns six weeks later to find the dog dead of starvation. The house-sitter explains, "You never said there actually *was* a dog or that if there was one I should feed it, just that I shouldn't let it out or feed it dry food. I did neither."

Would that explanation satisfy the owner?

Well, many of our most cherished rights are guaranteed in the kind of language the homeowner uses. For example, the First Amendment does not say, "everybody has freedom of speech and of religion"; it prohibits Congress from making laws infringing on religious freedom and our freedom of speech. But you would not say that it does not *guarantee* free speech and religion.

What, then, about the right to vote? It has appeared once in the Constitution already, but whatever Section Two of the Fourteenth Amendment means, it really can't mean that everyone must be allowed to vote. It penalizes states that withhold the ballot but does not require them to grant it. In the Fifteenth Amendment, this right is now explicitly mentioned under a new label: "the right of citizens of the United States to vote."

In this form, it will appear a total of three more times, each time now protected against abridgment, as an individual right "of citizens," one that can be enforced by both courts and Congress. Yet courts and citizens remain oddly ambivalent about it; it is common to regard voting as a "privilege," an incident of citizenship granted to some but not all. The "privilege" over the years has been made dependent on literacy, or long residency in a community, or ability to prove identity, or lack of a criminal past. None of these conditions would be allowed to restrict free speech, or freedom from "unreasonable" searches, or the right to counsel. Each of those rights is mentioned once in the Constitution. The right to vote of citizens of the United States, however, remains a kind of stepchild in the family of American rights, perhaps because it is not listed in the Bill of

Rights, and perhaps because Americans still retain the Framers' ambivalence about democracy.

In the Fifteenth Amendment, the right to vote is not to be "denied or abridged on account of race, color, or previous condition of servitude." Note first the verb. Many things might "abridge" a right without "denying" it altogether. Whatever the status of the right as a right, it is apparently quite strictly protected from any kind of limit—any kind of limit, that is, based on "race, color, or previous condition of servitude." The target is clear—racial restrictions on voting, or restrictions of the voting rights of former slaves. It is commonplace, thus, to describe the amendment as aimed solely at racial restrictions on the right to vote.

But that description slights part of the text. The amendment mentions "race" and "color"; but those aren't the only grounds of discrimination it forbids. It also uses the word "servitude," echoing the Thirteenth Amendment's prohibition not only of slavery but of "involuntary servitude, except as a punishment for crime whereof the party shall have been duly convicted."

The choice of the word "servitude" interacts intriguingly with the text of the Thirteenth Amendment. That is, "slavery" is prohibited, as is "involuntary servitude *except as a punishment for crime*." This language certainly foresaw that in the future, convicts might be put to hard labor, as indeed they were. (One recent book remembered the conditions in the twentieth-century Parchman Farm prison in Mississippi as "worse than slavery.")[26] But that kind of "servitude" is not mentioned in the Fifteenth Amendment; the omission suggests that conviction of crime in and of itself would *not* be an acceptable reason for restricting "the right to vote." Even convicted criminals must be afforded the right in its fullest extent.

In this reading, only felons actively serving prison terms could be barred from voting—their "condition of servitude" would be present, not "previous." The laborious process of civil-rights restoration imposed by many states (in 2010, one southern governor briefly proposed a requirement that every free felon write him a personal letter outlining his or her contributions to society, permitting the governor to decide in his discretion whether to allow the offender to reclaim his right to vote and to serve on juries)[27] seems contrary not only to the spirit but also to the letter of the Fifteenth Amendment.

One can understand questions about felons on juries. But "the right of citizens of the United States to vote" is more strongly protected in the text than jury service. It is the only right in the Constitution to be protected in terms of "previous condition of servitude." These words demand that we give them a meaning commensurate with their extent.

SECTION TWO. Once again, Congress is given the power to enforce the amendment "by appropriate legislation." The Supreme Court has taken as narrow a view of this power as it has of the first two such grants. It is the Court that has repeatedly written of the right to vote in scare quotes, as "the right" to vote, as if it were somehow questionable or inferior to other rights. That reading seems as strained as the house-sitter's construction of a reference to a "dog" as forbidding certain kinds of dog food but permitting him to starve the dog to death.

CONCLUSION. The language, tempo, and tone of the Constitution have changed rapidly during this burst of amendment. One can easily read these three measures as creating a new Republic on the ashes of the old: a Republic with a strong, even radical, constitutional commitment to political participation, despite any obstacle the state governments may devise to restrict or burden it, and a tentative but genuine decision to move toward human equality

These amendments were written at a time when recalcitrant state governments, and the doctrines of state's rights, state sovereignty, and nullification, had nearly destroyed the entire constitutional structure. Many readers discern in the original Constitution a concern to protect state governments from the federal government. In the text of the 1787 document and the Bill of Rights, that concern is elusive, and overshadowed by an emphasis on the power and prerogatives of the federal government. In the Civil War Amendments, state governments, far from being an object of constitutional solicitude, seem to be the enemy, with Congress designated as the force to lead them toward what Walt Whitman, writing at about the time the Fifteenth Amendment was ratified, called "Democratic Vistas."

A Burst of Reform

Sixteenth, Seventeenth, Eighteenth, and
Nineteenth Amendments

After the Civil War, the text of the Constitution remained fixed for nearly half a century, as if the nation were trying to digest the new commitments—to liberty, equality, inclusion, and democracy—it had taken on. Then, between 1913 and 1920, the nation saw a startling burst of amendments—all the product, one way or the other, of the Progressive impulse to reform, democratize, and empower government. Some of these reforms (votes for women) were overdue; at least one (prohibition) was the product of a mistaken view of government's power to command virtue in the people. Taken together, however, they mark a constitutional watershed, one that should be carefully studied for the new chapter they write in the national epic. They are the legacy of the Progressive Era, an ill-understood period when the American people banded together to demand that their government, and their Constitution, reflect the demands of a democratic society and a modern form of government.

Sixteenth Amendment

The 1787 Constitution contained expansive power to lay federal taxes, with only one exception: "direct taxes," which must be "apportioned according to population." This meant that the amount of money collected by such a tax from the people of a state must amount only to a proportional share of the total amount collected. A state possessing 20 percent of the nation's population, then, must be required to pay 20 percent of the total amount raised, regardless of whether its people were the richest or the poorest in the Union.

At the time of the Constitution's adoption, no one was quite sure how to define "direct taxes." Those confident we can know what the Framers or ratifiers meant by their words might ponder this, the most edifying discussion of the "direct taxes" provision to be found in Madison's *Notes* from the Philadelphia Convention: "Mr. King asked what was the precise meaning of *direct* taxation? No one answ[ere]d."[1] A century later, this uncertainty sabotaged the government's effort to raise funds by taxing income.

The first income tax in American history was imposed by statute in 1861 and expired at the end of the Civil War. The Supreme Court upheld the wartime tax in 1881. At the Convention, it noted, "[i]t does not appear that an attempt was made by anyone to define the exact meaning of the language employed."[2] Since then, the Court continued, "the text writers of the country are in entire accord" that the term referred exclusively either to head taxes or to real-estate taxes. An income tax, the Court said, was an excise or a duty.[3]

In 1894, Congress for the first time enacted a peacetime income tax, and a different Supreme Court, the next year, invoked the "direct taxes" language to hold the tax unconstitutional. Chief Justice Melville Fuller, with the breezy confidence of a man who could read the minds of the dead, wrote, "It is apparent that the distinction between direct and indirect taxes was well understood by the framers of the constitution and those who adopted it."[4]

What followed that decision seems almost incomprehensible to residents of twenty-first-century America, where the only word more reviled than "government" is "taxes." But between 1894 and 1913, popular movements demanded that the government have the power to "soak the rich" by proportioning taxes to income. Progressives, populists, and Western free-silverites adopted the cry; more remarkably, so did President William Howard Taft. The Sixteenth Amendment was proposed by Congress in 1909. In 1912, all three major presidential candidates—Taft, Theodore Roosevelt, and Woodrow Wilson—actively supported it. It became part of the Constitution in 1913.

Under its terms, Congress can tax incomes "from whatever source derived without apportionment among the several States, and without regard to any census or enumeration." The amendment carefully adds that Congress can not only "lay" a tax on incomes, but may also "collect" the tax. The language is robust. It is the textual legacy of a remarkable historic moment in which the people and political leaders agreed that the federal government should have a new power, one that most citizens find formidable, and that the new power should be framed in the most sweeping terms possible.

Even with that sweeping language, figures on the contemporary legal fringe have found ways to insist that it doesn't mean what it says. Wages, they say, are not "income," and for that reason the income tax as we know it is actually a "direct tax" and thus must be apportioned among the states. One pair of tax protesters, Mr. and Mrs. Eugene Lonsdale, made that argument to a federal court in 1981. As for the "direct tax" argument, the Court noted that the requirement of apportionment "was eliminated by the Sixteenth Amendment."[5]

The Lonsdales also argued that wages cannot be "income": they told the court that "the exchange of services for money is a zero-sum transaction, the value of the wages being exactly that of the labor exchanged for them and hence containing no element of profit." Replied the court, "This contention is meritless." (The court also patiently noted that a number of the arguments advanced by the Lonsdales were "partly theological. The latter, being beyond our special competence or jurisdiction, we are unable to consider.")

The "direct tax" argument, however, lives on in many quarters, not all of them laughable. During arguments over the constitutionality of the Patient Protection and Affordable Care Act ("Obamacare"), lawyers challenging the "individual mandate" provision argued that this required payment by the uninsured was a "direct tax."

In an opinion by Chief Justice Roberts for a majority of the justices, the Court responded:

> Even when the Direct Tax Clause was written it was unclear what else, other than a capitation (also known as a "head tax" or a "poll tax"), might be a direct tax. After the framing, Congress passed a tax on ownership of carriages, over James Madison's objection that it was an unapportioned direct tax. This Court upheld the tax, in part reasoning that apportioning such a tax would make little sense, because it would have required taxing carriage owners at dramatically different rates depending on how many carriages were in their home State. The Court was unanimous, and those Justices who wrote opinions either directly asserted or strongly suggested that only two forms of taxation were direct: capitations and land taxes. . . . A tax on going without health insurance does not fall within any recognized category of direct tax.[6]

Seventeenth Amendment

After the 2008 election, Illinois Governor Rod Blagojevich faced a momentous choice: whom would he appoint as temporary senator to replace Barack Obama, who had just been elected president of the United States? Wiretaps of Blagojevich's phone conversations (under way as part of a larger bribery investigation) produced a remarkable summary of the nature of his power: a Senate seat "is a f***ing valuable thing, you just don't give it away for nothing."[7] Blagojevich first considered appointing himself, then offered to let Obama name the replacement in exchange for a Cabinet position for himself. Blagojevich was later impeached, convicted of bribery, and sent to federal prison; but his eventual appointee, Roland Burris, served the entire remainder of Obama's term.

The appointment provisions of the Seventeenth Amendment create a constitutional aberration, which seems out of keeping with the structure of the document. In no other instance in the American system is an important government
job filled by the sole decision of one human being. For any other such position,
either popular election, or presidential nomination and the advice and consent
of the Senate, is required. The tawdry saga of Blagojevich and Burris illustrates
how a constitutional change designed to enhance democracy has had the unintended effect of occasionally empowering governors to cash in, politically or
otherwise, on a Senate vacancy.

In Article I, Section Three, of the original Constitution, the Senate was "composed of two Senators from each State, chosen by the Legislature thereof." The
legislatures in the eighteenth century were not in continuous session; some met
only once every two years. (Even today, many state legislatures are in session
only for a very small part of the time.) So Section Three specified a means of
filling vacancies: "if Vacancies happen by Resignation, or otherwise, during the
Recess of the Legislature of any State, the Executive thereof may make temporary Appointments until the next Meeting of the Legislature, which shall then
fill such Vacancies." A "temporary appointment" then ended at "the next meeting
of the legislature," at which legislators were *required* to fill the Senate vacancy.

The original Senate was designed as a direct representative of state governments in the federal legislature. The House was to be the "popular branch." The
Seventeenth Amendment was adopted in 1913, at almost exactly the same time
as the Sixteenth. In effect, it creates a new Senate, consisting of two senators per
state, "elected by the people thereof," and repeats that "each Senator shall have
one vote." Because the amendment was proposed by Congress before ratification (as Article V required), it is a startlingly rare instance of a powerful legislative body in effect voting to put itself out of existence and subject its members
to a new and highly uncertain process for reelection. So much attention was
focused on inducing the Senate to abolish itself, and so many calculations went
into designing its text, that no one apparently noticed that it introduced a new
indeterminacy into the text. The amendment was inspired by enthusiasm for
popular democracy but accidentally opened up the opportunity for a new highly
undemocratic procedure when Senate seats become vacant.

For more than two decades before the amendment passed Congress, reformers had argued that the legislative appointment process had opened the
door for special interests to dominate the Senate and corrupt the state legislatures. In a 1909 book called *The Treason of the Senate*, muckraking journalist
David Graham Philips profiled the Senate of his time—disproportionately
wealthy and, he said, entirely subservient to the interests of giant corporations.[8]
"Treason" (by which he meant treason to the interests of the people) is a strong
word, but Phillips's work, and other writing on the Senate, amplified popular

outrage until nothing could stand in its way. The Seventeenth Amendment finally brought to fruition a reform first proposed in 1826.

The new Senate is "elected by the people" of each state just as the House is, and the voters, like voters for the House, "shall have the qualifications requisite for electors of the most numerous branch of the State legislatures." (This language was contested; when the proposed amendment was pending, the southern members of the Senate attempted to bargain their votes for language allowing them to exclude black voters from Senate elections. Popular anger, which steamrollered all objections, made this cynical ploy untenable.)

The Senate is now, at least in theory, also the people's house. While making selection of senators more democratic in one way, however, it inadvertently made it less so in another. When a member of the House resigns, as we have seen, "the executive authority," or governor, "shall issue writs of election to fill such vacancies." There is no authority to appoint a caretaker. House vacancies are often filled by special election in a matter of weeks.

The Seventeenth Amendment's provisions for filling vacancies begin with precisely the same language as does the previous provision regarding the House: "the executive authority of such State shall issue writs of election to fill such vacancies." But then there is a limitation on the principle. For vacant Senate seats, (1) "the executive authority ... *shall* issue writs of election"... (2) "*Provided* that (3) the legislature of any State may empower the executive thereof to make (4) temporary appointments *until* (5) the people fill the vacancies (6) by election (7) as the legislature may direct."

Many Americans believe that the Constitution "gives" governors power to name replacement senators. It's easy to understand their confusion. The original Constitution *did* give governors that power. But the words in (1), especially the mandatory word "shall," actually state that the norm in replacing elected senators is another election, not a temporary appointment.

The exception begins with (2), "provided that." This term instantly gets the attention of any lawyer. The text could have said, "however," or simply "or"; instead, it begins with a highly technical term. When "provided that" is used in a statute, it is usually read as what is called a "proviso," which is a limited exception to a general rule. In statutes, it is hornbook law that a proviso is to be "construed strictly," meaning that its limitation on the general rule should be as narrow as possible. The purpose of a statute, lawyers say, is often to remedy a "mischief." Reading provisos broadly might allow the exception to eviscerate or even swallow the rule, leaving the "mischief," whatever it is, untouched.

As we have said earlier, we aren't construing a statute, however, but a constitution, and the ordinary "canons" of statutory construction don't necessarily apply. Nonetheless, it is striking that the authors of the amendment chose this lawyers' term when introducing the exception; if a broader, more "constitutional" reading of the amendment as a whole is proper, that wouldn't necessarily mean that the exception should also be broadened; instead, it might be equally logical to conclude that the *entire amendment*, with its under-lying preference for election, should be broadly read, and the exception read more narrowly. (That reading, like so much in interpretation, spawns its own opposite, a "state's rights" reading, which I will set out after we finish analyzing the "proviso.")

To repeat, the amendment sets out an apparent requirement that the gover-nor issue a "writ of election," which means schedule a special election to fill the seat. But under (3), the legislature *may*, if it chooses, "empower" the governor (by state statute) to make (4) "*temporary* appointments." What does the word "temporary" mean here? Could the legislature "empower" the governor to ap-point a new senator to serve the old senator's entire unexpired term? That would be "temporary" in one sense—it wouldn't last more than last six years at the most, depending on how long the old senators had already served.

But that *can't* be what the word "temporary" means here, because no senator, elected *or* appointed, can hold a seat beyond the "term of six years" provided for in Section One of the Amendment. An appointment for the entire unexpired term would thus be, in constitutional terms, a "permanent" appointment, and a violation of the text. What marks the end of a "temporary" appointment? It ends when "(5) the people fill the vacancies (6) by election." Oh, wait, you may think—then appointing a senator for the entire unexpired term might be a "tem-porary" appointment; after all, the temporary appointment ends in an election. But wait again—that election does not "fill" the vacancy caused by death or res-ignation; that vacancy ceases to exist at the end of the previous six-year term, and the new election chooses someone to serve a new six-year term in the Senate. If that's right, then the writ of election must produce a new elected senator who will serve for at least some part of the old senator's unexpired term.

The point is worth belaboring because each state picks its own mode of "empower[ing] the executive" to make a temporary appointment. Some few states do not allow their governors to make "temporary" appointments at all; when a senator resigns, the state holds a special election as soon as it can and forgoes Senate representation until the election is held. In other states, the gov-ernor appoints until a special election, held as soon as possible. In yet others, however, the governor appoints until a "special" election, which not held until the next "regular" election. This can be as long as two years—as it was in the case of Roland Burriss, and two years was the entire remainder of Barack Obama's term. By the language of the statute, the Illinois legislature managed to take the norm of "election by the people" out of the process altogether.

Here's another textual conundrum. Suppose the legislature passed no legis-lation at all dealing with Senate vacancies—did not provide for temporary appointment and did not provide for special election. In that case, the text suggests, the governor would be obligated to issue a "writ of election." The state would have to hold an election regardless of its own law. But if the legislature *allows* temporary appointment, the picture changes. Vacancies, if they are preceded by a "temporary" appointment, are to be filled "by special election as the legislature may provide."

The permissiveness of the text about state legislation and executive appointment is important because they give rise to intricate dances of dueling party and personal ambition. Governors usually want to nominate a temporary senator of their own party. Legislatures sometimes wish to encourage this aim, and sometimes to thwart it. Legislatures quite commonly make changes in their law regarding executive appointment—changes inspired by their perception of what will help their party retain the seat. In Massachusetts, for example, the Democratic legislature repealed executive appointment when Republican Mitt Romney was governor; they later restored it when, with Democrat Deval Patrick in the statehouse, Senator Edward Kennedy could be replaced quickly with a reliable vote in favor of the health-care bill then pending in Congress.

(Ironically, the appointment probably cost them the seat in the end. Had there been a special election directly after Kennedy's death, a Democrat would almost certainly have won; but by the time the "temporary" appointment expired a year later, the Democrats' political troubles swept a Republican into that office for the first time in three decades. Whatever party one favors, there's something fitting in seeing politicians outsmart themselves as they try to manipulate seats in the Senate.)

If we think that a broad reading of the policy of election makes sense, then we might conclude two things: first, that a "temporary" appointment to the Senate should last as short a time as possible; and second, that a governor exercising the power to make temporary amendments ought not to consider himself the "owner" of a "f****ing valuable thing" to be auctioned for personal or party advantage, but a trustee of the people's office, responsible to maximize their representation and their electoral choice.

But as promised, there is at least one other way to read the amendment. If we come into it with a belief that the rest of the Constitution is about protecting state governments and their rights, then we could look at the whole situation very differently—the whole proviso might mean that states should have the maximum flexibility to fashion their own procedures for replacing senators. Executive appointment for the rest of the term would be permissible; appointment until a special election would also be fine. The proviso, to such a reader, would be the important part of this sentence; the "writ of election" language would be there only for one purpose—to set up a means of filling a Senate vacancy in the unlikely case that a state legislature passed no law at all to do so. I frankly think that interpretation is wrong; but I cannot say it is ridiculous. To me, it seems slightly strained; to other readers it may make more sense than mine.

As so often in constitutional interpretation, one's overall philosophy and view of the document powerfully shape the meaning one gives to the words. And this is an issue that political actors and voters have been forced to negotiate without a great deal of help from the courts. The only Supreme Court case in this area concerned a statute that awarded the entire remainder—twenty-nine months— of a Senate term to a temporary appointee. The lower court had held that the amendment "grants the states some reasonable degree of discretion concerning both the time of vacancy elections and the procedures to be used in selecting candidates for such elections."[9] When those who objected to the proceedings appealed to the Supreme Court, it affirmed the lower court without bothering to issue an opinion.[10]

But the issue is still alive, not settled by the Court's silence. In 2009, after the appointment of Burris, a group of Illinois voters brought suit against Blagojevich arguing that the "temporary appointment" language bars a system that awards the entire unexpired term to an executive appointee. The voters' lawyers (not to be coy, I was one) also argued that the "writ of election" language required the governor to issue a writ for some election instead of simply waiting for the next general election, which would happen without a writ.

The result was a glorious victory for close textual reading. The US Court of Appeals for the Seventh Circuit analyzed the proviso and the amendment as a whole for twenty pages of small print, and held that by the amendment's terms, the governor *was* required to issue a writ of election before the next regular election.[11] Unfortunately, by that time almost all of Obama's term was past, and there was only time to organize a special election at the same time as the 2010 general election. As a result, when Illinois voters went to the polls in November 2010, they were given ballots for two senatorial elections. The first, conducted pursuant to a writ, chose a replacement senator to serve the sixty-two days remaining on Burris's term; the second chose a senator to serve the entire six-year term beginning in January 2011.

This may seem a small victory; but there is no doubt that Senator Mark Kirk, who was elected to both seats, appreciates it. Because of the Seventh Circuit's decision, he was sworn in as a senator immediately. Thus he was senior to the five other Republicans elected that year, a small but crucial advantage to him and the people of Illinois—and perhaps a good reason that governors would do well to heed the words of the Seventeenth Amendment.

And even if they don't, they should profit from Blago's story. A vacant Senate seat, whatever the state legislature may provide, is never a governor's property. It belongs—so says the Seventeenth Amendment—to the people.

Eighteenth Amendment

"Future generations will marvel that there was a time when men drank poison for pleasure."

Those were the last words of an American history textbook I found on my grandmother's bookshelf when I was a child. The book was published in 1920, at the dawn of a dry utopia in which alcohol use was expected to become a faint, barbaric memory.

To contemporary readers, Prohibition doesn't seem like a reform; but in its inception, the prohibition movement was idealistic, optimistic, and future-oriented. It was supported by many of the same high-minded citizens who championed the income tax and direct election of senators.

The Eighteenth Amendment, which embodied their idealistic effort to make America a "dry" country, was adopted in 1919. It has a number of distinctions: it's the only amendment to prohibit (or even discuss) a specific product; it's the only amendment to grant additional power to state governments as well as to the federal government; it's the only amendment to contain a provision delaying its effects for a year after ratification; it's the first amendment to provide in its terms that it had to be ratified within a certain term of years after being proposed by Congress. It has today one other distinction it did not have when it was adopted: it is the only constitutional amendment ever to be explicitly and totally repealed.

The tone of the amendment reflects the rise of statutory diction, which will increasingly make its way into the text of new amendments. We need a statutory diagram to understand with what specificity it sets out its scope and jurisdictional reach: "(1) the (a) manufacture, (b) sale, or (c) transportation of (2) intoxicating liquors (3) (a) within, (b) the importation thereof into, (b) or the exportation thereof from (4) (a) the United States and (b) all territory subject to the jurisdiction (5) for beverage purposes (6) is hereby prohibited."

The amendment's target is not "alcohol"; it is not even "alcohol fit for or intended for human consumption." Doctors use alcohol for many purposes (and even in the depth of prohibition, many citizens were grateful for prescriptions from their physicians of various forms of spirits supposedly "for medicinal purposes only"). In addition, the Catholic Church, some Protestant denominations, and even Jewish congregations use wine for sacramental purposes. Occasionally, the wine was even "intoxicating"—on Purim, which celebrates the delivery of Israel from Amalek, some rabbis in temple still follow the traditional command to become so drunk that they do not know whether they are saying "Cursed be Haiman" or "Blessed be Mordechai."

The Volstead Act, which carried Prohibition into the US Code, carefully exempted "liquor for nonbeverage purposes and wine for sacramental purposes," though religious bodies were required to obtain government permits for them.[12] Could the federal government have forbidden alcohol distribution even without the amendment by use, say, of the Commerce Power? National Prohibition had in fact been introduced before the adoption of the Eighteenth Amendment, but under the War Power of Congress—the theory being that the use of grains and grapes to manufacture beverages interfered with the growing of food for the troops in France.

The act allowed the brewing of wine or beer at home for personal consumption. And that brings us to the Eighteenth Amendment's scope. It forbade "manufacture," "sale," "transportation," "importation," and "exportation" of "intoxicating liquors." Conspicuous by their absence were "possession" and "consumption," or even "distribution" if done without exchange of value—as in offering dinner guests a drink of homemade wine "for medicinal purposes only." The amendment was carefully drawn to avoid the spectacle of revenue agents invading the parlor to confiscate half-bottles of Aunt Dahlia's elderberry cordial, and statutes implementing it forbade the search of private homes for illicit alcohol.

But if that provided a small personal space exempt from the reach of Prohibition, the amendment applied everywhere else: its ban on importation and exportation applied to the territory of the United States "and all territory subject to the jurisdiction" of the government. This matches the stern language of the Thirteenth Amendment, which prohibits slavery "within the United States, or any place subject to their jurisdiction."

The amendment forbade the distribution of alcohol, but it did not forbid laying taxes on that same activity. Not long after its adoption, the federal government arrested a South Carolina auto dealer named Manly Sullivan. The sale of spirituous liquors, the government said, had netted him the princely sum of $10,000 a year—well over $100,000 in today's economy. He was charged with failing to file an income-tax return. At his trial, Sullivan protested that the tax laws could not apply to illegal income; such illicit gains, his lawyer argued, were "beneath the contempt of the law for purposes of taxation."[13]

The United States Supreme Court, in a pithy opinion by Justice Oliver Wendell Holmes, brushed aside Sullivan's protests. The Court did not see "any reason why the fact that a business is unlawful should exempt it from paying the taxes that if lawful it would have to pay." In that opinion, Holmes drew not on United States law, but on a decision by the Privy Council of England, and on an aphorism he had delivered in an earlier case: "Of course Congress may tax what it also forbids."[14]

The Thirteenth Amendment, as we noted earlier, forbade slavery of its own force, without any need for implementing legislation: "neither slavery nor involuntary servitude . . . shall exist within the United States." The Eighteenth has some of the same near-fanatical tone. It might have been expected to provide that "Congress shall have the power" to outlaw the trade in liquor; but it goes further, stating that all its incidents are "hereby prohibited." Future Congresses would have no power to tolerate the liquor business, or even to narrow the scope of Prohibition.

The Constitution by its terms does not prohibit murder, or prostitution, or fraud, or any number of other heinous offenses by private persons against peace and good order. As of the adoption of the Eighteenth Amendment, it prohibited two and only two private wrongs—holding slaves and selling alcohol. As central constitutional values, the two made an uneasy pair.

SECTION TWO. The amendment also gives Congress power to enforce Prohibition. Section Two, however, goes further. It gives "Congress and the several States . . . concurrent power to enforce this article by appropriate legislation." Many states already had their own Prohibition laws by the time the amendment was adopted. But this language was not needed to preserve those state laws, because there was little serious question that states, if they chose, could use their so-called police power to outlaw liquor and the liquor trade within their borders.

Section Two makes clear that federal Prohibition is of the highest constitutional priority. Not even the Thirteenth Amendment invited the states to join the crusade against slave masters. That may be because in abolishing slavery, the Constitution was annexing territory the states had always held and acting in opposition to many state laws. With Prohibition, however, the Constitution paired the federal government with the states, and invited them to become partners in what President Herbert Hoover (who had a gift for the unfortunate phrase) once called "a great social and economic experiment, noble in motive and far-reaching in purpose."[15]

SECTION THREE. The first sentence of Section One set out a date on which the amendment was to take effect: "one year from the ratification of this article." Section Three sets up another kind of limitation, in a new kind of provision that has become standard in proposed amendments. The amendment, proposed in 1919, would not be valid "unless it shall have been ratified as an amendment to the Constitution . . . within seven years from the date of the submission hereof to the States by the Congress." It was to be ratified "by the legislatures of the several States." This was and is the ordinary means of ratification. But Prohibition was a Progressive reform, and part of Progressivism was its desire to take power away from elected politicians (such as state legislators who had picked senators) and give it to the people.

The idea of "direct democracy"—referendum to approve or veto legislatively passed laws, initiative to enact laws without the legislature, and recall of public officials—had taken hold in the states beginning about 1900. Ohio had a new law allowing a certain number of voters to "refer" any legislative measure to a popular vote. When the Ohio Legislature ratified the proposed amendment, outraged drinkers there immediately gathered the requisite signatures—and the people voted to rescind ratification. The next year, in a case called *Hawke v. Smith*, the Supreme Court invalidated the referendum.[16] The language of Article V, the Court reasoned, provided only two means of ratification—by the state legislatures or by state conventions. Plebiscite was not permitted. This snub to majority will left lasting bitterness among Prohibition's opponents—one that would show up later as a small but significant part of the text of the Twenty-First Amendment repealing the Eighteenth.

The time limit was a new kind of provision as well. At the time, and today, a constitutional question persists as to whether an amendment, once proposed by Congress, simply radiates into space like a radio signal slowly journeying beyond the solar system, ready for ratification when intercepted by state legislatures no matter how far away in time. (The latest amendment to the Constitution, the Twenty-Seventh, was proposed in 1789 and ratified only in 1992.) Most of the amendments proposed by Congress since the Nineteenth have been proposed by resolutions limiting the time for ratification. These resolutions become law as soon as passed by two-thirds of both houses; the failure of the Equal Rights Amendment to meet the time limits doomed its ratification. The Eighteenth Amendment limited its eligibility for ratification in the text of the amendment itself. Of course, until ratified, the language of Section Three had no force—it was not a statute, just a proposed amendment.

Nineteenth Amendment

Just weeks before Independence was declared, Abigail Adams had written to her husband John asking that she and her sisters be included as constituent members of the new Republic: "I desire you would remember the ladies and be more generous and favorable to them than your ancestors,"[17] wrote this brilliant woman, one of the most remarkable figures of the Revolutionary generation, male or female. John Adams was the "colossus of Independence," who guided the idea through the Continental Congress; but history gives little evidence that he was thinking of independent ladies at the time.

The Declaration that was eventually enacted was the handiwork of the courtly Jefferson. History might have been different had Jefferson's beloved wife, Martha Wayles Skelton Jefferson, thought to beg him to choose some other form of words than "all *men* are created equal." Given the almost hypnotic effect the Declaration has had on generations of Americans, different words might have loosed different images of equality. (Equally likely, though, is the possibility that the Continental Congress, who were, so to speak, men to a man, might have taken out that language, as it did Jefferson's description of the slave trade as "execrable commerce" and "cruel war against human nature itself.")

In 1848, the first Women's Rights Convention in American history convened in Seneca Falls, New York, and tried to remedy Jefferson's omission. "We hold these truths to be self-evident," the convention's "Declaration of Sentiments" proclaimed: "that all men *and women* are created equal."[18] Even these radical feminists at first hesitated to ask for voting rights, though by convention's end they narrowly voted to do so. By one of history's cruel ironies, one and only one of the women present—a teenaged glovemaker named Charlotte Woodward— ever cast a legal vote in the land of equality. Seventy-two years after Seneca Falls, at ninety-one, Charlotte Woodward Pierce voted in the land of her birth because the Nineteenth Amendment said she could no longer be stopped from doing so.[19]

As we remarked above, the Constitution depicts a masculine nation, dominated by war and trade. Even to this day it never uses one of the most common English words—"she." That pronoun does not make it into the text even in the words bestowing the vote on Charlotte Woodward Pierce. "The right of citizens of the United States to vote," it says, "shall not be denied or abridged by the United States or by any State on account of sex." In practical terms, this has the same meaning as a provision saying, "women shall be allowed to vote," or "voting rights for women are hereby guaranteed." Those locutions, however, would have a kind of tone of liberation and equality that the Constitution almost entirely avoids.

Nowhere does it proclaim racial equality—only "equal protection"; nowhere does it proclaim "woman suffrage," the goal for which three generations of post– Seneca Falls women struggled. In its present form, it protects the Charlotte Woodwards of the nation but also solemnly forbids any future feminist political monolith from wresting the vote away from men. In this linguistic precision, it recalls the salute to law by the great French novelist Anatole France, who wrote that "the law, in its majestic equality, forbids the rich as well as the poor to sleep under bridges, to beg in the streets, and to steal bread."[20]

A familiar phrase reappears in the amendment: "the right of citizens of the United States to vote." This is the second affirmation of this phantom right (the third occurrence of the bare phrase "the right to vote") and as in the Fifteenth Amendment, Congress is given power to enforce the amendment and protect the right "by appropriate legislation."

The Nineteenth Amendment was the last product of this remarkable period of constitutional reform. Between 1913 and 1920, the people remade the government. After 1920, it was more powerful, more democratic, and more inclusive— much closer, in structure and constitutional values, to what we would today call an advanced democracy.

The right to vote and the power of Congress have now become motifs, Homeric formulas, in the amended Constitution. Over the course of years they have acquired a poetry that inspire ordinary citizens with visions of self-government and equality. Judges, however, tend to be sober and prosaic, and to be men—and to this poetry, judges so far have remained remarkably indifferent.

Hangover Remedies

Twentieth through Twenty-Second Amendments

After 1920, the energy behind amendments slowed. Three amendments were passed between 1920 and the last burst of reform in the 1960s. We might draw from Prohibition and call them hangover amendments. The Twentieth was a reaction to an obstinate habit of Congress; the Twenty-First woke the nation from the nightmare of Prohibition; the Twenty-Second threw cold water on the legacy of Franklin Roosevelt. None of them creates broad new vistas, but their text does illuminate the American habit of constitution-making and how it has changed with the passage of time.

Twentieth Amendment

In November 2000, just days after that year's presidential election dissolved into chaos, the TV series *The West Wing* aired an episode called "The Lame Duck Congress." In the episode, President Josiah Bartlet considers calling a special session of Congress during the weeks between the congressional off-year elections and the swearing in of the new Congress. His party has lost crucial seats in the election, and Senate approval of an arms-control treaty is in jeopardy. In the old Congress, Bartlet believes, he can muster the votes; in the new one, the treaty will fail.

Bartlet's aides approach one of the treaty's principal sponsors, who has just been defeated. He stops the plan cold: "I'm a lame duck senator. The people of Pennsylvania voted me out," he says. "I'm a senator for another 10 weeks and I'm going to choose to respect these people and what they want. You call a lame duck session now, and I've got to abstain."[1]

The West Wing was beloved because, for all its flip dialogue and apparent cynicism, it portrayed a political world that was far more noble than the real one.

Even as "The Lame Duck Congress" was airing, the aftermath of the real election was demonstrating a key fact of American history. Almost never has a party or politician given up the chance to win a vote on the mere grounds that winning would be democratically indefensible.

Consider 1998. The Republican Party had expected to win handy gains in Congress on the strength of a campaign centered on Bill Clinton's sexual peccadilloes and his lying about them under oath. But on election day, political professionals were shocked at the nationwide results. Instead of winning as many as fifteen seats in the House, the Republicans lost five. They picked up no seats in the Senate, and two powerful Republican incumbents—Alfonse D'Amato of New York and Lauch Faircloth of North Carolina—were defeated for reelection.

The public, pundits and polls suggested, was sick of the hypocritical spectacle of Bill Clinton being pursued for his sex life by the likes of Newt Gingrich, Henry Hyde, and Bob Livingston—all three of whom had been, or shortly would be, outed as adulterers themselves. People all over the country sighed with relief that the impeachment fever, like the "reign of witches" Thomas Jefferson described when speaking of the Alien and Sedition acts, had broken at last.

Except it hadn't. The 106th Congress had been chosen; but immediately after the election, the members of the outgoing 105th Congress reassembled. That House of Representatives would shortly go out of existence; in ordinarily legislative matters, bills passed by the House but not yet passed by the Senate also cease to exist when the old Congress adjourns. But the outgoing House eagerly voted Articles of Impeachment and then adjourned forever, leaving the new Senate to consider them, and acquit the president.

It was an extraordinary performance—an angry political faction refused to accept the verdict of the voters and persisted in their course until final defeat. But it was by no means unique. Over and over in American history, important decisions are made by presidents and Congresses repudiated by the voters, but clinging to power by the grace of a confusing political calendar.

This entire situation arose by the unforeseen interaction of constitutional text and historical accident. The Twentieth Amendment, which had been expected to fix it, hasn't solved the problem.

We've seen how the problem of the "lame duck" arose. For 150 years, lameduck Congresses, their electoral mandate expired, came to Washington within weeks of the elections and made important decisions. Some were good (approving John Marshall as chief justice, for example); some were bad (proposing an amendment, mercifully never ratified, that would have enshrined slavery forever in the Constitution). Twice, in 1800 and 1824, the lame-duck House of Representatives chose the president of the United States.

Elected officials don't have much legitimacy when their replacements have already been chosen. Some may be retiring and may never have to account to the voters for their actions. Others have been defeated, often over the very policies they seek to further after the election. (In 1800, voters replaced twenty-two of Jefferson's opponents—one-fifth of the House—with Jeffersonians; the old anti-Jefferson House then deadlocked, because those very defeated opponents then tried to block Jefferson's election.)

The people are often slow to anger, against the Constitution at least; but in 1922, popular anger at the lame-duck Congress finally boiled over after passage of an intensely unpopular set of subsidies to shipping companies, and agitation for a change began. In 1932, Congress proposed the Twentieth Amendment, and it was ratified unanimously by the state legislatures in a breathtaking ten months. As we'll see, a change in the constitutional mechanism of succession requires complex language, and even if carefully drafted can have unforeseen results.

SECTION ONE. The amendment's first section changes the terms of federal elected officials, and for the first time sets a specific date for the handover of power. First, the president: "The terms of the President and Vice President shall end at noon on the 20th day of January . . . of the years in which such terms would have ended if this article had not been ratified; and the terms of their successors shall then begin." That is, the president's term begins and ends in January of the year following each presidential election. The original Constitution had given the president a four-year term but had not explicitly said that the term ended at a specific time. (March 4 became the beginning date because it took the First Congress that long to assemble and set an inauguration date.) No president had ever tried to extend his term by refusing to yield the office; but the new language makes that impossible by saying that as of noon (no time zone specified, but Eastern Standard Time is used) the old president isn't president any more.

But does that mean that the president-elect *is* president at that moment, or simply that his term has begun? In January 2009, Chief Justice John Roberts Jr. and President-elect Barack Obama together garbled the text of the presidential oath. The best account of this minor imbroglio, by Jeffrey Toobin, finds that the error arose because communication between the Court's staff and the new White House staff went awry. Roberts did not know at what point in the oath Obama would begin repeating its words. When the president spoke up at a time Roberts did not expect, both men became slightly flustered, and each repeated a different, but equally wrong, version of the text.[2]

(As an aside, the Constitution does not say anything about who is to administer the oath. A president could choose any justice of the Court, though that would be a snub to the chief justice. Many vice presidents have been sworn in to the presidency in emergencies by nearby officials empowered to administer oaths. Calvin Coolidge was sworn in the first time by his father, a notary public, but then took the oath again when some suggested that the oath-giver should be a federal official.)

Was Obama president? The Twentieth Amendment says his term began at noon on January 20. That's not the same wording as "the President-elect becomes President." Article I, Section One, Clause Eight of the Constitution says that "Before he enter on the Execution of his Office, he shall take the following Oath or Affirmation," followed by the oath the two men muffed. So one could read the combined wording to say that even though his term had begun, even if he had become president, he was not yet permitted to "enter on the execution of his office."

Is that the best reading? As we'll see in a moment, Section Two does use the term "become President." If the president-elect dies before taking office, the vice president elect "shall become president." No mention of the oath there; and remember, the vice president hasn't taken the presidential oath upon becoming vice president. Would it make sense for a person to "become" president in the latter case, but not for the person actually elected to "become president" in the normal course of events?

Would it make sense then to say that he *had* become president by working of the Constitution and that the oath was merely a formality, necessary for record-keeping but not required immediately? The answer to the question, then, depends on the reader's attitude toward law and oaths. Oaths are what remains of magic in our secular age. It's possible to believe that legal forms that are not followed to the letter are like a wizard's spells wrongly recited: the sorcery fails. The more rational reading, to me, is that the term of the old president (Bush) ended, and the new president (Obama), having been duly chosen according to constitutional form, became president. Obama's decision to take the oath again was a wise nod by a leader to the sometimes superstitious faith of his people in the special efficacy of legal words.

Section One also specifies the beginning of congressional terms: January 3, seventeen days earlier than the presidential transition. This ends the possibility that an outgoing Congress of losers might defy the popular will in choosing the president and vice president after electoral deadlock. But nowhere in the Constitution is it required that the deadlock be broken by the new Congress. Both Article I, Section One, and the Twelfth Amendment provide that the electoral votes must be counted "in the presence of the Senate and House of Representatives." Until that happens, there has been no electoral deadlock, and a choice by the House would be impossible. If there is a deadlock, the House shall "immediately" begin voting for a president. Congress by statute requires that the official count take place on January 6, three days after the new Congress begins; thus, a lame-duck Congress cannot be involved in choosing the new president and vice president.

A congressional majority that saw defeat coming might, in theory, alter the statute and require the counting earlier. It would be unpopular and unwise, but not unconstitutional. That far-fetched scenario, however, underlines the paradox that the "lame duck amendment" did not outlaw lame-duck sessions. Between election day (the first Tuesday after the first Monday in November) and January 3, the old Congress remains in office. Congresses routinely meet between election day and January 3, and sometimes they pass important laws. The problem of legitimacy is no less in those cases simply because the lame-duck period is shorter.

The lame-duck problem can't be fixed by barring the old Congress from meeting at all. For one thing, that would take a constitutional amendment, and, for another, such an amendment would be a bad idea. A country needs a functioning Congress. Consider that the Japanese attack on Pearl Harbor might have occurred on December 7, 1940 (during the lame-duck period) rather than on the same date in 1941. The attacks on the World Trade Center might have happened in December 2000 instead of September 2001. If Congress could not assemble at once, the country would have been crippled, with no way to organize for war or defense. Whatever one thinks of the Clinton impeachment, a genuine emergency—involving presidential insanity, say, or treason—might require the removal of a president right away; in such a case, even a lame-duck Congress would be justified in acting, and derelict if it did not do so.

SECTION TWO. The second section amplifies the first. Not only do the terms of Congress begin on January 3, but the congressional session "shall" begin at noon that day of every year, "unless they shall by law appoint a different day"— which gives the Congress the option of assembling a day late if January 3 is a Sunday. In theory, Congress could actually postpone its opening until much later in the year; in practice, the need to start work as soon as possible—and the possibility of choosing a new president—have kept them to the date set in Section Two.

SECTION THREE. In Section Three, another set of constitutional drafters marches into the Valley of Death that is the election and succession to the presidency. In attempting to forestall potential problems, they introduce new ambiguities into this rickety structure.

First, Section Three provides that if the president-elect dies between election day and the Inauguration, the vice president-elect will become president. This seems straightforward. Candidates run as a slate. The voters pick a slate on election day, and if their first choice dies between then and the Inauguration, they get their second choice. In practice it would work cleanly if the death occurred between the casting of electoral votes (the Monday after the second Wednesday in December, more than a month after the election) and the Inauguration. This potential flaw arises because, in the Constitution's language, "President elect" and "Vice President elect" are terms that have meaning only in relation to the electoral votes mentioned in Article II and the Twelfth Amendment. (As the luckless Al Gore learned in 2000, "merely" winning a vote of the people works no change in a candidate's constitutional status.)

Thus, if a candidate won the electoral voting and then died, the amendment would make the vice president-elect, chosen at the same time, president. That would happen because the new Congress, meeting in January, would open and count the ballots and determine that a man who was president-elect had died. It would then announce the winner of the electoral vote for vice president, and that person would automatically become president.

But if the winner of the popular vote died between the November election and the December electoral voting, the successful presidential nominee might not become "president elect" in constitutional terms. Though they may "pledge" themselves to one candidate or another, electors can always vote for anyone they want, living or dead; no state law or private agreement can limit that constitutional power of choice.

If one were an elector, it would be tempting to refuse to vote for a dead man. A national party whose victorious candidate had died might be unhappy with its vice-presidential candidate. (Consider if these events had happened when Dan Quayle or Sarah Palin was the presumptive vice president-elect.) The party might convene a national committee meeting, name a new candidate, and ask all the party's electors to vote for the new candidate. Meanwhile, the defeated party would almost certainly begin discreetly sounding out the victorious electors about the advantages of switching their votes to the last candidate standing. Media and popular debate might produce new names as figures to step in during a crisis. The result of this ferment might eventually be a scattering of electoral votes among three or more candidates.

If that happened, there would be no president-elect when the votes were counted. By the strict text of the Constitution, then, the vice president-elect would not succeed; instead, the election would go to the House of Representatives.

Section Two also introduces a new term into the Constitution's language, when in the next sentence it sets out what should happen when the electoral vote system has not produced a president by January 20. If that happens, it says, "the Vice President elect shall act as president." When does that occur? In two conditions. First is the obvious one in which the electoral vote has been dead-locked, the House has been deadlocked, and the old president's term has ended. What it literally says is "a President shall not have been chosen." Now here is a confusion—how can the vice president-elect have been chosen if the president-elect has not been? Remember that under the Twelfth Amendment, the electors vote for president and vice president by separate ballot, so in theory a vice president might win a majority while a president does not. But what is more likely is that the electors will produce a majority neither for the president nor the vice president. In that case, the Twelfth Amendment splits the work in an effort to ensure at least one winner: the Senate chooses a vice president from between the top two candidates. There is no voting by states. Two-thirds of the Senate must show up, and the winner must get a majority of those present. We can imagine circumstances where this would not work (the senators refuse to show up, or show up but abstain from voting), but it's not very likely.

But there's another possibility that would make the vice president-elect the "acting president," and that arises "if . . . President elect shall have failed to qualify." What does it mean to say that a president has "failed to qualify"? The verb "qualify," as something a potential president must do, has not appeared before. The "qualifications" for the presidency are set out in Article II: "he" must (1) be "a natural born citizen"; (2) "have attained to the age of thirty-five years"; and (3) have "been fourteen years a resident within the United States." If a person meets those qualifications, has that person "qualified"?

The new term is more confusing because, as we'll see, later in the text the amendment suggests that someone who has not "qualified" at the beginning of the president's term may have "qualified" at some later point. How could that happen? A non-"natural born citizen" cannot subsequently become a natural born citizen. Perhaps it might be discovered that an electoral vote winner was actually thirty-four years and ten months old, and thus would "qualify" two months into his term; or that a winner had been a resident "within the United States" for thirteen years and seven months, and would thus "qualify" five months after Inauguration Day. That could happen, but it seems like a vanishingly small possibility.

It could refer to a situation in which members of Congress, having counted the electoral votes, vote that the candidate who is elected doesn't meet the qualifications. (To pick a far-fetched example, what if members of Congress began to argue that a president-elect was not a "natural born" citizen?) The Constitution is vague about who actually *certifies* an electoral-vote result. It only says that the president of the Senate shall "open" the ballots, and "the ballots shall then be counted." The federal statutes governing this process state that the vice president's announcement of the vote totals "shall be deemed a sufficient declaration of the persons, if any, elected President and Vice President of the United States."[3] However, after the announcement, an "objection" to specific votes may be brought if the objection is signed by one senator and one representative. If objections are made, the two houses separate to vote on them; if both houses vote to reject the challenged votes, they will not be counted, and others may be counted in their place.

Imagine a circumstance in which senators refused to approve the count pending some proof that the president elect was qualified. (What could they want? Perhaps a "long-form" birth certificate, though in today's atmosphere that probably would not be enough.) Then this bizarre language would become relevant. If a potential president can fail to "qualify," so can a potential vice president. Now the Republic is in danger indeed, with two impostors having duped the people—perhaps one is too young and the other cannot yet prove "natural birth."

In that case, Congress has the power (as it has always had in the case of succession after death of resignation of a president already in office) to designate by statute the line of those who will become "acting president"; and it has an entirely new power—the power to decide "the manner in which one who is to act shall be selected." Since Congress already by the previous clause has the power to do this in advance by statute, this language can only mean the power to specify in advance emergency election procedures for this situation, including the power to create some kind of council or committee to chose a specific individual to become acting president in this crisis. There is no other instance in the Constitution that allows even the possibility of a committee having the potential power to name any federal official, much less one so important.

In the event, Congress has used this power, blended with its power under Article II and the later-granted power under the Twenty-Fifth Amendment, to provide that the Speaker of the House will "act as president." To do this, the Speaker must resign as Speaker and as a member of Congress. If the House hasn't elected a Speaker, or the Speaker "fails to qualify," then the president pro tempore of the Senate "shall act." Neither official is given the formal option to refuse and retain his or her seat. The "acting president" line of succession ends there; in the event that all of the people named in it turn out to be foreign-born sleeper agents, too young, or (under the Twenty-Fifth Amendment) disabled, then Congress will have to improvise a procedure to choose an "acting president."

No matter what official is thrust into the gap in this bizarre crisis, the "acting president" status persists only until the president-elect or vice president-elect "qualifies" (or, in the case of Twenty-Fifth Amendment "disability," until "the removal of the disability").[4]

SECTION FOUR. Remarkably enough, the list of prospective disasters covered by Section Three is not complete. The anxious lawyers who drafted this amendment fell to contemplating the possibility that the election of the president will be thrown into the House (and that of the vice president thrown into the Senate) at the same time that one of those who can be selected dies. Since the House, under the Twelfth Amendment, can only choose one of the top three electoral vote-getters, there will almost always be two candidates to choose from. The Senate, meanwhile, must choose a vice president from one of the top two electoral vote-getters in the vice-presidential voting. The death of one candidate for either office would not make the task of electing a president or vice president impossible; but Congress might conclude that it would make the elections a sham. That's even more true because there will almost always be only two serious electoral-vote contenders for president; the number three vote-getter, in today's world, would be at best the candidate of a third-party movement (imagine Congress facing a choice between, say, Bill Clinton and Ross Perot in 1992) and possibly a fringe one (imagine Al Gore versus Ralph Nader in 2000). Section Four empowers Congress to provide for this possibility by statute; that's a power Congress has been unwilling to exercise, trusting to the luck of the Republic.

In both Section Three and Section Four, as I said, there is a tone of anxiety, a desire to cover all the bases that is rarely found earlier in the Constitution. And the greater specificity also reflects a change in the style with which lawyers draft legislation. When the original Constitution was written, most of law and procedure was founded on common law, on unwritten precedents that every lawyer was presumed to know. Statutes (and even written constitutions) were a departure from the norm, used mostly to vary the existing structure of case law and the general sense of how things were done. The unity of the common law has long since disappeared. Most law is written law, often complex and technical; it is interpreted using close grammatical analysis and application of specialized rules and vocabulary incomprehensible to most lay people.

But historically it also probably reflects a change in the world. As government has become more powerful and more central to daily life, the consequences of presidential illness or assassination have become, even if unlikely, potentially more malign and more immediate.

When the Republic began, no one panicked when Washington, distracted by spring planning, was unable to make it to New York to take the oath of office until a month after the date set. The General would show up sooner or later and would designate the few dozen officials who would run the government. There wouldn't even be a session of Congress until the following December; there was no need to hurry.

Today, such a delay would at a minimum spark stock market collapse and public panic; Congress, which would already be in session, could not function without the president, and the massive machinery of government would need supervision. If the nation were at war or rocked by disaster, the delay might be fatal.

SECTIONS FIVE AND SIX. On February 15, 1933, an assassin tried to shoot President-elect Franklin Roosevelt, who was visiting Miami. (Chicago Mayor Anton Cermak, shaking hands with Roosevelt, caught the bullet and died.) Had Roosevelt been killed by his would-be assassin in 1933, a full-blown succession crisis would have occurred, even though the amendment had been ratified. That's because its framers, again imagining specific disasters, provided in Section

Five that no matter on what date it was ratified, it would not take effect until the following October 15.

Under Article II and the Twelfth Amendment, House Speaker John N. Garner, the vice president-elect, would have taken the oath on Inauguration Day, and the "powers and duties" of the presidency would have then "devolved" upon him the way they had "devolved" on other vice presidents from time of John Tyler.

In Section Four, the amendment requires ratification within seven years of proposal.

There is something strangely futuristic about the succession language of the Twentieth Amendment. In tone, it sounds a bit like the humanoid robot in a Star Trek film, who valiantly attempts to foresee any contingency and resolve it in advance by the use of logic. That tone will reappear when a new generation tackles the problem of presidential succession in the Twenty-Fifth Amendment. This amendment sits uneasily amid the general provisions of the Constitution, showing clearly a different authorship and a different mind-set. God only knows how it would work in practice; God be thanked, it has never yet become relevant.

Twenty-First Amendment

The earliest known law code, that of Hammurabi, takes note that human beings like to drink of the fruit of the grape. It required innkeepers to report criminal conspiracies hatched by their customers, prohibited priestesses from drinking in taverns, and made overcharging for drink a capital offense.[5]

Turns out Americans really like a drink too. The experiment may have been noble; but nobility is not always effectual, and in the case of Prohibition it might only generously be called quixotic. The widespread contempt for the liquor laws had spawned a culture of organized crime and lawlessness, cost the government millions in tax revenue, and generally repulsed ordinary Americans who believed then as now that government ought to stay out of their personal habits unless it had a good reason to get involved. At almost precisely the same time that they were tinkering with the presidential succession, the people gratefully freed themselves from Prohibition.

The reaction against Prohibition spawned an amendment that contains a couple of features not found anywhere else in the Constitution.

SECTION ONE. "The eighteenth article of amendment to the Constitution of the United States is hereby repealed." No other section of the Constitution—not the Three-Fifths Clause, the Fugitive Slave Clause or the legislative election of senators—has ever been explicitly repealed. The Eighteenth Amendment is gone as if it had never been, remaining only as the title of a tavern on Washington's Capitol Hill. Over the past eighty years, few have mourned its passing.

SECTION TWO. Even in the wave of disgust that powered what is still known simply as Repeal, some states wished to stay dry. Section Two gives them the authority to do so in terms almost as broad as those repealing the Eighteenth Amendment. It directly prohibits the "transportation or importation . . . of intoxicating liquors" into any state, "in violation of the laws thereof, for delivery or use therein." In other words, states could prohibit liquor for their own citizens; they could not, however, bar its shipment through their territory in interstate commerce if it wasn't going to be delivered or consumed inside the state.

Also empowered to enact prohibitions were United States territories and "possession[s]." The latter language is the first and only explicit recognition in the Constitution that the United States, in the years after 1896, had become master of a worldwide empire. A United States "territory" is a term implying an area being run by the federal government while it prepares for statehood. But by 1933, the United States had seized control of the Philippines, had bought the Canal Zone, had entered into a perpetual "leasehold" of Guantanamo, Cuba, and had made a colony of Puerto Rico. Today the Philippines are independent and the Canal Zone has reverted to Panama, but the United States still governs the Commonwealth of Puerto Rico, as well as places like American Samoa, Micronesia, and the Marianas Islands.

The Constitution has no provisions discussing colonies. In the Eighteenth Amendment they were referred to as "territory subject to the jurisdiction" of the United States. Just as slavery spawned a vocabulary of euphemisms that sounded odd in the language of liberty, the remnants of colonialism have an odd tone in a republican constitution.

But the language does more than empower states, territories, and possessions to enact their own prohibition laws. It makes violations of those laws independent violations of the Constitution; importation of liquor into dry places "in violation of the laws thereof" is "*hereby* [that is, by the Constitution] prohibited." Even in death, Prohibition still rules us from the grave, with sweeping language that subsequently proved problematic more than half a century later.

After repeal, each state enacted a patchwork of laws to govern what alcohol could be sold there, who could sell it, how it could be marketed, and how it could be delivered. Some states continued to ban "liquor by the drink" outside private clubs; Mississippi was the last of these to legalize dram-shops, in 1966. Some states permit individual counties to remain "dry," and a few still do. But as time went on the laws began to concern themselves increasingly not with discouraging drinking but at encouraging local booze.

After Prohibition, the American wine industry slowly revived, until by the 1970s American wines were a powerful force in the world market, respected even in France. As wine prices increased, vineyards and wineries sprang up in states where they had never been before. Today, there is at least one winery in every state of the union. Some states found a way to boost their homegrown wines: they required all out-of-state wine to be sold through state-approved distributors, while allowing in-state wineries to ship their bottles direct to customers.

This is rank discrimination against interstate commerce. With any other product, it would have been facially invalid under court interpretation of the Interstate Commerce Clause. But alcohol has its own amendment, and that amendment "prohibited" its "transportation or importation . . . for delivery or use" in any state "in violation of the laws thereof." It didn't say that those laws had to ban all alcohol. It didn't say they had to be even-handed. It didn't say they couldn't favor local wineries. In broad language, it seemed to incorporate all state liquor laws, no matter how mean-spirited or stupid, into the Constitution itself. Why shouldn't states favor their own vintners?

In a pair of cases in 2005, the Court, by one vote, held that states could regulate alcohol, but not use those regulations to force consumers to deal with instate businesses. In lawyers' language, the justices "harmonized" the Twenty-First Amendment and the Interstate Commerce Clause. "The Twenty-first Amendment did not give the States complete freedom to regulate where other constitutional principles are at stake," Justice Anthony Kennedy wrote.[6] It seems likely that the drafters of the amendment had in mind allowing states to prevent their citizens from buying liquor at all; forcing them to buy in-state wine seems a bit far from the amendment's subject matter. Broad constitutional language, however soothing it may be to state sensibilities, can give rise to unforeseen difficulties later. Who in 1933 would have thought that rock-ribbed Prohibition states Mississippi, Iowa, or Utah would one day be more eager to foist their own "intoxicating liquors" on the public than to ban alcohol altogether?

SECTION THREE. At first glance, Section Three seems like the standard boilerplate requiring ratification within seven years. But constitution-reading requires a sharp eye for the intended as well as the unintended anomaly. This provision, unlike other time-limit provisions, requires approval "by conventions in the several states" rather than, as all the rest do, by "the legislatures." The language is there, at least in part, to cock a snook at the Eighteenth Amendment's sponsors and the Supreme Court.

Recall that during ratification of the Eighteenth Amendment, Ohio voters used their new referendum laws to vote to rescind their legislature's ratification. The Court rebuffed this, holding that when Congress proposed ratification by legislatures, only the legislature itself could grant or withhold approval. Popular resentment at this snub to majority will persisted, and the sponsors of the Twenty-First Amendment took their revenge by insisting that approval for this amendment bypass the legislatures. Accordingly, the amendment was approved by bodies of citizens elected by the voters for that sole purpose, which met, voted, and adjourned.

These were not the high-minded deliberative bodies the Framers might have foreseen—the New Hampshire convention met, voted, and adjourned in seventeen minutes. New Mexico's convention had three delegates, who met on November 3, voted to approve, adjourned forever and (presumably) went to have a beer. Squabbling had broken out about whether Congress could pass a statute setting out detailed rules for these conventions; many eminent authorities argued that it could. The state of New Mexico, land of small conventions, passed a statute preemptively proclaiming any such statute null and void. Congress did nothing, and the question remains unsolved. But the fate of Prohibition was unambiguous. The necessary thirty-seven conventions ratified the proposed amendment within less than ten months. Only one convention, South Carolina's, met and rejected repeal. (North Carolina selected delegates at a statewide vote, but, in the same vote, decided not to bother with a convention.)[7]

The convention route ran smoothly and produced a result no one quarreled with. And yet it has never been used again. In proposing the remaining six amendments, Congress has followed the conventional legislative-approval mechanism.

An apocryphal tale illustrates the potential of the convention route to appear again, however. In 1972, Congress (after decades of consideration) approved the Equal Rights Amendment, which, if adopted, would have provided that "Equality of rights under the law shall not be denied or abridged by the United States or by any State on account of sex." The amendment was overwhelmingly popular at the time, but at the end of the seven-year period, opposition by religious and conservative groups had bottled it up in key legislatures, and only thirty-five of the thirty-eight states required had ratified. Subsequently Congress voted to extend the period.

The story goes that a key group of feminist leaders met to consider strategy during the debate over extension. One person present suggested that the state legislative opposition could be finessed by changing the ratification method to conventions. A second person objected that reviving conventions would open the way to other, less desirable amendments.

"Like what?" the group's chair asked.

"Like banning abortion."

"That's not a problem," the chair responded. "We can block that in at least thirteen states."

"What about school prayer?"

A silence ensued. Finally, the chair said thoughtfully, "Well, it won't hurt the little bastards to pray every now and then."

Twenty-Second Amendment

In 1796, George Washington set a durable precedent by declining to run for a third term as president. By some historians' assessment, it marked the first time in Western history that a head of state had voluntarily and peacefully relinquished power. It cemented Washington's reputation and set a durable precedent.

Washington's successor, John Adams, was roundly defeated in 1800. For most presidents, a second term is difficult to win; a third is out of reach. Between Washington's retirement and 1932, only eight of the thirty-one presidents won a second term, and only six served eight consecutive years in office. Abraham Lincoln served only a few weeks of his second term. Ulysses S. Grant served two full terms and declined to run for a third in 1876. He did, however, encourage a movement to nominate him for a third term in 1880; the Republican Convention instead nominated James A. Garfield. Grover Cleveland served one term, was defeated, and was then reelected as a nonincumbent four years later. Theodore Roosevelt served nearly eight years but had never been elected to a first term because he succeeded William McKinley after McKinley's assassination. Upon election to a term of his own in 1904, Roosevelt publicly committed himself not to seek a third term, and retired in 1909; but he came out of retirement in 1912 to seek that third term, in vain, as the nominee of the Progressive Party. Woodrow Wilson was elected twice and left office a broken man after a second term. The two-term tradition was nowhere in the Constitution; but it seemed unbreakable.

Enter Franklin D. Roosevelt, probably the most brilliant electoral politician ever to sit in the White House. First as "Dr. New Deal," and then as "Dr. Win the War," he convinced the voters that he was indispensable to the nation's survival. In so doing he shattered the hopes of a generation of his rivals. "No Crown for Franklin," was a motto of the Republican 1940 ticket of Wendell Willkie and Charles McNary; but Roosevelt defeated them handily, and then defeated New York Governor Thomas Dewey and Ohio Governor John Bricker in 1944. By the time he died, less than three months into his fourth term, those who could not defeat him in life were determined to prevent his reincarnation.

The Twenty-Second Amendment provides for two situations; together they might be called "the Roosevelt phenomenon." The first is the Franklin situation: "No person shall be elected to the office of President more than twice." Unlike some state constitutions, which permit two-term governors to run again after a four-year hiatus, the amendment imposes a lifetime presidential disability on anyone elected twice.

The second part covers the Teddy situation: no person who has "held the office of President or acted as President" for more than two years can be elected more than once more. This means that a vice president who succeeds a president beyond midway in the president's term *could* be elected twice, and thus, unlike any other eligible figure, serve more than eight years as president. Lyndon B. Johnson succeeded John F. Kennedy when Kennedy's term had fifteen months to run; Johnson was preparing to run for a second full term when the catastrophic failure of his war policy in Vietnam drove him to renounce reelection. Gerald Ford could not muster one election, but, had he done so, he would not have been eligible to run again, as he took over before Nixon had served half his term.

The rest of the language makes clear that the amendment will not apply to whoever was holding office when it was proposed by Congress or when ratified by the legislatures. In both cases, that was Harry S. Truman. The amendment was proposed in 1947 and ratified in 1951. Truman, whose election in 1948 still ranks as the greatest electoral shock in American history, remained eligible for reelection in 1952. Had he won another term, he would have served eleven years, nearly as long as FDR. But by the usual political logic of the presidency, Truman declined to run again. His motive was probably not Washingtonian reticence but the simple fact that with the war in Korea stalemated, he was by most modern metrics one of the least popular presidents in American history.

Section Two imposes the customary timetable and leaves ratification to the legislatures, not conventions, this time. The people had reelected Roosevelt four times. When politicians decided to make sure they would never have the chance to do it again, they left them out of the process.

Dreams and Nightmares

The Twenty-Third through Twenty-Sixth Amendments

The 1960s were a long march through a strange new landscape by a nation that wondered frequently whether it would survive: the doomsday terror of the 1962 Cuban Missile Crisis, the national epiphany of the 1963 March on Washington, the recurrent horror of assassination, the flare of urban rioting, the carnage of Vietnam. It was a time of daily shocks for which neither the American people nor their system of government felt fully prepared. Those shocks left behind an ambiguous constitutional legacy.

After the 1960s agitation, the text of the Constitution was altered. In one way, the alterations were specific and detailed: the events of November 1963 focused public attention on the dangers of chaos at the top of our government and convinced the public that the still-flawed provisions for presidential succession needed detailed refinement. On the other hand, the insistent demands for inclusion by African Americans and young people were written into the text.

Like other reform periods, the 1960s left the text altered and in some ways deformed. The dangers of nuclear disaster were confronted strongly, but the result reads strangely, written in stilted language. The ballot was opened further, but in a half-hearted and shameful way reminiscent of the ambiguity of previous steps forward in voting and representation.

Twenty-Third Amendment

In early 2009, Eric Holder, the new attorney general, placed his support behind a federal statute that would have given the District of Columbia a voting member of the House of Representatives. Holder initially sought an opinion from the Justice Department's Office of Legal Counsel (OLC) about the measure's constitutionality. OLC, which usually makes judgments binding on the executive branch, replied that the statute would be unconstitutional: Article I states that House members are to be elected by "the people of the several states," and the District is not a state. Holder, undaunted, then made an end-run around OLC, asking the acting solicitor general (SG) whether he could *defend* the statute if it were passed. A good lawyer can defend many causes that he or she does not personally embrace, and the solicitor general, required by statute to be "learned in law," is almost always one of the best lawyers in America. The SG said he could muster a case for the law. Holder announced administration support for the bill. It failed anyway.[1]

This was sharp practice, and arguably improper. But it illustrates the persistence of a problem the Framers did not foresee. What do we do when the nation's capital has more people than the state of Wyoming, but those people have no voice in national affairs?

The very notion of a federal enclave at the nation's capital was an invention of the Constitution, which in Article I, Section Eight, gives to Congress full control of what was then a hypothetical capital district. Congress is empowered "to exercise exclusive legislation in all cases whatsoever" over a district "not exceeding ten miles square" that might be given to the nation by willing states in order to "become the seat of government." This authority is specifically equated—it is "like [or identical] authority" over any territory purchased from states "for the erection of forts, magazines, arsenals, dock-yards and other needful buildings."

The negotiations over the site of a permanent capital were complex and prolonged. The result was what we know as the District of Columbia, relatively unpromising lowlands along the Potomac River given to the government by Virginia and Maryland (Originally ten miles square, the District was reduced in 1846 when Virginia took back its gift of territory out of fear that slavery would be abolished in the District. It is now roughly 68 square miles.) John Adams was the first president to govern from the District. Three generations later, in 1850, his great-grandson Henry Adams, arriving there to serve as private secretary to his father, Representative Charles Francis Adams, found the capital almost as deserted as the ruins of a lost civilization. In *The Education of Henry Adams*, a classic of American autobiography, he recalled "the white marble columns and fronts of the Post Office and Patent Office, which faced each other in the distance, like white Greek temples in the abandoned gravel-pits of a deserted Syrian city." The most interesting landmark was merely a promise of what was to come: "an unfinished square marble shaft"—a monument to George Washington that would not be completed for another thirty-five years.[2]

This strange mock-capital began life as slave territory, and on the eve of the shelling of Fort Sumter, human property was still being auctioned off within view of the Capitol. Like the nation that created it, it was transformed forever by the Civil War—its own slave population, freed by law only after a year of the war, was joined by thousands of freed slaves seeking refuge from the fighting and the real possibility of recapture and reenslavement by Confederate forces. The black population today Forms the core of the city.

By 1960 the District had a population of 840,000—more than Alaska, North or South Dakota, Delaware, Hawaii, Idaho, Montana, Nevada, or Wyoming. (Today, with the movement of population west, the District remains ahead only of Wyoming.)

These 840,000 people had no elected city or state government, no senators, no representatives, and no voice in the selection of their city's most prominent resident, the president. Congress—including members sent by the nine states less populous than DC—made all decisions for them. The Twenty-Third Amendment partially (and somewhat grudgingly) addresses this democratic deficit. Under its terms, the District has three electoral votes in every presidential election. But its people do not, by constitutional mandate, necessarily *elect* those electors. Instead, they are "appoint[ed] in such manner as Congress may direct." This language tracks the language of Article II, which gives the state legislatures the sole power to determine how state electors are appointed; as we noted earlier, voting for president nationwide is carried out only by legislative largesse rather than constitutional right. The Twenty-Third Amendment, ratified nearly 175 years after the Constitution was written in Philadelphia, embodies in fresh text the Framers' horror of democracy.

That fear is expressed in another clause. In 1960, had it been a state, the District would have had as many as four electoral votes, more than Alaska, Delaware, Hawaii, Nevada, Vermont, or Wyoming. But the amendment devalues District voters: its total shall be "in no event more than the least populous state." In 1964, and in every election since, the District has cast three electoral votes. The drafters prudently added that the District's electors "shall be considered, for the purposes of the election of President and Vice President, to be electors appointed by a State." The modern legal imagination seems to foresee some future desperate electoral-vote struggle in which one side might be tempted by textual ambiguity to claim that the Constitution gave the District the right to "appoint" electors, but did not require Congress to count their votes.

District voters go to the polls every four years. DC's three electoral votes are never in contention. It is solidly Democratic. It is suggestive to note that the DC voting amendment was proposed and ratified around the time that Alaska and Hawaii were admitted as states. Congress tends to be careful to keep a "balance" of power in matters of representation between the two parties, for all the world as if the Constitution took note of partisan matters or guaranteed the nation a two-party system. The admission of Alaska and Hawaii, of course, was achieved by the simple passage of a statute. Even a partial federal enfranchisement of the nation's capital, however, required a formal amendment.

That enfranchisement remains partial, despite repeated proposals for reform. The District sends a nonvoting "delegate" to the House of Representatives; that delegate, Eleanor Holmes Norton, is equal in rank to delegates from American Samoa, Guam, the United States Virgin Islands, and the Northern Mariana Islands. (Delegates can actually vote in the House when it sits in what's called the "Committee of the Whole"—but only if their votes don't change the result of the vote; that is, delegates can vote in the Committee any time their votes don't count.)

Reformers have proposed making the District a state, with at least one representative and two senators. There's no *constitutional* reason that couldn't happen—and by statute. Article I, Section Eight does not require that the nation's capital be a federal enclave; it simply gives Congress that option, which Congress could reverse.

However, if the District is not made a state, giving it a voting representative would almost certainly require a formal amendment, because the Constitution, as noted, requires House members to be elected by "the people of the several states."

Twenty-Fourth Amendment

In 1787, as we've seen, the Constitution recognized that states might limit voting to holders of property, as well as to males and to whites. The Fifteenth Amendment made it impossible to limit the vote explicitly to whites, and formal property qualifications fell out of favor.

Southern white supremacy, however, was a tenacious and creative force. After the passage of the Fifteenth Amendment, it contrived a new "poll," or head tax. Each adult must pay a set amount per year—somewhere around one dollar, which was a full day's pay for a white working man. There was no penalty for failing to pay; but an adult who could not produce receipts for the past three years' taxes could not vote. Even a voter who had the money in hand could not pay the tax on the spot; it had to be paid in advance.

It worked brilliantly. At the height of this period, eleven former Confederate states employed poll tax schemes to cleanse the voting rolls. Poor voters dropped off the rolls; combined with intimidation and terror, poll tax laws reduced the southern black vote to almost zero.

Beginning in 1939, northern members of Congress tried to eliminate the poll tax by legislation. Not until the nation was confronted by the civil rights movement of the 1950s and 60s, however, did the political will develop to limit the poll tax by constitutional amendment.

We are getting near the end of the Constitution; by this point the eye may be gliding somewhat glassily over the page, noting familiar phrases and legal

boilerplate like the time-limit sections. It is easy to conclude that this amendment "outlaws" the poll tax, nod with satisfaction, and move on to the forbidding
specificity of the Twenty-Fifth Amendment.

But compare the language of the Twenty-Fourth Amendment with, say, that
of the Fifteenth and the Nineteenth. The earlier amendments use the same
language—neither race nor sex may be used to deny the vote "by the United
States or by any State." In the Twenty-Fourth Amendment, however, "failure to
pay any poll tax or other tax" may not be used to deny the vote "in any primary
or other election for President or Vice President, for electors for President or
Vice President, or for Senator or Representative in Congress."

The Fifteenth and Nineteenth Amendments straightforwardly ban race and
sex distinctions in *any* election, state or federal. The Twenty-Fourth carefully
limits its applicability to elections for federal office. States remained free to impose
the poll tax on their own people as a condition—not to put too fine a point on it,
a fee—for the "privilege" of choosing governors, legislators, and mayors. Those
without money to pay are guaranteed a "right to vote"—but a second-class one,
not equal in extent to that of their more prosperous neighbors.

The leading historian of the amendment process, David Kyvig, recounts the
formulation and passage of the Twenty-Fourth Amendment. It involved careful
drafting and parliamentary wiliness to get past the opposition of racist southern
committee chairs, whose power came from seniority, and whose seniority came
from never having to face real elections—thanks, in part, to the poll tax. The
measure had to be worded carefully, with respect for the sensibilities of southern
"moderates" who treasured their state governments' "rights" to decide which of
their citizens was "fit" to vote.

The amendment had "great symbolic importance," he writes. It set the legislative table for the passage soon after of the Civil Rights Act of 1964 and
the Voting Rights Act of 1965, which transformed American life. In addition,
by the time of ratification, only five of the eleven southern states retained a
poll tax.[3]

All this is true. Yet there is symbolism and symbolism, and the shadow cast by
this amendment half a century later is small, but dark indeed. Having blurted
out, in a moment of great need, that "all men are created equal," America as a
nation has been unable for more than two centuries to utter those words again.
Every step toward equality has left in the Constitution a trace of its own denial.
The Constitution provides a representative form of government, and prissily
defines what percentage of a person shall stand for each slave. The Fourteenth
Amendment provides equal protection but countenances denying votes to
women and to blacks. Now, at the dawn of a legal revolution, the Constitution
has enshrined forever the idea that some Americans are worthy only of national
votes, if their local masters so conclude.

That exclusion is symbolic only; two years after the amendment was ratified, the Supreme Court seized the privilege, declined by Congress and the people, of declaring that "wealth or fee paying has, in our view, no relation to voting qualifications; the right to vote is too precious, too fundamental to be so burdened or conditioned."[4] After that case, no state may impose a poll tax as a condition for voting in any election.

The Twenty-Fourth Amendment remains in the text, however, as yet another half-hearted commitment to free elections. Once again, faced with an opportunity to proclaim equality from the housetops, the nation chose to mumble.

Twenty-Fifth Amendment

Three great American films of the 1960s capture the deepest nightmare of this time. Two are by the great director John Frankenheimer: *The Manchurian Candidate* (1962) and *Seven Days in May* (1964). The third, *Fail-Safe* (1964), is directed by Sidney Lumet. In *The Manchurian Candidate*, a hypnotized assassin is programmed to kill a presidential candidate in circumstances arranged to propel a Communist sleeper agent into the White House with powers that, as the coup-plotter's wife exults, "will make martial law look like anarchy." In *Fail-Safe*, an errant American bomber vaporizes Moscow without authorization; to convince the Soviets not to launch a global holocaust, the American president, played by Henry Fonda, atones by sending another US bomber to destroy New York. In *Seven Days in May*, the Joint Chiefs of Staff, outraged by a projected nuclear-arms reduction treaty, plot a coup d'état to kill the president and install a military junta.

All three movies are dark, claustrophobic, all but hopeless in tone. The viewer finishes each feeling like a patient who has just received a fatal diagnosis. After the coup plot has been defused, the beleaguered president in *Seven Days in May* explains that the renegade generals are not the enemy. "The enemy is an age, a nuclear age. It happens to have killed man's faith in his ability to influence what happens to him."[5] That brute fact—that at every moment of every day, each of us faced instant death if our leaders miscalculated—defined the age we call the Cold War.

From the time of Washington on, America's presidents had wielded the power of life or death over some of their people. Now they were no longer mere humans; they were gods, holding the entire species in their hands. Being mortal, they could be killed, as Jack Kennedy had; they could fall sick, as Dwight Eisenhower had, or become disabled; they could even go mad. (Fletcher Knebel, the author of *Seven Days in May*, evoked this possibility in another novel called *Night of Camp David*, imagining a deranged president who tries to annex Canada and Scandinavia and form a new nation called "Aspen.")

The Twenty-Fifth Amendment represents a gallant attempt to foresee the un-foreseeable. At 396 words, it is nearly as long as the Fourteenth Amendment, but it deals with only one subject—permanent and temporary succession to the presidency. It was clearly written by twentieth-century lawyers; as a result, readers often find it opaque. It deals with one of the most stirring questions in history and literature—who shall rule?

In Shakespeare's hands, this question produced Richard II's famous soliloquy:

> For God's sake, let us sit upon the ground
> And tell sad stories of the death of kings;
> How some have been deposed; some slain in war,
> Some haunted by the ghosts they have deposed;
> Some poison'd by their wives: some sleeping kill'd;
> All murder'd: for within the hollow crown
> That rounds the mortal temples of a king
> Keeps Death his court . . .[6]

In the hands of modern lawyers, that story sounds considerably different.

SECTION ONE. If the president is removed, resigns, or dies, "the Vice President shall become President." Nothing surprising here, except that it needed to be said. As we noted above, inartful drafting in the original Constitution had created confusion about whether a vice president became president upon a vacancy or simply assumed the "powers and duties" of the office in an acting capacity. That issue had been settled in Tyler's time; but careful modern lawyers are trained not to leave threads dangling.

This precision was perhaps prudent because presidential succession was now governed by the Twentieth Amendment as well, and that amendment created a new shadow office of "acting president" for officials who filled in until a president was chosen by the House, or (in whatever fashion) "qualified." Since its enactment, Harry S. Truman had succeeded Franklin Roosevelt without noises about acting status; but a lawyer is usually the most nervous and annoying person in the room—in part because a lawyer must try to imagine the unlikely and in part because a lawyer must insist on stating the obvious. At any rate, Section One is the easiest to understand; like the man who had been speaking prose his whole life without knowing it, the Republic had been following this rule for a century and a half.

SECTION TWO. Until the enactment of the Twenty-Fifth Amendment, the death of a president meant there would be no vice president until the next election. Section Two addresses this problem by creating an entirely new procedure for filling a federal post. The vice president is the only office that is filled by presidential nomination and the approval of *both* houses of Congress, not just that of the Senate. Since the vice president will be president of the Senate, it may make sense to allow the "people's house" some role in approval; on the other hand, it could be argued that the two-house approval measure simply introduces a new complication into a measure designed to fill a vacancy on close to an emergency basis.

At any rate, on the only occasions it has been used, Section Two worked slowly, but that had no bad effect. Vice President Spiro T. Agnew resigned in October 1973 after pleading no contest to corruption charges. Two days later, President Nixon nominated House Minority Leader Gerald Ford to replace him. It took the two houses more than two months to confirm Ford as vice president. A year later, when Nixon resigned, Ford appointed Nelson Rockefeller to the vice presidency, and his confirmation took three months. In both cases, confirmation by the Senate alone might have been quicker—and that should matter in the operation of a measure that is designed for emergencies.

The Democratic Congress certainly did not hurry. But the leadership did not insist that the new president name a Democrat instead of his own choice. That would be something close to a coup d'état and calculated to provoke a constitutional crisis. In the case of the Ford and Rockefeller appointments, the out party showed a certain political honor in accepting the president's nominees without filibuster or undue delay. In the poisonous atmosphere of today's Washington, it's easy to imagine scenarios much more frightening. No matter how hard lawyers try, the unforeseen continues to tap at our doors and windows, trying to force its way in.

SECTION THREE. Presidential mortality has long been the dirty secret of national politics. Presidents have often been sick, confused, and even (as was the case with Andrew Johnson) sometimes drunk. William Henry Harrison and Zachary Taylor, both seemingly vigorous military figures, died within weeks of taking office. Chester Arthur was diagnosed in the White House with Bright's disease. His successor, Grover Cleveland, underwent secret cancer surgery aboard a yacht. Woodrow Wilson suffered a stroke in 1919 and was unable to meet with his Cabinet or anyone else for the rest of his term.[7] Calvin Coolidge was "silent Cal" in part because of a crippling depression triggered in 1924, when his beloved son Calvin Jr. died of blood poisoning.

The public knew little or nothing of these events. News media helped maintain the silence, as if physical health were a private matter, of no concern to the voters. Franklin Roosevelt had been disabled with polio in 1921 and never regained use of his legs; even photographers and newsreel camera operators collaborated in keeping from the public the sight of their president being pushed in a wheelchair.

The luxury of ignoring presidential disability ended on August 6, 1945, when the first American atomic bomb destroyed Hiroshima, Japan. From then on, the most important single duty of a president has been managing potential nuclear conflict. And as bombers grew faster and missiles more accurate, the amount of time that could be spared grew shorter.

The issue became acute during Dwight Eisenhower's two terms in the White House. Seemingly a sturdy father figure, Eisenhower suffered a serious heart attack, a bout of Crohn's disease, and a mild stroke. He made no attempt to conceal his condition, and he sent a letter to his vice president, Richard Nixon, authorizing Nixon to assume the duties and powers of president whenever Eisenhower indicated he could not do so; Nixon was to yield them back when Eisenhower reported that he was now all right again.

That was an improvised solution. Section Three makes this procedure constitutional and involves Congress in the arrangement. A president who is or shortly will become disabled—for example, by undergoing anesthesia for surgery—may formally pass power to the vice president. The letter, however, can't be a secret between them—he must send it to the president pro tempore of the Senate and the Speaker of the House. The letter must explicitly say that the president "is unable to discharge the powers and duties of his office." The vice president will then "discharge" those duties as "Acting President."

His coach will turn into a pumpkin, however, as soon as the president sends the same officials "a written declaration to the contrary." The initiative at all times remains with the president. Section Three contains no provision for a vice president to refuse to return the "powers and duties" and return to insignificance.

SECTION FOUR. This brings us to the hardest problem—one that, if improperly solved, could bring a country to the edge of civil war. It attempts to deal with the nightmare scenario—a president who is unable to function but refuses to admit it. The situation could arise in relation to physical illness, as in the case of Woodrow Wilson's prolonged recovery from a stroke. Or, even more ominously, it might stem from mental illness, in which an unstable president, with formal control of the American military and its nuclear arsenal, becomes a danger to the country and the planet.

Section Four takes up two-thirds of the amendment and sets up a complex system for addressing a claim of presidential disability. Essentially, the amendment empowers the vice president, after consultation with another group of leaders, to proclaim himself acting president and require the president to give Congress an account of his fitness. An acting presidency can last up to about three weeks. It's easy to see the danger of such a period, when the United States might have two presidents, like rival popes in medieval Christendom. The machinery has never been tried, and a reader who wades carefully through them might conclude that they are unlikely to work as advertised.

If officials around the president begin to think he is unable to function, they can in essence suspend him. The vice president must agree, and so must either a majority of (1) the Cabinet or (2) "such other body as Congress may by law provide." As in Section Three of the Twenty-Second Amendment, the drafters considered that Congress might want to set up a special council to take this decision away from the president's own appointees. (Congress has not yet exercised this option.)

If the vice president and a majority of the Cabinet (or council) agree, they transmit a "written declaration" to the Speaker and president pro tempore of the Senate. There can be no palace coup; the suspension of the president must be a matter of record, with names signed to the document. The "declaration" must state that "the President is unable to discharge the powers and duties of his office." Once the declaration is transmitted, the suspension begins, and the vice president "shall immediately assume the powers and duties of the office as Acting President."

The president, in other words, is suspended without any further procedure. If he agrees with this suspension, there the matter will rest, with the vice president as acting president. When the president is ready to return to his functions, he will transmit to the congressional leaders his own "written declaration that no disability exists," and he goes back to work—unless, that is, the vice president and a majority of the Cabinet (or other body designated by Congress) disagree. In that case, they have four days to submit a counter-declaration that he is still unable to serve. If they serve such a declaration, the president will remain suspended.

Now the showdown begins, with Congress as the referee. As soon as the counter-declaration is received, Congress must convene (if it is not in session, "within forty-eight hours"). Once assembled, Congress has three weeks to confirm the suspension of the president. If the houses split, or less than two-thirds of *either* vote against him, he returns to the "powers and duties" of the office. If they don't decide at all, the president will resume his duties; if, however, both houses hold a vote, and if two-thirds of the members of each house vote that the president is unfit, he then remains suspended. Note, however, that he can renew the process whenever he wishes, simply by transmitting a new declaration, setting off another emergency session of Congress and in effect submitting his health and sanity to public trial yet again.

One can admire the earnestness of the amendment's drafters without being convinced that their handiwork will ever function as intended. Just at the most niggling level, what happens if the president, suspended by the vice president and Cabinet, sends a declaration of fitness? He shall resume his duties "unless" the original body submits a new declaration "within four days." But it does not say that the president must wait four days before resuming. A situation could arise in which the president sends his declaration (in fact, one could read the language to say that the declaration does not need to have even reached the congressional leadership, just that it have been "transmit[ted]") and immediately seizes the reins of power, only to be confronted with a second declaration by the advisers that he is still unfit, and a second suspension.

Early in Ronald Reagan's second term, as reported by journalists Jane Mayer and Doyle McManus, the president became deeply withdrawn and depressed—symptoms that in hindsight seem to have been early warnings of the Alzheimer's disease that disabled him after he left office. White House Chief of Staff James Baker actually discussed invoking Section Three until doctors could examine the president.[8] Nothing came of it—for in Reagan's time, as in Wilson's, the careers of most of those around the president depend on the success of the presidency. Once the Twenty-Fifth Amendment is invoked, the potential for chaos—and what is worse for politicians, of public disgrace—are too great to be used. One suspects that the Twenty-Fifth Amendment will, over the life of the Constitution, stand as a monument to the futility of trying to control the unpredictable and foresee the unforeseeable.

Twenty-Sixth Amendment

The Twenty-Sixth Amendment, last of the 1960s amendments, is the constitutional residue of that aching generational divide. For millions of men of the baby-boom generation, turning eighteen offered two major life changes: a chance to go to war, and the legal right to buy extremely weak beer in a saloon. Eighteen-year-old men were required to register for the draft—a draft that was not theoretical but quite real, and that swept thousands into the Army and off to Vietnam. "Old enough to fight? Old enough to vote!" read a popular bumper-strip slogan at the time.

It's not clear what difference a vote would have made. The voters were never given a choice about the war in Vietnam. But at the level of symbolism, the American system responded to the anger of its young. In 1971, the Twenty-Sixth Amendment required every state to lower its voting age to eighteen.

Once again, the "right of citizens of the United States to vote," like Harvey the Giant Rabbit, makes an ambiguous appearance in the text. And unlike the right of the poor to vote without tax receipts in hand, this is a first-class right, guaranteed against abridgment or denial by "by the United States or by any State."

Young American voters are better protected in the text of the Constitution than are the poor. Young people turning eighteen today may vote freely and may volunteer to fight and die in their country's wars.

But in most places, they can't buy beer any more.

CONCLUSION. With the Twenty-Sixth Amendment, the 1960s reforms ground to a halt. The Equal Rights Amendment, which would have been the first explicit guarantee of equality for any group, was halted by grassroots opposition. Since its failure, the major use of the Article V process has been as a political tool to offer angry voters the opportunity to withdraw rights they dislike. Proposed amendments would have empowered the government to punish flag-burners, forced dissenting children to pray in school, blocked pregnant women from choosing abortion, narrowed Bill of Rights guarantees to criminal suspects, and barred same-sex couples from gaining the right to marry. All have failed.

One is tempted to take this failure as a tribute to the wisdom of the Framers and the cumbersome amendment process they designed. But it is also a devastating comment on the gathering darkness of American politics. In the past four decades, the national dialogue has turned away from the quest for equality and focused more and more on which groups to punish.

Madison's Return

The Twenty-Seventh Amendment

James Madison, principal author of the original Constitution and its Bill of Rights, has the last word in the text. Even though it was added to the Constitution in 1992, the Twenty-Seventh Amendment was proposed by Madison in 1789 and wandered the new country like a mendicant ghost for two centuries before being welcomed home under very strange circumstances by members of Congress too terrified of immediate political disadvantage to concern themselves with the possible consequences of what they were doing.

After the legalisms of amendments like the Twentieth and the Twenty-Fifth, the Twenty-Seventh speaks in the elevated tones of the original document: "No law, varying the compensation for the services of the Senators and Representatives, shall take effect, until an election of representatives shall have intervened."

Congress must approve all appropriations and all expenditures. This means that it must set its own rate of pay. Under the Twenty-Seventh Amendment, no pay raise can take effect until after the next election, giving the people the right to express their feelings about it by defeating those who supported it. (With the fine objectivity of constitutional text, the amendment by its terms bars Congress from voting itself an immediate pay cut as well.)

Madison originally proposed not ten but thirteen amendments in his original Bill of Rights. The one he considered most important would have forbidden states, as well as the federal government, to "violate the equal rights of conscience, or the freedom of the press, or the trial by jury in criminal cases." This proposal did not even make it through Congress; even if it had, it would have faced an uphill fight among state legislatures more eager to restrain the federal government than themselves.

Two others were approved by the necessary two-thirds of Congress but failed of ratification in the months after approval. One of those would have required at least one member of the House of Representatives for every 50,000 people (today's

House, had this passed, would have more than 5,500 members). The second eventually became the Twenty-Seventh Amendment. "There is a seeming impropriety in leaving any set of men without controul their hand into the public coffers, to take out money to put in their pockets," Madison told the First Congress.[1]

When first proposed by Congress in 1789, the salary amendment was rejected by legislatures in Hew Hampshire, New Jersey, New York, Pennsylvania, and Rhode Island. For two centuries, then, it slept fitfully in the public imagination. Congress never approved it again. But from time to time, various state legislatures would seize upon it and approve it as a painless way to show hometown disapproval of the distant Washington elite. Ohio's legislature approved it in 1873, and Wyoming's in 1978. But the proposed amendment remained a beggar outside the gates until 1982, when an earnest twenty-year-old college undergraduate, Gregory Watson, proposed ratification as part of a term paper. Watson's professor thought the idea untenable, but the student took his quest to state legislatures and members of Congress, and ratifications began to pile up.

Obviously there is a conceptual problem with the idea of ratifying a proposed amendment over a 200-year period. Many of the states approving the measure in the 1980s were not even dreamed of in 1789. (Who at Philadelphia would have predicted that the nation would make states out of part of Russia or the independent nation of the Sandwich Islands?) The nation had changed, and the nature of Congress itself had been transformed. A limit on pay increases might be a good idea; but it was not this generation's idea, or that of its parents or grandparents. The approvals with which the measure began its final approach to ratification were the "dead hand of the past" at its deadest, voted by men long buried, whose very names are forgotten.

But political cowardice overwhelms theoretical concerns. The final burst of approvals came during the House banking scandal of 1992, in which it was revealed that members of Congress had access to a special bank that would often hold their checks for payment even when the members' accounts could not cover them. In May 1992, five new states approved, and Madison's rough beast slouched toward the National Archives to be born. Senator Robert Byrd of West Virginia sharply warned the archivist—charged by statute with certifying the passage of new amendments—that the process was improper. But the statute prescribed a duty, which the archivist followed, and when certification was challenged in Congress, only three members of either House voted against incorporating it into the Constitution.[2]

As policy, the Twenty-Seventh Amendment does no harm, or very little. Salaries today range from $174,000 for an ordinary representative or senator to $223,000 for the Speaker of the House. Under law, members receive a regular cost-of-living adjustment, though some who can afford to choose not to accept it. And of course, as in past times, a certain number of members find ways to allow grateful citizens to supplement their wages with gifts, kickbacks, and bribes. Whether their creativity in this regard would be lessened if their salaries were higher is at best open to dispute.

But as stewardship of the Constitution, the approval of the Twenty-Seventh Amendment is troubling. During the twentieth century, amendment proponents, as we've seen, began proposing time limits for ratification. This was seemly; ratification was seen as a single act of political decision, rather than as the slow accumulation of fossilized approval, like the geological growth of a stalactite in a constitutional cavern. The living would propose change, and the living would approve or reject it, and the nation would move on. That view had also been endorsed by the Supreme Court in the 1922 case of *Dillon v. Gloss*, in which it wrote that in Article V "we do not find anything . . . which suggests that an amendment once proposed is to be open to ratification for all time, or that ratification in some of the states may be separated from that in others by many years and yet be effective. We do find that which strongly suggests the contrary."[3] The Court, however, decided that setting those limits was a matter for Congress, not the courts; which is wise because it's also hard to find anything in Article V that suggested the courts should have power to approve or reject amendments to the Constitution. That prospect, I suspect, would given even the most hawkish fan of judicial review pause.

As the Twenty-Seventh Amendment's approval shows, however, Congress is not a firm wall of protection when its members' immediate political advantage conflicts with the value of textual integrity. If during some future spasm of popular anger, activists and college students begin hectoring state legislatures about Madison's other proposed amendment, might we not wake up one day to find that some obscure act of legislative approval has overnight changed the House of Representatives from an assembly of 435 members into a small city of 5,500 or so? And would that really be a constitutional amendment, or a revolution in fancy dress?

Americans like to think of the Constitution as a fixed law that holds down the preferences of the leaders and the led, that channels them into paths set down over the years by wise figures in clear text. The Twenty-Seventh Amendment can be seen as an inconsequential homage to the Constitution's father. It can also be seen as a warning that the text, which so many revere and so many fewer have read, remains unfixed, permeable to the winds of popular passion, and open to unsettling changes by irregular procedure.

As a whole, its composition spanning two centuries, the Constitution forges a complex language, its words drawing meaning from their interrelation and the gloss of new uses. Whatever the political implications of this latest and oddest amendment, it has at least the poetic virtue of allowing the Constitution to come full circle.

It began with an invocation of the people, its mythical authors; in that invocation, the Framers portrayed their words as ours. Now, like a sestina, it finishes with what poets call an "envoi," a short final stanza in the voice of its greatest bard. In this last amendment, after two centuries, Madison's words have become our own.

Appendix

THE UNITED STATES CONSTITUTION*

We the People of the United States, in Order to form a more perfect Union, establish Justice, insure domestic Tranquility, provide for the common defence, promote the general Welfare, and secure the Blessings of Liberty to ourselves and our Posterity, do ordain and establish this Constitution for the United States of America.

Article I

Section 1

All legislative Powers herein granted shall be vested in a Congress of the United States, which shall consist of a Senate and House of Representatives.

Section 2

The House of Representatives shall be composed of Members chosen every second Year by the People of the several States, and the Electors in each State shall have the Qualifications requisite for Electors of the most numerous Branch of the State Legislature.

No Person shall be a Representative who shall not have attained to the Age of twenty five Years, and been seven Years a Citizen of the United States, and who shall not, when elected, be an Inhabitant of that State in which he shall be chosen.

Representatives and direct Taxes shall be apportioned among the several States which may be included within this Union, according to their respective Numbers, which shall be determined by adding to the whole Number of free Persons, including those bound to Service for a Term of Years, and excluding Indians not taxed, three fifths of all other Persons. The actual Enumeration shall be made within three Years after the first Meeting of the Congress of the United

* National Archives, "Charters of Freedom: 'A New World is at Hand,'" www.archives.gov/exhibits/charters

States, and within every subsequent Term of ten Years, in such Manner as they shall by Law direct. The Number of Representatives shall not exceed one for every thirty Thousand, but each State shall have at Least one Representative; and until such enumeration shall be made, the State of New Hampshire shall be entitled to chuse three, Massachusetts eight, Rhode-Island and Providence Plantations one, Connecticut five, New-York six, New Jersey four, Pennsylvania eight, Delaware one, Maryland six, Virginia ten, North Carolina five, South Carolina five, and Georgia three.

When vacancies happen in the Representation from any State, the Executive Authority thereof shall issue Writs of Election to fill such Vacancies.

The House of Representatives shall chuse their Speaker and other Officers; and shall have the sole Power of Impeachment.

Section 3

The Senate of the United States shall be composed of two Senators from each State, chosen by the Legislature thereof for six Years; and each Senator shall have one Vote.

Immediately after they shall be assembled in Consequence of the first Election, they shall be divided as equally as may be into three Classes. The Seats of the Senators of the first Class shall be vacated at the Expiration of the second Year, of the second Class at the Expiration of the fourth Year, and of the third Class at the Expiration of the sixth Year, so that one third may be chosen every second Year; and if Vacancies happen by Resignation, or otherwise, during the Recess of the Legislature of any State, the Executive thereof may make temporary Appointments until the next Meeting of the Legislature, which shall then fill such Vacancies.

No Person shall be a Senator who shall not have attained to the Age of thirty Years, and been nine Years a Citizen of the United States, and who shall not, when elected, be an Inhabitant of that State for which he shall be chosen.

The Vice President of the United States shall be President of the Senate, but shall have no Vote, unless they be equally divided.

The Senate shall chuse their other Officers, and also a President pro tempore, in the Absence of the Vice President, or when he shall exercise the Office of President of the United States.

The Senate shall have the sole Power to try all Impeachments. When sitting for that Purpose, they shall be on Oath or Affirmation. When the President of the United States is tried, the Chief Justice shall preside: And no Person shall be convicted without the Concurrence of two thirds of the Members present.

Judgment in Cases of Impeachment shall not extend further than to removal from Office, and disqualification to hold and enjoy any Office of honor, Trust or Profit under the United States: but the Party convicted shall nevertheless be liable and subject to Indictment, Trial, Judgment and Punishment, according to Law.

Section 4

The Times, Places and Manner of holding Elections for Senators and Representatives, shall be prescribed in each State by the Legislature thereof; but the Congress may at any time by Law make or alter such Regulations, except as to the Places of chusing Senators.

The Congress shall assemble at least once in every Year, and such Meeting shall be on the first Monday in December, unless they shall by Law appoint a different Day.

Section 5

Each House shall be the Judge of the Elections, Returns and Qualifications of its own Members, and a Majority of each shall constitute a Quorum to do Business; but a smaller Number may adjourn from day to day, and may be authorized to compel the Attendance of absent Members, in such Manner, and under such Penalties as each House may provide.

Each House may determine the Rules of its Proceedings, punish its Members for disorderly Behaviour, and, with the Concurrence of two thirds, expel a Member.

Each House shall keep a Journal of its Proceedings, and from time to time publish the same, excepting such Parts as may in their Judgment require Secrecy; and the Yeas and Nays of the Members of either House on any question shall, at the Desire of one fifth of those Present, be entered on the Journal.

Neither House, during the Session of Congress, shall, without the Consent of the other, adjourn for more than three days, nor to any other Place than that in which the two Houses shall be sitting.

Section 6

The Senators and Representatives shall receive a Compensation for their Services, to be ascertained by Law, and paid out of the Treasury of the United States. They shall in all Cases, except Treason, Felony and Breach of the Peace, be privileged from Arrest during their Attendance at the Session of their respective Houses, and in going to and returning from the same; and for any Speech or Debate in either House, they shall not be questioned in any other Place.

No Senator or Representative shall, during the Time for which he was elected, be appointed to any civil Office under the Authority of the United States, which shall have been created, or the Emoluments whereof shall have been encreased during such time; and no Person holding any Office under the United States, shall be a Member of either House during his Continuance in Office.

Section 7

All Bills for raising Revenue shall originate in the House of Representatives; but the Senate may propose or concur with Amendments as on other Bills.

Every Bill which shall have passed the House of Representatives and the Senate, shall, before it become a Law, be presented to the President of the United States: If he approve he shall sign it, but if not he shall return it, with his Objections to that House in which it shall have originated, who shall enter the Objections at large on their Journal, and proceed to reconsider it. If after such Reconsideration two thirds of that House shall agree to pass the Bill, it shall be sent, together with the Objections, to the other House, by which it shall likewise be reconsidered, and if approved by two thirds of that House, it shall become a Law. But in all such Cases the Votes of both Houses shall be determined by yeas and Nays, and the Names of the Persons voting for and against the Bill shall be entered on the Journal of each House respectively. If any Bill shall not be returned by the President within ten Days (Sundays excepted) after it shall have been presented to him, the Same shall be a Law, in like Manner as if he had signed it, unless the Congress by their Adjournment prevent its Return, in which Case it shall not be a Law.

Every Order, Resolution, or Vote to which the Concurrence of the Senate and House of Representatives may be necessary (except on a question of Adjournment) shall be presented to the President of the United States; and before the Same shall take Effect, shall be approved by him, or being disapproved by him, shall be repassed by two thirds of the Senate and House of Representatives, according to the Rules and Limitations prescribed in the Case of a Bill.

Section 8

The Congress shall have Power To lay and collect Taxes, Duties, Imposts and Excises, to pay the Debts and provide for the common Defence and general Welfare of the United States; but all Duties, Imposts and Excises shall be uniform throughout the United States;

To borrow Money on the credit of the United States;

To regulate Commerce with foreign Nations, and among the several States, and with the Indian Tribes;

To establish an uniform Rule of Naturalization, and uniform Laws on the subject of Bankruptcies throughout the United States;

To coin Money, regulate the Value thereof, and of foreign Coin, and fix the Standard of Weights and Measures;

To provide for the Punishment of counterfeiting the Securities and current Coin of the United States;

To establish Post Offices and post Roads;

To promote the Progress of Science and useful Arts, by securing for limited Times to Authors and Inventors the exclusive Right to their respective Writings and Discoveries;

To constitute Tribunals inferior to the supreme Court;

To define and punish Piracies and Felonies committed on the high Seas, and Offences against the Law of Nations;

To declare War, grant Letters of Marque and Reprisal, and make Rules concerning Captures on Land and Water;

To raise and support Armies, but no Appropriation of Money to that Use shall be for a longer Term than two Years;

To provide and maintain a Navy;

To make Rules for the Government and Regulation of the land and naval Forces;

To provide for calling forth the Militia to execute the Laws of the Union, suppress Insurrections and repel Invasions;

To provide for organizing, arming, and disciplining, the Militia, and for governing such Part of them as may be employed in the Service of the United States, reserving to the States respectively, the Appointment of the Officers, and the Authority of training the Militia according to the discipline prescribed by Congress;

To exercise exclusive Legislation in all Cases whatsoever, over such District (not exceeding ten Miles square) as may, by Cession of particular States, and the Acceptance of Congress, become the Seat of the Government of the United States, and to exercise like Authority over all Places purchased by the Consent of the Legislature of the State in which the Same shall be, for the Erection of Forts, Magazines, Arsenals, dock-Yards, and other needful Buildings;—And

To make all Laws which shall be necessary and proper for carrying into Execution the foregoing Powers, and all other Powers vested by this Constitution in the Government of the United States, or in any Department or Officer thereof.

Section 9

The Migration or Importation of such Persons as any of the States now existing shall think proper to admit, shall not be prohibited by the Congress prior to the Year one thousand eight hundred and eight, but a Tax or duty may be imposed on such Importation, not exceeding ten dollars for each Person.

The Privilege of the Writ of Habeas Corpus shall not be suspended, unless when in Cases of Rebellion or Invasion the public Safety may require it.

No Bill of Attainder or ex post facto Law shall be passed.

No Capitation, or other direct, Tax shall be laid, unless in Proportion to the Census or enumeration herein before directed to be taken.

No Tax or Duty shall be laid on Articles exported from any State.

No Preference shall be given by any Regulation of Commerce or Revenue to the Ports of one State over those of another; nor shall Vessels bound to, or from, one State, be obliged to enter, clear, or pay Duties in another.

No Money shall be drawn from the Treasury, but in Consequence of Appropriations made by Law; and a regular Statement and Account of the Receipts and Expenditures of all public Money shall be published from time to time.

No Title of Nobility shall be granted by the United States: And no Person holding any Office of Profit or Trust under them, shall, without the Consent of the Congress, accept of any present, Emolument, Office, or Title, of any kind whatever, from any King, Prince, or foreign State.

Section 10

No State shall enter into any Treaty, Alliance, or Confederation; grant Letters of Marque and Reprisal; coin Money; emit Bills of Credit; make any Thing but gold and silver Coin a Tender in Payment of Debts; pass any Bill of Attainder, ex post facto Law, or Law impairing the Obligation of Contracts, or grant any Title of Nobility.

No State shall, without the Consent of the Congress, lay any Imposts or Duties on Imports or Exports, except what may be absolutely necessary for executing it's inspection Laws: and the net Produce of all Duties and Imposts, laid by any State on Imports or Exports, shall be for the Use of the Treasury of the United States; and all such Laws shall be subject to the Revision and Controul of the Congress.

No State shall, without the Consent of Congress, lay any Duty of Tonnage, keep Troops, or Ships of War in time of Peace, enter into any Agreement or Compact with another State, or with a foreign Power, or engage in War, unless actually invaded, or in such imminent Danger as will not admit of delay.

Article II

Section 1

The executive Power shall be vested in a President of the United States of America. He shall hold his Office during the Term of four Years, and, together with the Vice President, chosen for the same Term, be elected, as follows:

Each State shall appoint, in such Manner as the Legislature thereof may direct, a Number of Electors, equal to the whole Number of Senators and Representatives to which the State may be entitled in the Congress: but no Senator or Representative, or Person holding an Office of Trust or Profit under the United States, shall be appointed an Elector.

The Electors shall meet in their respective States, and vote by Ballot for two Persons, of whom one at least shall not be an Inhabitant of the same State with themselves. And they shall make a List of all the Persons voted for, and of the Number of Votes for each; which List they shall sign and certify, and transmit sealed to the Seat of the Government of the United States, directed to the President of the Senate. The President of the Senate shall, in the Presence of the Senate and House of Representatives, open all the Certificates, and the Votes shall then be counted. The Person having the greatest Number of Votes shall be the President, if such Number be a Majority of the whole Number of Electors appointed; and if there be more than one who have such Majority, and have an equal Number of Votes, then the House of Representatives shall immediately chuse by Ballot one of them for President; and if no Person have a Majority, then from the five highest on the List the said House shall in like Manner chuse the President. But in chusing the President, the Votes shall be taken by States, the Representation from each State having one Vote; A quorum for this purpose shall consist of a Member or Members from two thirds of the States, and a Majority of all the States shall be necessary to a Choice. In every Case, after the Choice of the President, the Person having the greatest Number of Votes of the Electors shall be the Vice President. But if there should remain two or more who have equal Votes, the Senate shall chuse from them by Ballot the Vice President.

The Congress may determine the Time of chusing the Electors, and the Day on which they shall give their Votes; which Day shall be the same throughout the United States.

No Person except a natural born Citizen, or a Citizen of the United States, at the time of the Adoption of this Constitution, shall be eligible to the Office of President; neither shall any Person be eligible to that Office who shall not have attained to the Age of thirty five Years, and been fourteen Years a Resident within the United States.

In Case of the Removal of the President from Office, or of his Death, Resignation, or Inability to discharge the Powers and Duties of the said Office, the Same shall devolve on the Vice President, and the Congress may by Law provide for the Case of Removal, Death, Resignation or Inability, both of the President and Vice President, declaring what Officer shall then act as President, and such Officer shall act accordingly, until the Disability be removed, or a President shall be elected.

The President shall, at stated Times, receive for his Services, a Compensation, which shall neither be increased nor diminished during the Period for which he shall have been elected, and he shall not receive within that Period any other Emolument from the United States, or any of them.

Before he enter on the Execution of his Office, he shall take the following Oath or Affirmation:—"I do solemnly swear (or affirm) that I will faithfully execute the Office of President of the United States, and will to the best of my Ability, preserve, protect and defend the Constitution of the United States."

Section 2

The President shall be Commander in Chief of the Army and Navy of the United States, and of the Militia of the several States, when called into the actual Service of the United States; he may require the Opinion, in writing, of the principal Officer in each of the executive Departments, upon any Subject relating to the Duties of their respective Offices, and he shall have Power to grant Reprieves and Pardons for Offences against the United States, except in Cases of Impeachment.

He shall have Power, by and with the Advice and Consent of the Senate, to make Treaties, provided two thirds of the Senators present concur; and he shall nominate, and by and with the Advice and Consent of the Senate, shall appoint Ambassadors, other public Ministers and Consuls, Judges of the supreme Court, and all other Officers of the United States, whose Appointments are not herein otherwise provided for, and which shall be established by Law: but the Congress may by Law vest the Appointment of such inferior Officers, as they think proper, in the President alone, in the Courts of Law, or in the Heads of Departments.

The President shall have Power to fill up all Vacancies that may happen during the Recess of the Senate, by granting Commissions which shall expire at the End of their next Session.

Section 3

He shall from time to time give to the Congress Information of the State of the Union, and recommend to their Consideration such Measures as he shall judge necessary and expedient; he may, on extraordinary Occasions, convene both Houses, or either of them, and in Case of Disagreement between them, with Respect to the Time of Adjournment, he may adjourn them to such Time as he shall think proper; he shall receive Ambassadors and other public Ministers; he shall take Care that the Laws be faithfully executed, and shall Commission all the Officers of the United States.

Section 4

The President, Vice President and all civil Officers of the United States, shall be removed from Office on Impeachment for, and Conviction of, Treason, Bribery, or other high Crimes and Misdemeanors.

Article III

Section 1

The judicial Power of the United States shall be vested in one supreme Court, and in such inferior Courts as the Congress may from time to time ordain and establish. The Judges, both of the supreme and inferior Courts, shall hold their Offices during good Behaviour, and shall, at stated Times, receive for their Services a Compensation, which shall not be diminished during their Continuance in Office.

Section 2

The judicial Power shall extend to all Cases, in Law and Equity, arising under this Constitution, the Laws of the United States, and Treaties made, or which shall be made, under their Authority;—to all Cases affecting Ambassadors, other public Ministers and Consuls;—to all Cases of admiralty and maritime Jurisdiction;—to Controversies to which the United States shall be a Party;—to Controversies between two or more States;— between a State and Citizens of another State,—between Citizens of different States,—between Citizens of the same State claiming Lands under Grants of different States, and between a State, or the Citizens thereof, and foreign States, Citizens or Subjects.

In all Cases affecting Ambassadors, other public Ministers and Consuls, and those in which a State shall be Party, the supreme Court shall have original Jurisdiction. In all the other Cases before mentioned, the supreme Court shall have appellate Jurisdiction, both as to Law and Fact, with such Exceptions, and under such Regulations as the Congress shall make.

The Trial of all Crimes, except in Cases of Impeachment, shall be by Jury; and such Trial shall be held in the State where the said Crimes shall have been committed; but when not committed within any State, the Trial shall be at such Place or Places as the Congress may by Law have directed.

Section 3

Treason against the United States, shall consist only in levying War against them, or in adhering to their Enemies, giving them Aid and Comfort. No Person shall be convicted of Treason unless on the Testimony of two Witnesses to the same overt Act, or on Confession in open Court.

The Congress shall have Power to declare the Punishment of Treason, but no Attainder of Treason shall work Corruption of Blood, or Forfeiture except during the Life of the Person attainted.

Article IV

Section 1

Full Faith and Credit shall be given in each State to the public Acts, Records, and judicial Proceedings of every other State. And the Congress may by general Laws prescribe the Manner in which such Acts, Records and Proceedings shall be proved, and the Effect thereof.

Section 2

The Citizens of each State shall be entitled to all Privileges and Immunities of Citizens in the several States.

A Person charged in any State with Treason, Felony, or other Crime, who shall flee from Justice, and be found in another State, shall on Demand of the executive Authority of the State from which he fled, be delivered up, to be removed to the State having Jurisdiction of the Crime.

No Person held to Service or Labour in one State, under the Laws thereof, escaping into another, shall, in Consequence of any Law or Regulation therein, be discharged from such Service or Labour, but shall be delivered up on Claim of the Party to whom such Service or Labour may be due.

Section 3

New States may be admitted by the Congress into this Union; but no new State shall be formed or erected within the Jurisdiction of any other State; nor any State be formed by the Junction of two or more States, or Parts of States, without the Consent of the Legislatures of the States concerned as well as of the Congress.

The Congress shall have Power to dispose of and make all needful Rules and Regulations respecting the Territory or other Property belonging to the United States; and nothing in this Constitution shall be so construed as to Prejudice any Claims of the United States, or of any particular State.

Section 4

The United States shall guarantee to every State in this Union a Republican Form of Government, and shall protect each of them against Invasion; and on

Application of the Legislature, or of the Executive (when the Legislature cannot be convened), against domestic Violence.

Article V

The Congress, whenever two thirds of both Houses shall deem it necessary, shall propose Amendments to this Constitution, or, on the Application of the Legislatures of two thirds of the several States, shall call a Convention for proposing Amendments, which, in either Case, shall be valid to all Intents and Purposes, as Part of this Constitution, when ratified by the Legislatures of three fourths of the several States, or by Conventions in three fourths thereof, as the one or the other Mode of Ratification may be proposed by the Congress; Provided that no Amendment which may be made prior to the Year One thousand eight hundred and eight shall in any Manner affect the first and fourth Clauses in the Ninth Section of the first Article; and that no State, without its Consent, shall be deprived of its equal Suffrage in the Senate.

Article VI

All Debts contracted and Engagements entered into, before the Adoption of this Constitution, shall be as valid against the United States under this Constitution, as under the Confederation.

This Constitution, and the Laws of the United States which shall be made in Pursuance thereof; and all Treaties made, or which shall be made, under the Authority of the United States, shall be the supreme Law of the Land; and the Judges in every State shall be bound thereby, any Thing in the Constitution or Laws of any State to the Contrary notwithstanding.

The Senators and Representatives before mentioned, and the Members of the several State Legislatures, and all executive and judicial Officers, both of the United States and of the several States, shall be bound by Oath or Affirmation, to support this Constitution; but no religious Test shall ever be required as a Qualification to any Office or public Trust under the United States.

Article VII

The Ratification of the Conventions of nine States, shall be sufficient for the Establishment of this Constitution between the States so ratifying the Same.

Amendment I

Congress shall make no law respecting an establishment of religion, or prohibiting the free exercise thereof; or abridging the freedom of speech, or of the press; or the right of the people peaceably to assemble, and to petition the Government for a redress of grievances.

Amendment II

A well regulated Militia, being necessary to the security of a free State, the right of the people to keep and bear Arms, shall not be infringed.

Amendment III

No Soldier shall, in time of peace be quartered in any house, without the consent of the Owner, nor in time of war, but in a manner to be prescribed by law.

Amendment IV

The right of the people to be secure in their persons, houses, papers, and effects, against unreasonable searches and seizures, shall not be violated, and no Warrants shall issue, but upon probable cause, supported by Oath or affirmation, and particularly describing the place to be searched, and the persons or things to be seized.

Amendment V

No person shall be held to answer for a capital, or otherwise infamous crime, unless on a presentment or indictment of a Grand Jury, except in cases arising in the land or naval forces, or in the Militia, when in actual service in time of War or public danger; nor shall any person be subject for the same offence to be twice put in jeopardy of life or limb; nor shall be compelled in any criminal case to be a witness against himself, nor be deprived of life, liberty, or property, without due process of law; nor shall private property be taken for public use, without just compensation.

Amendment VI

In all criminal prosecutions, the accused shall enjoy the right to a speedy and public trial, by an impartial jury of the State and district wherein the crime shall have been committed, which district shall have been previously ascertained by law, and to be informed of the nature and cause of the accusation; to be confronted with the witnesses against him; to have compulsory process for obtaining witnesses in his favor, and to have the Assistance of Counsel for his defence.

Amendment VII

In Suits at common law, where the value in controversy shall exceed twenty dollars, the right of trial by jury shall be preserved, and no fact tried by a jury, shall be otherwise re-examined in any Court of the United States, than according to the rules of the common law.

Amendment VIII

Excessive bail shall not be required, nor excessive fines imposed, nor cruel and unusual punishments inflicted.

Amendment IX

The enumeration in the Constitution, of certain rights, shall not be construed to deny or disparage others retained by the people.

Amendment X

The powers not delegated to the United States by the Constitution, nor prohibited by it to the States, are reserved to the States respectively, or to the people.

Amendment XI

Passed by Congress March 4, 1794. Ratified February 7, 1795.
    Note: Article III, section 2, of the Constitution was modified by amendment 11.
    The Judicial power of the United States shall not be construed to extend to any suit in law or equity, commenced or prosecuted against one of the United States by Citizens of another State, or by Citizens or Subjects of any Foreign State.

Amendment XII

Passed by Congress December 9, 1803. Ratified June 15, 1804.

Note: A portion of Article II, section 1 of the Constitution was superseded by the 12th amendment.

The Electors shall meet in their respective states and vote by ballot for President and Vice-President, one of whom, at least, shall not be an inhabitant of the same state with themselves; they shall name in their ballots the person voted for as President, and in distinct ballots the person voted for as Vice-President, and they shall make distinct lists of all persons voted for as President, and of all persons voted for as Vice-President, and of the number of votes for each, which lists they shall sign and certify, and transmit sealed to the seat of the government of the United States, directed to the President of the Senate;—the President of the Senate shall, in the presence of the Senate and House of Representatives, open all the certificates and the votes shall then be counted;—The person having the greatest number of votes for President, shall be the President, if such number be a majority of the whole number of Electors appointed; and if no person have such majority, then from the persons having the highest numbers not exceeding three on the list of those voted for as President, the House of Representatives shall choose immediately, by ballot, the President. But in choosing the President, the votes shall be taken by states, the representation from each state having one vote; a quorum for this purpose shall consist of a member or members from two-thirds of the states, and a majority of all the states shall be necessary to a choice. [And if the House of Representatives shall not choose a President whenever the right of choice shall devolve upon them, before the fourth day of March next following, then the Vice-President shall act as President, as in case of the death or other constitutional disability of the President. —]* The person having the greatest number of votes as Vice-President, shall be the Vice-President, if such number be a majority of the whole number of Electors appointed, and if no person have a majority, then from the two highest numbers on the list, the Senate shall choose the Vice-President; a quorum for the purpose shall consist of two-thirds of the whole number of Senators, and a majority of the whole number shall be necessary to a choice. But no person constitutionally ineligible to the office of President shall be eligible to that of Vice-President of the United States.

Amendment XIII

Passed by Congress January 31, 1865. Ratified December 6, 1865.

---

* *Superseded by section 3 of the 20th amendment.*

Note: A portion of Article IV, section 2, of the Constitution was superseded by the 13th amendment.

Section 1

Neither slavery nor involuntary servitude, except as a punishment for crime whereof the party shall have been duly convicted, shall exist within the United States, or any place subject to their jurisdiction.

Section 2

Congress shall have power to enforce this article by appropriate legislation.

Amendment XIV

Passed by Congress June 13, 1866. Ratified July 9, 1868.
   Note: Article I, section 2, of the Constitution was modified by section 2 of the 14th amendment.

Section 1

All persons born or naturalized in the United States, and subject to the jurisdiction thereof, are citizens of the United States and of the State wherein they reside. No State shall make or enforce any law which shall abridge the privileges or immunities of citizens of the United States; nor shall any State deprive any person of life, liberty, or property, without due process of law; nor deny to any person within its jurisdiction the equal protection of the laws.

Section 2

Representatives shall be apportioned among the several States according to their respective numbers, counting the whole number of persons in each State, excluding Indians not taxed. But when the right to vote at any election for the choice of electors for President and Vice-President of the United States, Representatives in Congress, the Executive and Judicial officers of a State, or the members of the Legislature thereof, is denied to any of the male inhabitants of such State, being twenty-one years of age,* and citizens of the United States, or in any way abridged, except for participation in rebellion, or other crime, the basis of representation

---

* *Changed by section 1 of the 26th amendment.*

therein shall be reduced in the proportion which the number of such male citizens shall bear to the whole number of male citizens twenty-one years of age in such State.

Section 3

No person shall be a Senator or Representative in Congress, or elector of President and Vice-President, or hold any office, civil or military, under the United States, or under any State, who, having previously taken an oath, as a member of Congress, or as an officer of the United States, or as a member of any State legislature, or as an executive or judicial officer of any State, to support the Constitution of the United States, shall have engaged in insurrection or rebellion against the same, or given aid or comfort to the enemies thereof. But Congress may by a vote of two-thirds of each House, remove such disability.

Section 4

The validity of the public debt of the United States, authorized by law, including debts incurred for payment of pensions and bounties for services in suppressing insurrection or rebellion, shall not be questioned. But neither the United States nor any State shall assume or pay any debt or obligation incurred in aid of insurrection or rebellion against the United States, or any claim for the loss or emancipation of any slave; but all such debts, obligations and claims shall be held illegal and void.

Section 5

The Congress shall have the power to enforce, by appropriate legislation, the provisions of this article.

Amendment XV

Passed by Congress February 26, 1869. Ratified February 3, 1870.

Section 1

The right of citizens of the United States to vote shall not be denied or abridged by the United States or by any State on account of race, color, or previous condition of servitude—

Section 2.

The Congress shall have the power to enforce this article by appropriate legislation.

Amendment XVI

Passed by Congress July 2, 1909. Ratified February 3, 1913.

   Note: Article I, section 9, of the Constitution was modified by amendment 16.

   The Congress shall have power to lay and collect taxes on incomes, from whatever source derived, without apportionment among the several States, and without regard to any census or enumeration.

Amendment XVII

Passed by Congress May 13, 1912. Ratified April 8, 1913.

   Note: Article I, section 3, of the Constitution was modified by the 17th amendment.

   The Senate of the United States shall be composed of two Senators from each State, elected by the people thereof, for six years; and each Senator shall have one vote. The electors in each State shall have the qualifications requisite for electors of the most numerous branch of the State legislatures.

   When vacancies happen in the representation of any State in the Senate, the executive authority of such State shall issue writs of election to fill such vacancies: *Provided*, That the legislature of any State may empower the executive thereof to make temporary appointments until the people fill the vacancies by election as the legislature may direct.

   This amendment shall not be so construed as to affect the election or term of any Senator chosen before it becomes valid as part of the Constitution.

Amendment XVIII

Passed by Congress December 18, 1917. Ratified January 16, 1919. Repealed by amendment 21.

Section 1

After one year from the ratification of this article the manufacture, sale, or transportation of intoxicating liquors within, the importation thereof into, or the exportation thereof from the United States and all territory subject to the jurisdiction thereof for beverage purposes is hereby prohibited.

Section 2

The Congress and the several States shall have concurrent power to enforce this article by appropriate legislation.

Section 3

This article shall be inoperative unless it shall have been ratified as an amendment to the Constitution by the legislatures of the several States, as provided in the Constitution, within seven years from the date of the submission hereof to the States by the Congress.

Amendment XIX

Passed by Congress June 4, 1919. Ratified August 18, 1920.
The right of citizens of the United States to vote shall not be denied or abridged by the United States or by any State on account of sex.
Congress shall have power to enforce this article by appropriate legislation.

Amendment XX

Passed by Congress March 2, 1932. Ratified January 23, 1933.
Note: Article I, section 4, of the Constitution was modified by section 2 of this amendment. In addition, a portion of the 12th amendment was superseded by section 3.

Section 1

The terms of the President and the Vice President shall end at noon on the 20th day of January, and the terms of Senators and Representatives at noon on the 3rd day of January, of the years in which such terms would have ended if this article had not been ratified; and the terms of their successors shall then begin.

Section 2

The Congress shall assemble at least once in every year, and such meeting shall begin at noon on the 3d day of January, unless they shall by law appoint a different day.

Section 3

If, at the time fixed for the beginning of the term of the President, the President elect shall have died, the Vice President elect shall become President. If a President shall not have been chosen before the time fixed for the beginning of his term, or if the President elect shall have failed to qualify, then the Vice President elect shall act as President until a President shall have qualified; and the Congress may by law provide for the case wherein neither a President elect nor a Vice President shall have qualified, declaring who shall then act as President, or the manner in which one who is to act shall be selected, and such person shall act accordingly until a President or Vice President shall have qualified.

Section 4

The Congress may by law provide for the case of the death of any of the persons from whom the House of Representatives may choose a President whenever the right of choice shall have devolved upon them, and for the case of the death of any of the persons from whom the Senate may choose a Vice President whenever the right of choice shall have devolved upon them.

Section 5

Sections 1 and 2 shall take effect on the 15th day of October following the ratification of this article.

Section 6

This article shall be inoperative unless it shall have been ratified as an amendment to the Constitution by the legislatures of three-fourths of the several States within seven years from the date of its submission.

Amendment XXI

Passed by Congress February 20, 1933. Ratified December 5, 1933.

Section 1

The eighteenth article of amendment to the Constitution of the United States is hereby repealed.

Section 2

The transportation or importation into any State, Territory, or Possession of the United States for delivery or use therein of intoxicating liquors, in violation of the laws thereof, is hereby prohibited.

Section 3

This article shall be inoperative unless it shall have been ratified as an amendment to the Constitution by conventions in the several States, as provided in the Constitution, within seven years from the date of the submission hereof to the States by the Congress.

Amendment XXII

Passed by Congress March 21, 1947. Ratified February 27, 1951.

Section 1

No person shall be elected to the office of the President more than twice, and no person who has held the office of President, or acted as President, for more than two years of a term to which some other person was elected President shall be elected to the office of President more than once. But this Article shall not apply to any person holding the office of President when this Article was proposed by Congress, and shall not prevent any person who may be holding the office of President, or acting as President, during the term within which this Article becomes operative from holding the office of President or acting as President during the remainder of such term.

Section 2

This article shall be inoperative unless it shall have been ratified as an amendment to the Constitution by the legislatures of three-fourths of the several States within seven years from the date of its submission to the States by the Congress.

Amendment XXIII

Passed by Congress June 16, 1960. Ratified March 29, 1961.

Section 1

The District constituting the seat of Government of the United States shall appoint in such manner as Congress may direct:

A number of electors of President and Vice President equal to the whole number of Senators and Representatives in Congress to which the District would be entitled if it were a State, but in no event more than the least populous State; they shall be in addition to those appointed by the States, but they shall be considered, for the purposes of the election of President and Vice President, to be electors appointed by a State; and they shall meet in the District and perform such duties as provided by the twelfth article of amendment.

Section 2

The Congress shall have power to enforce this article by appropriate legislation.

Amendment XXIV

Passed by Congress August 27, 1962. Ratified January 23, 1964.

Section 1

The right of citizens of the United States to vote in any primary or other election for President or Vice President, for electors for President or Vice President, or for Senator or Representative in Congress, shall not be denied or abridged by the United States or any State by reason of failure to pay poll tax or other tax.

Section 2

The Congress shall have power to enforce this article by appropriate legislation.

Amendment XXV

Passed by Congress July 6, 1965. Ratified February 10, 1967.
Note: Article II, section 1, of the Constitution was affected by the 25th amendment.

Section 1

In case of the removal of the President from office or of his death or resignation, the Vice President shall become President.

Section 2

Whenever there is a vacancy in the office of the Vice President, the President shall nominate a Vice President who shall take office upon confirmation by a majority vote of both Houses of Congress.

Section 3

Whenever the President transmits to the President pro tempore of the Senate and the Speaker of the House of Representatives his written declaration that he is unable to discharge the powers and duties of his office, and until he transmits to them a written declaration to the contrary, such powers and duties shall be discharged by the Vice President as Acting President.

Section 4

Whenever the Vice President and a majority of either the principal officers of the executive departments or of such other body as Congress may by law provide, transmit to the President pro tempore of the Senate and the Speaker of the House of Representatives their written declaration that the President is unable to discharge the powers and duties of his office, the Vice President shall immediately assume the powers and duties of the office as Acting President.

Thereafter, when the President transmits to the President pro tempore of the Senate and the Speaker of the House of Representatives his written declaration that no inability exists, he shall resume the powers and duties of his office unless the Vice President and a majority of either the principal officers of the executive department or of such other body as Congress may by law provide, transmit within four days to the President pro tempore of the Senate and the Speaker of the House of Representatives their written declaration that the President is unable to discharge the powers and duties of his office. Thereupon Congress shall decide the issue, assembling within forty-eight hours for that purpose if not in session. If the Congress, within twenty-one days after receipt of the latter written declaration, or, if Congress is not in session, within twenty-one days after Congress is required to assemble, determines by two-thirds vote of both Houses that the President is unable to discharge the powers and duties of his office, the Vice President shall continue to discharge the same as Acting President; otherwise, the President shall resume the powers and duties of his office.

Amendment XXVI

Passed by Congress March 23, 1971. Ratified July 1, 1971.
Note: Amendment 14, section 2, of the Constitution was modified by section 1 of the 26th amendment.

Section 1

The right of citizens of the United States, who are eighteen years of age or older, to vote shall not be denied or abridged by the United States or by any State on account of age.

Section 2

The Congress shall have power to enforce this article by appropriate legislation.

Amendment XXVII

Originally proposed Sept. 25, 1789. Ratified May 7, 1992.
No law, varying the compensation for the services of the Senators and Representatives, shall take effect, until an election of representatives shall have intervened.

NOTES

Preface

1. E. L. Doctorow, "A Citizen Reads the Constitution," in *Jack London, Hemingway, and the Constitution* (New York: Random House, 1993), p. 117.
2. Brown v. Allen, 344 U.S. 443, 540 (1953)(Jackson, J., concurring).
3. "First Inaugural Address," Abraham Lincoln, *Speeches and Writings 1859–1865*, ed. Don E. Fehrenbacher (New York: Library of America, 1989), pp. 215, 221.
4. William Martin, *The Lost Constitution* (New York: Forge Books 2008).
5. Martin Luther King Jr., *A Call to Conscience: The Landmark Speeches of Dr. Martin Luther King, Jr.*, ed. Clayborne Carson and Kris Shepard (New York: Warner Books, 2001), p. 10.
6. Ibid., p. 100.
7. The essays were published in twelve volumes between 1910 and 1915. They are available in one volume as R. A. Torrey et al., eds., *The Fundamentals: The Famous Sourcebook of Foundational Biblical Truths* (Grand Rapids, MI: Kregel, 1990).
8. Karl N. Llewellyn, "Remarks on the Theory of Appellate Decision and the Rules or Canons about How Statutes Are to Be Construed," 3 *Vanderbilt Law Review* 395, 422 (1949).
9. Antonin Scalia, *A Matter of Interpretation: Federal Courts and the Law* (Princeton University Press, 1997), p. 23.
10. Ibid., p. 31.
11. Ibid., p. 37.
12. Ibid.
13. Guido Calabresi, *A Common Law for the Age of Statutes* (Cambridge, MA: Harvard University Press, 1985).
14. Jefferson to Madison, November 18, 1788, in James Morton Smith, ed., *The Republic of Letters: The Correspondence between Thomas Jefferson and James Madison 1776–1826* (1995), Vol. 1, p. 567.
15. Anthony A. Peacock, *How to Read the Federalist Papers* (Washington, DC: Heritage Foundation, 2010), p. 5.
16. Ibid., p. 81.
17. "Law Like Love," in W.H. Auden, *Collected Poems* (Edward Mendelson, ed., New York: Modern Library, 2007), 260.
18. Gary Lawson and Guy Seidman, "Originalism as a Legal Enterprise," 23 *Constitutional Commentary* 47 (2006).
19. Christopher L. Eisgruber, "The Living Hand of the Past: History and Constitutional Justice," 5 *Fordham Law Review* 1611, 1617 (2007).
20. Lewis Putnam Turco, *The Book of Forms: A Handbook of Poetics Including Odd and Invented Forms* (Lebanon, NH: University Press of New England, 2012), p. 117.
21. "Howl," in Allen Ginsberg, *Howl and Other Poems* (San Francisco: City Lights Books, 1956), p. 9.

22. Harold Bloom, *The Art of Reading Poetry* (New York: HaperCollins, 2004) p. 1.
23. Walt Whitman, "Song of Myself," *Complete Poetry and Selected Prose*, ed. Justin Kaplan (New York: Library of America, 1982), p. 87.
24. Whitman, "By Blue Ontario's Shore," Ibid., p. 469.
25. Whitman, "When I Heard the Learn'd Astronomer," Ibid., p. 409.
26. Vladimir Nabokov, "Good Writers and Good Readers," *Lectures on Literature*, ed. Fredson Bowers (New York: Harcourt Brace Jovanovich, 1980), p. 3.

Chapter 1

1. James Madison, *Notes of Debates on the Federal Convention of 1787* at 385 (August 6), ed. Adrienne Koch (New York: Norton, 1966), hereinafter *notes*.
2. Homer, *The Iliad*, trans. Robert Fagles (New York: Viking Penguin, 1990), 1:1.
3. Virgil, *The Aeneid*, trans. Robert Fagles (New York: Viking Penguin, 2006), 1:8–9.
4. Walt Whitman, "By Blue Ontario's Shore," *Complete Poetry and Selected Prose*, ed. Justin Kaplan (New York: Library of America, 1982) p. 469.
5. Charles Olson, "Projective Verse," in *Twentieth Century American Poetics: Poets on the Art of Poetry*, ed. Dana Gioia et al. (New York: McGraw-Hill Higher Education, 2004), p. 174.

Chapter 2

1. On the role of the assembly in epic, see Albert B. Lord, *The Singer of Tales*, ed. Stephen Mitchell and Gregory Nagy (Cambridge, MA: Harvard University Press, 2000), pp. 146–47.
2. Powell v. McCormack, 395 U.S. 486 (1969).
3. See David P. Currie, *The Constitution in Congress: The Federalist Period, 1789–1801* (Chicago: University of Chicago Press, 1997), pp. 3–4.
4. Norman Davies, *Europe: A History* (Oxford: Oxford University Press, 1996), p. 551.
5. Akhil Reed Amar, *The Bill of Rights: Creation and Reconstruction* (New Haven, CT: Yale University Press, 1998), p. 24.
6. J. Howard B. Masterman, *A History of the British Constitution* (1912) (Farmington Hills, MI: Gale, 2010), p. 162.
7. Whitman, *Complete Poetry and Collected Prose* (New York: Library of America, 1982), p. 174.
8. Homer, *The Iliad*, trans. Robert Fagles (New York: Viking Penguin, 1990), 18:564–708, passim.
9. McCulloch v. Maryland, 17 U.S. 316 (1819).
10. Her Fictional Grace, the Duchess of Carbondale, is a memorable character from C.M. Kornbluth's 1956 science-fiction short story, "The Cosmic Charge Account," which attempts to create a completely ridiculous world by suggesting that an American might actually style herself with a title of nobility. C. M. Kornbluth, *Eight Worlds of C.M. Kornbluth* (Rockville, MD: Wildside Press, 2010), p. 15.

Chapter 3

1. Judges 9: 7–15.
2. Harvey C. Mansfield, Jr., *Taming the Prince: The Ambivalence of Modern Executive Power* (New York: Free Press, 1989).
3. Youngstown Sheet & Tube Co. v. Sawyer, 343 U.S. 579, 634 (1952)(Jackson, J., concurring).
4. *See generally* Joseph Chitty Jun., *A Treatise on the Law of the Prerogatives of the Crown; and the Relative Duties and Rights of the Subject* (1820, reprint ed. Classics of English Legal History of the Modern Era No. 72, 1978); on the contemporary prerogative, see House of Commons, Public Administration Select Committee, "PASC Publishes Government Defense of Its Sweeping Powers" (Press Notice No. 19, Session 2002-03)(available at http://www.parliament.uk/parliamentary_committees/public_administration_select_committee/pasc_19.cfm) (accessed August 28, 2009).

5. "president, n," *The Oxford English Dictionary Online*, 3d ed. (March 2007; online version June 2012). http://www.oed.com/view/Entry/150742 (accessed 14 June 2012).
6. Akhil Reed Amar, *America's Constitution: A Biography* (New York: Random House, 2005), p. 133.
7. Ibid., p. 134.
8. Bush v. Gore, 531 U.S. 98, 104 (2000)(per curiam).
9. See Ron Chernow, *Alexander Hamilton* (New York: Penguin Books, 2004), pp. 508–9.
10. 25 Edw. III. st. 2.
11. An Act to Establish an Uniform Rule of Naturalization, 1 Stat. 103 (1790).
12. An Act to Establish an Uniform Rule of Naturalization, and to Repeal the Act Heretofore Passed on that Subject, 1 Stat. 214 (1795).
13. Henry F. Graff, ed., *The Presidents: A Reference History*, 2nd ed. (New York: Macmillan Library Reference, 1997), pp. 144–47.
14. Letter from John Adams to Abigail Adams, 19 December 1793 [electronic edition]. Adams Family Papers: An Electronic Archive. Massachusetts Historical Society. Available online at http://www.masshist.org/digitaladams/aea/cfm/doc.cfm?id=L17931219ja&mode=popup sm&pop=L17931219ja_2 (accessed July 12, 2012).
15. O. C. Fisher, *Cactus Jack* (Waco: Texian Press, 1982), p. 118.
16. 5 USC § 3331.
17. Brian C. Kalt, *Constitutional Cliffhangers: A Legal Guide for Presidents and Their Enemies* (New Haven: Yale University Press, 2012), p. 96.
18. Andrea Seabrook, "Oath of Office: To Swear or to Affirm," *All Things Considered*, National Public Radio, January 18, 2009.
19. Stanley Elkins and Eric McKitrick, *The Age of Federalism: The Early American Republic, 1788–1800* (Oxford: Oxford University Press, 1993), p. 55.
20. Noel Canning v. National Labor Relations Board, ___ F.3d ___ (Nos. 12–1115, 12–1153, January 23, 2013).
21. Louis Fisher, "The 'Sole Organ' Doctrine," Studies on Presidential Power in Foreign Relations No. 1, Law Library of Congress, August 2006.
22. Youngstown Sheet & Tube, Inc. v. Sawyer, 100 U.S. 1 (1952).
23. David Currie, *The Constitution in Congress*, (Chicago: University of Chicago Press, 1997), pp. 275–81.
24. U.S. Congress. Congressional Record. 1970. 91st Cong., 2d sess. Vol. 116, p. 11913. Washington, DC.
25. Brian Kalt, "The Constitutional Case for the Impeachability of Former Federal Officials: An Analysis of the Law, History, and Practice of Late Impeachment," 6 *Texas Review of Law and Politics* 13, 125 (2001).
26. "Thirteen Ways of Looking at a Blackbird," Wallace Stevens, *The Collected Poems of Wallace Stevens* (New York: Vintage, 1990), p. 93.

Chapter 4

1. Kings 3:9.
2. I Kings 3:16–28.
3. Martin H. Redish, "Response: Good Behavior, Judicial Independence, and the Foundations of American Constitutionalism," 116 *Yale Law Journal* 139 (2006).

Chapter 5

1. Loughran v. Loughran, 292 U.S. 216 (1934), p. 222.
2. 28 U.S.C. § 1738C.
3. 7 U.S.C. § 7.
4. Wilson v. Ake, 354 F. Supp. 2d 1298 (M.D. Fla. 2005), pp. 1304-05.
5. Loving v. Virginia, 388 U.S. 1, 13 (1967).
6. Articles of Confederation, Art. IV.

7. *Fraser's Magazine* LVI. 161 (1857), quoted in "extradition," *The Oxford English Dictionary*, http://dictionary.oed.com.proxy-bl.researchport.umd.edu/cgi/entry/50081014?query_type=word&queryword=extradition&first=1&max_to_show=10&sort_type=alpha&result_place=1&search_id=wI58-CS9Umf-4414&hilite=50081014 (accessed September 18, 2009).
8. Theodore Bolema, "A Governor Cries 'Treason,'" Mackinac Center for Public Policy (July 14, 2005—note that this is Bastille Day) http://www.mackinac.org/article.aspx?ID=7163 (accessed September 18, 2009).
9. Kentucky v. Dennison, 65 U.S. 66 (1860).
10. 1 Stat. 302.
11. 9 Stat. 462.
12. Sidney Greenbaum, *The Oxford English Grammar* § 11.17 at 527–28 (1996).
13. Id. at 528.
14. Texas v. White, 74 U.S. 700 (1869).
15. S.J.R. 9, 28th Congress, 2d Sess., 5 Stat. 797, 798 (March 1, 1845),
16. Northwest Ordinance of 1787, 1 Statutes at Large 52.
17. "To John C. Breckinridge (August 12, 1803)," in Thomas Jefferson, *Writings*, ed. Merrill D. Peterson (New York: Library of America,1984), pp. 1137, 1138.
18. "To Wilson Cary Nicholas (September 7, 1803)," in Jefferson, *Writings*, pp. 1139, 1140.
19. Ibid., p. at 1140.
20. Ibid.
21. Luther v. Borden, 48 U.S. 1 (1849).
22. Nebraska Const, Art. III § 1.
23. US Bureau of the Census. Heads of Families at the First Census of the United States Taken in the Year 1790 (Washington, DC: Bureau of the Census, 1908). Available at http://www.census.gov/prod/www/abs/decennial/1790.html.

Chapter 6

1. Hollingsworth v. Virginia, 3 U.S. 378 (1798).
2. David P. Currie, *The Constitution in Congress, The Federalist Period, 1789–1801* (Chicago: University of Chicago Press, 1997), p. 115.
3. David E. Kyvig, *Explicit and Authentic Acts: Amending the U.S. Constitution* (Lawrence: University Press of Kansas, 1996), p. 162.
4. Garrett Epps, *Democracy Reborn: The Fourteenth Amendment and the Fight for Equal Rights in Post–Civil War America* (New York: Henry Holt, 2006), p. 245.
5. Kyvig, *Explicit and Authentic Acts*, p. 362.
6. David A. Strauss, *The Irrelevance of Constitutional Amendments*, 114 *Harvard Law Review* 1457 (2001).
7. Michael Vorenberg, "Imagining a Different Reconstruction Constitution," *Civil War History*, 51 (December 2005), 416–26.

Chapter 7

1. Missouri v. Holland, 252 U.S. 416 (1920).
2. Matt. 5:33–37.

Chapter 8

1. Sir John Harington, "Of Treason," *The Epigrams of Sir John Harington*, ed. Gerard Kilroy (1605) (London: Ashgate, 2009), III:43, p. 148.

Chapter 10

1. Jaroslav Pelikan, *Interpreting the Bible and the Constitution* (New Haven, CT: Yale University Press, 2004), p. 7.

2. Leonard W. Levy, *Origins of the Bill of Rights* (New Haven, CT: Yale University Press,1999), p. 23.
3. Googling "organic constitution" initiates a dizzying tour through the alternate reality of the militia and "sovereign citizen" movements, including detailed discussions of which parts of the Constitution are unconstitutional. For a good sample, see this explanation for why subsequent amendments such as the Fourteenth, Sixteenth, and Seventeenth are largely invalid:

> Since the constitution—state or federal—is a document of negative authority, meaning that if a power or authority is not specifically delegated to government in the constitution, then that same power or authority is specifically withheld from government. Further, all government officials are creations of the constitution, since the constitution lays down the structure of the government itself. So the question we should ask is, from where did any government officials obtain lawful authority to change the constitution that created those same officials in the first place? Lacking authority to alter the constitution means that any such alterations are invalid, as if they never occurred.

BarnacleBob, "The Organic Constitution," http://goldismoney.info/forums/archive/index.php/t-18582.html (Feb. 22, 2005, accessed September 28, 2009).
4. Barron v. Baltimore, 32 U.S. 243 (1833).
5. Constitution of Iraq, Art. 16, English text available from United Nations Assistance Mission for Iraq, http://www.uniraq.org/documents/iraqi_constitution.pdf.
6. The Constitution of Japan, Art. 25, English text provided by the Prime Minister and His Cabinet, http://www.kantei.go.jp/foreign/constitution_and_government_of_japan/constitution_e.html.
7. James Madison, "Speech in Congress Proposing Constitutional Amendments," June 8, 1789, in Madison, *Writings*, ed. Jack N. Rakove (New York: Library of America, 1999), pp. 437, 443.
8. Roger Williams, "Mr. Cottons Letter Lately Printed, Examined and Answered," London, 1644, in *The Complete Writings of Roger Williams*, ed. Reuben Aldridge Guild (New York: Russell & Russell, 1963), Vol. 1, p. 108.
9. Akhil Reed Amar, *The Bill of Rights: Creation and Reconstruction* (New Haven: Yale University Press, 1998), p. 25.
10. Henry Winthrop Ballantine, *Blackstone Commentaries* (Chicago: Blackstone Institute, 1915), p. 465.
11. New York Times Co. v. Sullivan, 376 U.S. 254, 280 (1964).
12. The Riot Act (1713) (1 Geo.1 St.2 c.5)
13. Militia Act of 1792. Act of May 8, 1792, ch. XXXIII, 1 Stat. 271.
14. Commonwealth v. Davis, 140 Mass. 485 (MA 1895), aff'd Davis v. Comm., 167 U.S. 43 (1897).
15. Hague v. CIO, 307 U.S. 496, 515 (1939) ("Wherever the title of the streets and parks may rest, they have immemorially been held in trust for the use of the public and, time out of mind, have been used for purposes of assembly, communicating thoughts between citizens, and discussing public questions. Such use of the streets and public places has, from ancient times, been a part of the privileges, immunities, rights, and liberties of citizens.") See also Harry Kalven Jr. "The Concept of the Public Forum: Cox v. Louisiana," 1 *Supreme Court Review* 13 (1965). "On this view the matter is perhaps not quite so clear, but there is the aura of a large democratic principle. When the citizen goes to the street, he is exercising an immemorial right of a free man, a kind of First-Amendment easement." (emphasis added).
16. Emily Dickinson, [Revolution Is the Pod], No. 1044, *The Poems of Emily Dickinson* (1865), ed. R.W. Franklin (Cambridge, MA: Harvard University Press, 1999), p. 427.
17. regulator, n. *Oxford English Dictionary*, 3rd ed., December 2009; online version June 2012. http://www.oed.com/view/Entry/161429; accessed August 8, 2012. An entry for this word was first included in *New English Dictionary*, 1905.
18. Sanford Levinson, "The Embarassing Second Amendment," 99 *Yale Law Journal* 637 (1989).
19. Levy, *Origins of the Bill of Rights*, p. 135.

20. The Bill of Rights, 1 W. & M. sess. 2. c. 2.
21. District of Columbia v. Heller, 554 U.S. 570 (2008).
22. McDonald v. City of Chicago, 561 U.S. 3025 (2010).
23. Custer County Action Ass'n v. Garvey, 256 F.3d 1024 (10th Cir. 2001).
24. Jones v. U.S. Secretary of Defense, 346 F.Supp. 97 (D.Minn.1972).
25. Engblom v. Carey, 677 F.2d 957 (2c Cir. 1982).
26. "Warrant," Oxford English Dictionary Online, http://dictionary.oed.com.proxy-bl.researchport.
    umd.edu/cgi/entry/50280999?query_type=word&queryword=warrant&first=1&max_
    to_show=10&sort_type=alpha&search_id=iRF2-kML5Xf-1509&result_place=1 (accessed
    October 10, 2009).
27. Matthew Hale, Historia Placitorum Coronæ [The History of the Pleas of the Crown], II. xviii.
    150 (1736): They are not to be granted without oath made before the justice of a felony com-
    mitted, and that the party complaining hath probable cause to suspect they are in such a
    house or place, and do shew his reasons of such suspicion.
28. William Shakespeare, *Hamlet*, II:ii, 529–31.
29. People v. Defore, 150 N.E. 585, 587 (N.Y. 1926).
30. Blair v. United States, 250 U.S. 273, 282 (1919).
31. United States v. R. Enterprises, Inc., 498 U.S. 292, 297, 111 S.Ct. 722, 112 L.Ed.2d 795
    (1991).
32. Hurtado v. California, 110 U.S. 516 (1884).
33. Stuart P. Green, *Deceit and the Classification of Crimes: Federal Rule of Evidence 609(a)(2)
    and the Origins of Crimen Falsi*, 90 Journal of Criminal Law and Criminology 1087, 1105
    (2000).
34. "Punishment," Black's Law Dictionary, WESTLAW Database, http://web2.westlaw.com/
    result/default.wl?mt=Westlaw&origin=Search&tempinfo=BLACKS%7cTEMPLATE
    %7cDefine%3aInTxt%3dpunishment%7cQueryTemplate0%7cctn%3dQT_BLACKS&
    srch=TRUE&qttab=QT_BLACKS&db=BLACKS&rlt=CLID_QRYRLT806214835613&
    method=ConcordTemplate&service=Search&eq=search&rp=%2fSearch%2fdefault.wl
    &query=CA(PUNISHMENT)&vr=2.0&dups=false&action=Search&rltdb=CLID_DB73
    204135613&sv=Split&qtrcc=QueryTemplate&fmqv=s&fn=_top&rs=LAWS2.0> (accessed
    March 1, 2013).
35. Ex parte Wilson, 114 U.S. 417 (1885).
36. Ibid., p.422.
37. Ibid., p. 427–28.
38. United States v. Moreland, 258 U.S. 433 (1922).
39. Ibid., p. 441–51.
40. Robert Sherrill, *Military Justice Is to Justice as Military Music Is to Music* (New York: Harper &
    Row, 1970), p. 2.
41. Callins v. Collins, 510 U.S. 1141 (1994) (Scalia, J., concurring).
42. 13 Edw. III 3 c. 3 (1354).
43. Pennsylvania Coal Co. v. Mahon, 260 U.S. 393 (1922).
44. Kelo v. City of New London, 545 U.S. 469 (2005).
45. Joseph William Singer, "Legislative Responses to *Kelo*," http://blogs.law.harvard.edu/
    jsinger/2009/09/26/legislative-responses-to-kelo/ (accessed March 12, 2013).
46. Batson v. Kentucky, 476 U.S. 79, 89 (1986); J.E.B. v. Alabama, 511 U.S. 127, 129 (1994).
47. William H. Burgess and Douglas G. Smith, "Proper Remedy for a Lack of Batson Findings:
    The Fall-Out from Snyder v. Louisiana," 101, 1 *Journal of Criminal Law & Criminology* 2–3
    (Winter 2011).
48. Gideon v. Wainwright, 372 U.S. 335 (1963).
49. Anthony Lewis, *Gideon's Trumpet* (New York: Random House, 1964).
50. Gideon, 372 U.S. at 336.
51. Johnson v. Zerbst, 304 U.S. 458 (1938).
52. Miranda v. Arizona, 384 U.S. 436 (1966).
53. Coffin v. United States, 156 U.S. 432 (1895).
54. Commonwealth v. Webster, 59 Mass. (5 Cush.) 295, 320 (1850).
55. In re Winship, 397 U.S. 358 (1970).

56. James Q. Whitman., *The Origins of Reasonable Doubt: Theological Roots of the Criminal Trial* (New Haven, CT: Yale University Press, 2008), p. 3.

57. "Relative Values—US $ Calculator," Measuring Worth http://www.measuringworth.com/ uscompare (accessed August 10, 2012). This online calculator determined that $20 in 1789 equaled $527 in real price, $8,110 in labor value in 2011.

58. Reed was quoted in Thurman W. Arnold, "Criminal Attempts: The Rise and Fall of an Abstraction," 40 *Yale Law Journal* 58 (1930).

59. Southern Pacific Co. v. Jensen, 244 U.S. 205, 222 (1917) (Holmes, J., dissenting).

60. See, e.g., John J. McCusker, *How Much Is That in Real Money? A Historical Price Index for Use as a Deflator of Money Values in the Economy of the United States* (Chapel Hill: University of North Carolina Press, 1991).

61. L. P. Hartley, *The Go-Between* (London: Hamis Hamilton, 1953).

62. William Shakespeare, *Hamlet* V:1: 96–98.

63. Hearing before the United States Senate Judiciary Committee, 110th Cong., 1st Sess, January 18, 2007, p. 52 (Committee Print, Serial No. J-110-3)(Testimony of Attorney General Albert Gonzales).

64. Biographical details about Gödel's life and work are supplied by an excellent intellectual biography, Rebecca Goldstein, *Incompleteness: The Proof and Paradox of Kurt Gödel* (New York: Norton, 2005). The story of Einstein's explanation for coming to Princeton is found in id. at 33. My understanding (if such is the correct term) of Gödel's proofs comes from laborious plodding through Ernest Nagel and James R. Newman, "Goedel's Proof," in *The World of Mathematics: A Small Library of Mathematics from A'h-mosé the Scribe to Albert Einstein*, 3 vols., ed. Philip and Phyllis Morrison (1988), Vol. 3, pp. 1641–67. If there is even the slightest tinge of truth in my observations on Gödel, it is due to Professors Goldstein, Nagel, and Newman. But they are not responsible for my naiveté and errors.

65. George Eliot, *Middlemarch* (New York: Penguin Classics, 2003), p. 58.

66. "Power," *Black's Law Dictionary*, 8th ed., ed. Bryan Garner (St. Paul: West, 2004).

67. United States v. Darby, 312 U.S. 100, 124 (1941).

Chapter 11

1. Abraham Lincoln, "Speech in the U.S. House of Representatives on Internal Improvements," *Lincoln: Speeches and Writings, 1832–1858*, ed. Don E. Fehrenbacher (New York: Library of America, 1989), p. 196.

2. "construe, v.," *Oxford English Dictionary*, 2nd ed., 1989; online version June 2012. http:// www.oed.com/view/Entry/39912 (accessed August 12, 2012). Earlier version first published in *New English Dictionary*, 1893.

3. The controversy is laid out in Thomas Colby, "The Federal Marriage Amendment and the False Promise of Originalism," 108 Columbia Law Review 529 (2008).

4. Ibid., p. 547.

5. Chisholm v. Georgia, 2 U.S. 419 (1793).

6. "construe, n.," *Oxford English Dictionary*.

7. Seminole Tribe of Florida v. Florida, 517 U.S. 44 (1996).

8. Seminole Tribe of Florida v. Florida, 517 U.S. 44, 102 (1996) (Souter, J., dissenting).

9. Regents of the University of Alabama v. Garrett, 531 U.S. 356 (2001).

Chapter 12

1. George Orwell, "In Front of Your Nose," *In Front of Your Nose*, Vol. 2 of *The Collected Essays, Journalism, and Letters of George Orwell*, ed. Sonia Orwell and Ian Argus (New York: Harcourt Brace Jovanovich, 1968), p. 125.

2. Micah 4:3–4.

3. Bailey v. Alabama, 219 U.S. 219, 244 (1910). ("The state may impose involuntary servitude as a punishment for crime, but it may not compel one man to labor for another in payment of a debt, by punishing him as a criminal if he does not perform the service or pay the debt.")

4. Maryland Declaration of Rights § 38 (1776), *The Complete Bill of Rights*, ed. Neil H. Cogan (New York: Oxford University Press, 1997), p. 94.

5. Thurgood Marshall, "The Constitution's Bicentennial: Celebrating the Wrong Document?" 40 *Vanderbilt Law Review* 1340–41 (May 1987).

6. Tony Mauro, "Early Line on the Next Justice," *Legal Times*, May 18, 1987.

7. Garrett Epps, *Democracy Reborn: The Fourteenth Amendment and the Fight for Equal Rights in Post–Civil War America* (New York: Henry Holt, 2006), p. 251.

8. Dr. John C. Eastman, Professor of Law, Chapman University School of Law, Director, Claremont Institute Center for Constitutional Jurisprudence, "Dual Citizenship, Birthright Citizenship, and the Meaning of Sovereignty," Testimony, US House of Representatives, Committee on the Judiciary, Subcommittee on Immigration, Border Security and Claims (September 29, 2005)

9. Dred Scott v. Sandford, 60 U.S. 393, 406–07 (1856).

10. Slaughter-House Cases, 83 U.S. 36, 78 (1872).

11. John Hart Ely, *Democracy and Distrust* (Cambridge, MA: Harvard University Press, 1980), p. 18.

12. Jacobellis v. Ohio, 378 U.S. 184, 197, 84 St. Ct. 1676, 1683 (1964)(Stewart, J., concurring).

13. Declaration of the Rights of Man and of the Citizen, Art. I (1789).

14. William Blake, "A Memorable Fancy," *The Marriage of Heaven and Hell*, ed. Michael Phillips (Oxford: Bodleian Library, 2011).

15. Johnson's reorganization orders restricted the vote to voters who had been eligible under the former Confederate states' prewar constitutions—which naturally restricted the franchise to whites. See, e.g., Andrew Johnson, "Proclamation 135—Reorganizing a Constitutional Government in North Carolina" (May 29, 1865).

16. Andrew Johnson, "Proclamation 167—Offering and Extending Full Pardon to All Persons Participating in the Late Rebellion" (September 7, 1867).

17. Amnesty Act of 1872, 17 Stat. 142 (1872).

18. Michael Abramowicz, "Beyond Balanced Budgets, Fourteenth Amendment Style," 33 *Tulsa Law Journal* 561, 562 (1997), quoting Irvin Molotsky, "Lafayette Park: Not Just Another Pretty Postcard," *New York Times*, Sept. 7, 1984, p. A13.

19. Perry v. United States, 294 U.S. 330, 354 (1935).

20. Garrett Epps, "The Speech Obama Could Give: The Constitution Forbids Default," theatlantic. com, April 28, 2011, http://www.theatlantic.com/politics/archive/2011/04/the-speech-obama-could-give-the-constitution-forbids-default/237977/.

21. Adam Liptak, "Legal Memo: The 14th Amendment, the Debt Ceiling and a Way Out," *New York Times*, July 24, 2011.

22. David A. Strauss, "The Irrelevance of Constitutional Amendments." 114 *Harvard Law Review* 1457, 1479 (2001).

23. City of Boerne v. Flores, 521 U.S. 507, 520 (1997).

24. Civil Rights Cases, 109 U.S. 3 (1883).

25. Lewis Carroll, *Alice's Adventures in Wonderland*, in Martin Gardner, ed., *The Annotated Alice: The Definitive Edition* (New York: W.W. Norton & Co., 2000), p. 213.

26. David M. Oshinsky, *Worse than Slavery: Parchman Farm and the Ordeal of Jim Crow Justice* (New York: Free Press, 1997).

27. Anita Kumar, "McDonnell in Hot Water over Nonviolent Felons' Rights," *Washington Post*, April 11, 2010.

Chapter 13

1. James Madison, *Notes of Debates in the Federal Convention of 1787*, Gaillard Hunt and James Brown Scott, eds., (New York: W.W. Norton & Co., 1987), p. 494.

2. Springer v. United States, 102 U.S. 586 (1880), p. 596.

3. Ibid., p. 602.

4. Pollock v. Farmers' Loan & Trust Co., 157 U.S. 429 (1895), p. 573.

5. Lonsdale v. Commissioner of Internal Revenue, 661 F.2d 71 (1981).

6. National Federation of Independent Business v. Sebelius, 572 U.S. ___ (2012) slip op. at 40–41 (citations omitted).
7. CBS News, "Blago: A Senate Seat is a f****ing Valuable Thing," June 29, 2009, http://www.cbsnews.com/2100-501563_162-4657414.html. Jeff Coen, Rick Person, John Chase, and David Kidwell, "Illinois Gov. Rod Blagojevich Arrested on Federal Charges," *Chicago Tribune*, December 10, 2008.
8. David Graham Phillips, *The Treason of the Senate*, ed. George E. Mowry and Judson A. Grenier (Chicago: Quadrangle Books, 1964).
9. Valenti v. Rockefeller, 292 F.Supp. 851, 856 (1968).
10. Valenti v. Rockefeller, 393 U.S. 405 (1969).
11. Judge v. Quinn, 612 F.3d 537 (7th Cir. 2010).
12. National Prohibition Act, 27 U.S.C.A. § 40, Repealed Aug. 27, 1935.
13. United States v. Sullivan, 15 F.2d 809 (1926).
14. United States v. Sullivan, 274 U.S. 259 (1927).
15. Glen Jeansome, *The Life of Herbert Hoover: Fighting Quaker, 1928–1933* (New York: Palgrave Macmillan, 2012), p. 33.
16. Hawke v. Smith, 253 U.S. 221, 231 (1920).
17. Abigail Adams to John Adams, April 14, 1776. Abigail Adams and John Adams, *My Dearest Friend: Letters of Abigail and John Adams*, Margaret Hogan and C. James Taylor eds. (Cambridge, MA: Harvard University Press, 2007), p. 110.
18. Seneca Falls Convention, "Declaration of Sentiments," Elizabeth Cady Stanton, Susan B. Anthony, Matilda Joslyn Gage, and Ida Husted Harper, *A History of Woman Suffrage*, Vol. 1 (Rochester, NY: Fowler and Wells, 1889), pp. 70–71.
19. Judith Wellman, "Charlotte Woodward Pierce," Women's Rights National Historical Park, http://www.nps.gov/wori/historyculture/charlotte-woodward.htm (accessed August 3, 2012).
20. Quoted in Griffin v. Illinois, 351 U.S. 12 (1956), p. 23 (Frankfurter, J., concurring).

Chapter 14

1. "The Lame Duck Congress," *The West Wing: The Complete Second Season*, episode 6, DVD, directed by Jeremy Kagan (2000; Burbank, CA: Warner Home Video, 2004).
2. "Jeffrey Toobin, *The Oath: The Obama White House and the Supreme Court* (New York: Doubleday, 2012), p. 110.
3. 3 U.S.C. § 15.
4. 3 U.S.C. 19.
5. Robert Francis Harpert, trans., *The Code of Hammurabi King of Babylon* (Chicago: University of Chicago Press, 1902; Holmes Beach, FL: WM. M. Gaunt & Sons, 1994), p. 37.
6. Granholm v. Heald, 544 U.S. 460, 488 (2005).
7. Donald Kyvig, *Explicit and Authentic Acts* (Lawrence, KS: The University Press of Kansas, 1996), p. 285 ; Everett S. Brown, "The Ratification of the Twenty-First Amendment," 29.6 *American Political Science Review* 1005–1017 (December 1935).

Chapter 15

1. Carrie Johnson, "A Split at Justice on DC Vote Bill; Holder Overrode Ruling That Measure Is Unconstitutional," *Washington Post*, April 1, 2009, sec. A1.
2. Henry Adams, *The Education of Henry Adams* (New York: Modern Library, 1996), p. 44.
3. David E. Kyvig, *Explicit and Authentic Acts* (Lawrence: University Press of Kansas, 1996), p. 356.
4. Harper v. Virginia Board of Elections, 383 U.S. 663 (1966).
5. *Seven Days in May*, directed by John Frankenheimer (1964; Burbank, CA: Warner Home Video, 2000).
6. Richard II, III:155–62.
7. John Milton Cooper, Jr., *Woodrow Wilson: A Biography* (New York: Alfred A. Knopf, 2009), pp. 535–43.
8. Jane Mayer and Doyle McManus, Land side: The Unmaking of the President, 1984–1988 (Boston: Houghton Mifflin, 1988), p. x.

Chapter 16

1. James Madison, "Speech in Congress Proposing Constitutional Amendments," June 16, 1789, in Madison, *Writings*, ed. Jack N. Rakove (New York: Library of America, 1999), 437, 450.
2. John Heltman, "27th Amendment or Bust!" *American Prospect*, May 25, 2012, http://prospect.org/article/27th-amendment-or-bust.
3. Dillon v. Gloss, 256 U.S. 368 (1921).

INDEX